SLA in Plain English

Understanding and Applying SLA for Teachers of English as a Second or Foreign Language

From Practice to Theory

Dennis Murphy Odo

About this book

SLA in Plain English: Understanding and Applying SLA for Teachers of English as a Second or Foreign Language can help pre-service and in-service teachers of English as a second or foreign language and possibly teachers of other languages. This book provides readers with an introduction to how to plan lessons on the four skills as well as guidance on examples of activities that they could include for each part of a skills-based lesson. The second half of the book discusses the key theories, concepts and principles from second language acquisition research that most influence current practice in second and foreign language education pedagogy.

Author

Dennis Murphy Odo is an associate professor of English Education at Pusan National University in South Korea where he teaches courses in second language acquisition and TESOL instructional methods. His main research interests are in second language literacy instruction and teacher education. He has 20 years of experience teaching TESOL methods in Korea and Canada and well as an assistant professor of ESOL/ Reading education in the US.

Dennis Murphy Odo

SLA in Plain English

Understanding and Applying SLA for Teachers of English as a Second or Foreign Language

From Practice to Theory

PNU Press

Table of Contents

SLA in Plain English

Chapter 1
Introduction

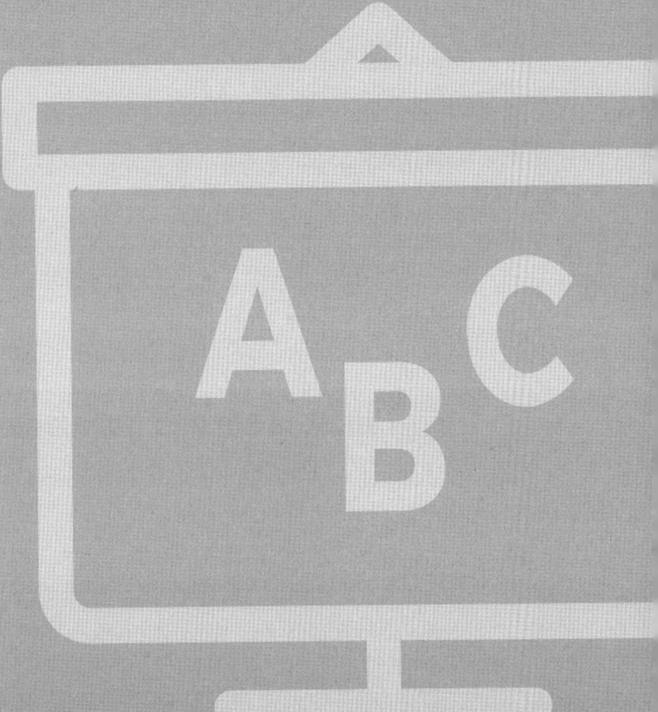

Chapter 1

Introduction

1.1 About this book

The primary aim of this book is to teach novice second and foreign language teachers the basics of how to teach a second language. I have tried to focus mostly on the essentials so those just entering the field can start with what is important and hopefully feel a little less overwhelmed. This book offers an introduction to the practicalities of preparing to teach the four skills in a second/foreign language context. It also provides generally non-technical explanation of key SLA concepts and theories which should help readers better connect their understanding of how L2 learning happens to their second language teaching practices.

1.2 What is second language acquisition (SLA)?

SLA is basically the mental processes that occur inside of the learner's mind that allow her to learn an additional language. SLA can naturalistically or in a classroom setting. Naturalistic learning usually refers to "picking up" a second language without any formal classroom instruction while classroom-based learning typically entails at least some formal instruction. Of course, this is a somewhat simplistic distinction because ordinarily most learners have a more complex L2 learning trajectory that involves exposure to both kinds of learning.

This topic will receive more attention in the second half of the book.

The words second language learning and second language acquisition will be used interchangeably through this book so the distinction between learning and acquisition hypothesized by researchers like Stephen Krashen (1982) is not made here. As well, the abbreviation L2 will be used instead of writing out second or foreign language. For those who might not be familiar with the distinction, second language learning happens in contexts where the L2 is widely used so that learners have more opportunities to practice using it. In contrast, foreign language learning occurs in places where the L2 is not widely used. As with naturalistic and classroom-based learning, with the advent of ubiquitous access to many languages through global media, the distinction of second and foreign language has become somewhat blurred. I have also opted to use the term second language (or L2) throughout the book but this term also includes third, fourth (and so forth) languages.

1.3 Connecting L2 instruction with SLA research

Although there are many clear connections between L2 instruction and SLA research, there is also plenty of information about L2 teaching that does not attempt to connect to SLA research and vice versa. Those who are relatively unfamiliar with the field may not realize that SLA research is not necessarily directed at informing L2 teaching practice. Indeed, there are some scholars who contend that SLA findings often do not directly relate to language pedagogy (Block, 2000; Ellis, 2001).

Efforts have been made toward connecting L2 pedagogy with second language acquisition research but, in some sense, the worlds of SLA and L2 pedagogy may never be completely aligned given SLA's scientific and L2 pedagogy's practice focus. The SLA subfield that most directly relates SLA research findings and L2 classroom pedagogy is known as instructed second language acquisition (ISLA). This subfield has grown substantially in recent years but, as many doing research in this area would attest, there is still much to learn about exactly how the findings from ISLA can translate smoothly into classroom practice.

Although ISLA offers many valuable insights to practicing teachers, in many cases, not enough is known about the effectiveness of some widely-used teaching approaches. For example, the present-practice-produce (PPP) paradigm presented in this book has been criticized by some (Lewis, 1996) and praised by others (Ur, 2018). However, the reality is that not enough research has been conducted on PPP to make a final determination regarding its effectiveness either way (Loewen, 2014).

If teachers wait only for SLA research to tell them what to do in their practice, they may have to wait for a long time. The issue is that SLA's research agenda often overlooks the investigation of teaching methods, techniques and practices that are widely used but for whatever reason have not been high on the research agenda of Applied Linguists. Thus, while we should certainly keep abreast of the major developments in SLA as language teachers, we should also be willing to look beyond SLA research for techniques that we can use in our classes.

A second justification for the present volume has to do with a limitation shared by a number of the existing resources available. That is, they tend to lack a suitable balance given to both theory and practice. Some books that try to connect SLA and L2 pedagogy are written from the perspective of the applied linguist or SLA researcher and thus tend to place more of an emphasis on theory. Accordingly, the advice they give can be somewhat challenging to put into practice. The reader may have to sift through technical explanation to find the more practical suggestions. Sometimes, classroom suggestions are relegated to a chapter at the end that may not go into the level of detail novice teachers need to clearly understand the steps necessary to plan lessons and teach the four skills.

Conversely, there are resources that are written primarily from the perspective of an experienced practitioner. These resources usually focus more on the "classroom tested" methods that new teachers need. However, they also often have limited theoretical support and so they function like a recipe book that tells the reader what to do but not why they should do it that way. However, teachers need to understand the reasons for their actions because they often have to extrapolate the advice given to novel circumstances or with unfamiliar groups of learners. They also have to be prepared to occasionally justify their instructional decisions to other stakeholders. At least some theoretical understanding is essential to be able to explain why some methods or techniques are superior to others in light of what we know about L2 learning. Thus, familiarity with the basics of L2 learning theories is vital to be able to effectively adjust one's instruction and defend one's instructional decisions.

1.4 Specific challenges for novice L2 teachers

Novice teachers face many demands while adjusting to their new careers. One significant hurdle is learning how to plan different lessons for the various L2 skills. Lesson planning can be particularly daunting to a novice because each lesson has a different structure depending on the skill (e.g., reading vs. writing) being taught. Therefore, new teachers need straightforward guidance on how to plan lessons for the various skills. They should also understand the main SLA concepts, principles and theories that they can draw on as an L2 teacher to develop the beginnings of a personal theory of how second languages are learned. This theory can then inform their instructional decisions and choice of materials.

I hope that after reading this book new teachers will feel more confident in planning lessons that address the four skills. More specifically, I hope that you will be able to write lesson objectives and plan well-structured lessons that include appropriate activities. I also hope that the SLA topics discussed here will help form a firm basis upon which you will be able to provide justifications for why you use the methods that you do. As part of this experience, I urge you to examine your own tacit beliefs and theories about L2 learning so that you can develop a coherent personal theory of L2 learning that reflects modern understandings and that connects with your core values.

1.5 Contents of the book

The book can be roughly divided into two main parts. The first seven chapters generally deal with the more practical aspects of planning and teaching English lessons. Chapters 7 through 9 relate more to the concepts and theories in SLA. First, chapter 2 begins with a discussion of lesson planning that includes an overview of how to write instructional objectives as well as how to structure lessons for the various 4 language skills. Chapter 3 reviews a number of ways of teaching grammar including implicit and explicit as well as deductive and inductive approaches. Several strategies for presenting new vocabulary and recycling previously taught vocabulary are suggested as well. Chapter 4 covers approaches to teaching listening and speaking. This includes discussion of the basic pre, during, post structure of a listening lesson. The present, practice, produce model for teaching a speaking lesson is also discussed as well as to how teachers can integrate cooperative learning activities into their lessons.

Chapter 5 looks at teaching reading and writing and explores the pre, during, post structure of a reading lesson as well as a structure for teaching writing. The writing lesson structure is based on the gradual release of responsibility model that involves teacher modeling, teacher-student co-construction, small-group collaboration and individual creation of a target genre. Chapter 6 on multicompetence and professional development discusses suggestions for how teachers can continue to develop professionally and how those who speak English as an additional language can begin to see their bilingualism in a more positive light. Chapter 7 on providing comprehensible input several steps that teachers can take to better ensure that their learners understand them more easily when they use the L2 during lessons.

Chapter 8 begins to explore several of the more influential theories of second language acquisition including the monitor model, information processing, and sociocultural theory among several others. Chapter 9 reviews many of the individual differences that learners have that can influence L2 acquisition including learning strategies, aptitude, intelligence, anxiety, and motivation among others. Finally, chapter 10 finishes with a brief discussion of age and L2 learning that examines several of the key themes related to age and second language learning such as the critical period hypothesis as well as the relationship between age and the acquisition of phonology and grammatical ability.

1.6 Suggestions for using the book

This book is likely to be most useful for pre-service teachers in MATESOL programs that focus on teacher preparation. It probably works best in a class that tries to connect SLA theory to teaching practice. In-service teachers who would like to refresh their knowledge a bit and be introduced to some of the more recent theories of SLA may also find it to be useful. The organization of the chapters is a bit unusual for books in this genre. Typically, they are organized so that the theory sections come first and are followed by the more teaching oriented parts.

I chose to organize the book this way because, in my own classes, I have included a micro-teaching component that gives the teachers the chance to put some of the ideas that we have been discussing into practice. However, in order for all of the students to have enough time to do their lesson, they have to begin early in the semester. I have found that to give them a solid foundation to use in their teaching, the organization of chapters used here works best. I also find that a theory tends to make more sense to students after they have had the chance try out some of the methods and techniques that have been derived from that theory in their microteaching. Having said this, no chapter depends on the others to be understood so they can be read in any order. However, if you want to do that, I would recommend at least reading chapter one on lesson planning first.

Finally, I hope that you enjoy the book and that it helps you reach a clearer understanding of the fundamentals of lesson planning as well as the key theories and concepts in SLA. That way, you can forge a clearer connection between theory and practice which in turn improves understanding of what you are doing in your language classes as well as why you are doing it.

Chapter 2
Lesson Planning

Chapter 2

Lesson Planning

2.1 Introduction

This chapter covers the important facets of instructional planning including course and lesson planning. In the process of talking about lesson planning, lesson objectives and activities are discussed. Other important considerations related to planning such as lesson enrichment and remediation as well as assessment are also discussed.

Effective planning is the foundation of effective teaching. It enables you to move from slavishly following a textbook or finding random activities to kill time toward becoming a professional who fulfills her duty to educate those in her charge. Understanding how to structure lessons is also the essential foundation upon which we can build our ability to structure lessons for the four skills discussed in the upcoming chapters. In addition to setting objectives, you must also be able to use valid methods to assess whether your objectives have been met. Objectives and assessments are the vital tools that allow you to guide your students' efficient learning.

With the information presented in this chapter, you will be able to plan lessons more efficiently and consider appropriate activities that your learners could do for remediation or enrichment. This chapter's content will also help you to tailor and adjust your lessons to meet the specific needs of your students as you continuously assess the achievement of your lesson goals.

2.2 Reasons for planning

Farrell (2002) defines a lesson plan as "...a systematic record of a teacher's thoughts about what will be covered during a lesson"(p. 30). In other words, it can be described as your relatively detailed description of your aims and intended activities to meet those aims for a given lesson of instruction. The lesson plan should be written before the actual lesson is given because it is supposed to be an aid to helping you think about what activities to include in the lesson as well as structure and sequence those activities.

You have probably heard the old adage that "failing to plan is planning to fail." That is, if we do not plan in advance, we are often setting ourselves up for unnecessary problems when we actually start teaching. So, let's reflect a bit more on why it is such a good idea to spend some time planning our lessons. First, we want to make the most efficient use of the class time possible so having a realistic plan will allow us to avoid wasting time making too many instructional decisions during the actual lesson. That way, we will not give our students the impression that we are just improvising and that we actually know what we are doing. Another obvious reason for planning our lessons is that the plan can serve as a guide to our lesson (J. C. Richards, 1998). It reminds us of what we are trying to do (i.e., the aims) and how we are trying to do it (i.e., the procedures). We can always refer back to it when we feel the lesson is beginning to go a bit off course.

In addition to these more practical reasons, there are also some other important purposes for lesson planning. For instance, our plans also push us to carefully consider the value and feasibility of our objectives and whether our classroom activities meet those objectives (Farrell, 2002). Our previous lesson plans can also remind us of what we have already taught so we can decide on what content or skills remains to be covered in a unit of material (Purgason, 1991). Thus, on a macro level, lesson plans provide greater structure and coherence to our courses. As well, our written lesson plans can provide record of our teaching for future reference. Such documentation could be valuable when we want to offer a somewhat more factual basis upon which to discuss our class with interested stakeholders such as parents or administrators (Purgason, 1991).

Despite the unquestionable value of engaging in thoughtful lesson planning, we nevertheless do not want to be too rigid in our planning. Inflexible adherence to your lesson plan can have some negative consequences (Scrivener, 2011). For example, a teacher who is overly focused on completing all of the activities scheduled in the plan is may miss students' signals that the pace of the lesson is too fast and consequently leave a several students struggling to keep up. This sort of unproductive classroom dynamic is likely to eventually present problems for classroom management (J. C. Richards & Renandya, 2002). It is important to remember that we are teaching people, not content. So, we do not have to worry so much about whether we have covered all of the content that we wanted to but rather that the content we did cover was understood by the maximum number of students.

While we must plan our course and lessons carefully, we must be flexible in our implementing the plan to allow for unplanned teachable moments and productive diversions (Scrivener, 2011). For example, we might have a listening activity followed by a speaking activity planned but we noticed that learners were especially engaged and benefiting from an extended work with the listening text. It would probably be worthwhile to allow them to continue with that task for longer than planned to capitalize on their high level of engagement. You could then either do the speaking task in the next lesson or, if pressed for time, eliminate it altogether. Such action can only be taken if you are willing to let go of adhering to your lesson plan too rigidly.

Lesson "white space" is another important lesson planning consideration (Lydon, 2017). We should plan our lessons so that there are not too many activities for the time available thereby allowing time for these teachable moments that do not derail our lesson objectives. So, when considering the timing of your lesson, you should not fill it with so many activities that students never have the chance to collect themselves and catch their breath. That being said, it is usually a good idea to havc an extra activity ready just in case. That way you will always have something to fall back on when the lesson proceeds a bit faster than you anticipated. It can be a disconcerting experience to finish your lesson and realize that you still have ten minutes of class time remaining.

Formal lesson plans like those prepared during pre-service teacher training or for a teaching practicum are not commonly written in many educational contexts. With experienced teachers, most of the lesson planning occurs in their mind with no more than a few notes on required materials and textbook page numbers written down as a memory aid (Scrivener, 2011). Nevertheless, it is essential for beginning teachers to learn how to plan in a more formal manner because it helps you to think like a teacher. It also gives colleagues and evaluators a record of your thought process that they can use to provide you with feedback and guidance. Thus, when more of the planning begins to take place inside your head chances are better it will be more effectively guided by the input and feedback of more practiced colleagues.

2.3 Course planning

An extended discussion of course planning is beyond the scope of the present text but, in general, planning should proceed in the manner outlined below. Start by planning the overall structure of your course and crafting the syllabus. When constructing your syllabus, you will need to decide the type of syllabus you will use (e.g., notional, functional, task based, content-based etc.) (McDonough & Shaw, 2012). Many teachers today use multi-dimensional syllabus comprised of several other components of other syllabus types (Mohseni Far, 2008). Upon choosing your syllabus type, decide what topics and skills will be covered in the course. As you do this, consider the curriculum or the local curricular guidance documents of the school where you are working. Also keep in mind the learners that you will be teaching. As you choose your textbook and materials and develop your units of instruction, you will need to consider their age, language proficiency, stage of intellectual development, background knowledge and attitudes among other factors (McGrath, 2002). As well, you should take into account the materials and resources that you can gain access to. For example, are there flashcards, books, computer software or other ancillary materials that you can use to supplement the textbook? If you have some control over your textbook selection, you will want to make sure that whatever you choose as your textbook can be used without an inordinate amount of supplementation. You do not want to spend too much time having to create materials that should have already been included in the textbook.

At the planning stage, you will also need to decide on the teaching principles that you will adopt in your course. Findings from extensive educational research suggest the use of the following principles. First, try to incorporate student-centered tasks and activities into your lessons as much as possible to reduce teacher talk time and maximize student talk time (Nunan, 1988). These kinds of activities encourage learners to participate actively in the lesson by incorporating small group work and hands-on learning. Examples of these cooperative and communicative activities include information gap and role play tasks. Through these types of activities, learners are able to develop their communicative competence as they gradually learn how to navigate the hubbub of authentic conversation in the target language. They also are able to develop their accuracy and fluency in the process.

Use of digital audio-visual teaching materials should also be encouraged through access to software that can allow learners to practice and reinforce their L2 skills independently. To illustrate, a quality spaced-repetition based flashcard review app will allow learners to efficiently review new vocabulary without their having to waste time on words that they already know (Barr, 2016). These materials could include phonics games, grammar apps, or reading assistance software among many other types. Access to these materials also allow learners to engage in the autonomous learning that they will need to do to progress to advanced levels.

One final principle is to integrate the target language into lessons whenever possible. This is not to say that the mother tongue cannot be used as an occasional scaffold for language that is too time-consuming to explain. However, it is preferable to focus on giving your learners access to comprehensible input in the target language rather than spending excessive amounts of time explaining language, concepts and skills in the first language. Regular exposure to comprehensible input benefits learners especially at the beginning levels (Shintani, Li, & Ellis, 2013).

2.4 The Lesson planning process

The lesson planning process begins with the selection of its subject matter. As well, the topic and objectives for your lesson should tie back in with the broader aims of your syllabus. For instance, if your syllabus focuses on notions and functions, the topic of your lesson might be about apartment hunting (notion) and asking for directions (function). As with general course planning, you will also need to keep in mind the learners' age, grade level, language proficiency and other related factors as you decide what content is appropriate for the lesson.

As you begin plan the lesson, you will first want to consider what the learners will already need to know to successfully learn the content of the lesson – their pre-requisite knowledge. As an example, if the lesson is designed to teach the learner about the meaning of the written word "cat," the learner's prerequisite knowledge might be that he can decode the letters and sound out the word or that he has the concept of a cat in his L1.

2.5 Lesson objectives

After deciding the pre-requisite knowledge you will assume the learner has, you are ready to begin devising the objectives for the lesson. Clear and achievable objectives are the foundation of an effective lesson. They serve as the roadmap of the class that remind you what students are supposed to be learning (Scrivener, 2011). All lesson activities and assessments should clearly connect to the objectives.

Lesson objectives are comprised of three main components. The first is referred to as the condition which is the situation under which the desired behavior you want the learner to do will be observed. Examples of conditions include "given a short reading passage" or "given three sentences with grammar errors." The next component of the objective is the learner's performance. This is what the learner is expected to be able to do by the end of the lesson. It is important that this part includes an action verb that will allow the learner to clearly demonstrate for the teacher that she can perform the desired action. To illustrate, phrases such as "students will read aloud" or "students will list in writing" must be included in the objective. Also, note the observability of the verb in the objective. It is something that you can see and therefore evaluate that the student can in fact perform the action. You must start with an observable action verb and not a verb like learn or understand because we cannot actually watch someone learn. We have to infer their learning from their behavior. It is this behavior that we want to examine. The final component of the objective is the criterion. This element represents the accuracy with which the student must be able to perform the task. For instance, the student will summarize a story in five written sentences. It is usually best to have the learner demonstrate their ability to do the task more than once so that you can be certain that their performance was not a fluke occurrence. Here are a couple of examples of objectives with each of the components labelled:

Table 2.1 Parts of a lesson objective

	Condition	Performance	Criterion
Reading	Given a 100 word reading passage	Students will orally summarize the main ideas	In five sentences
Listening	After listening to a short dialog	Students will check	Four items mentioned in the dialog

A number of different types of objectives exist related to language teaching. However, we'll focus on three common objective types outlined below. The first is a cognitive objective which is used to plan and assess student knowledge (Winocur, 1985). That is, what you want them to *know* by the end of the lesson. Common types of verbs used in this objective include identify, describe, explain or paraphrase. An illustration of this sort of objective would be "given a picture of a school, students will be able to verbally identify five different rooms in the school."

A second category of lesson objective is psychomotor through which learners practice skills. The focus here is the skill you want learners to be able to *demonstrate* by the end of the lesson (Bixler, 2006). Examples of activities that would achieve these objectives in a language class include performing a grammar drill or participating in a role play. A psychomotor objective could be written as "given four pictures, students will arrange the pictures in order and tell a five sentence story."

A third type of objective relates to affective states. This objective typically receives less attention from teachers because affect is often difficult to measure (Holt & Hannon, 2006). The primary aim for this objective is to focus on what you want students to value or be concerned about. This focus can include "the manner in which we deal with things emotionally, such as feelings, values, appreciation, enthusiasms, motivations, and attitudes" (Clark, 2010, p. 2). Relevant actions during the lesson could include demonstrating appreciation or preference for something or showing interest, attention, or curiosity. An example of such an objective is "During a small group discussion, students will verbally identify three of their favorite benefits about speaking English."

2.6 Creating lesson objectives

Having outlined the various types of objectives that exist, let's now summarize the process that a teacher might follow when constructing an objective. What are the steps that you need to proceed through in coming up with objectives? This first step is to refer to the curricular standards that are being used to guide the English curriculum at your school. Next, choose a curriculum standard that you would like to address in your lesson and begin considering how you will turn the standard into lesson objectives.

You should begin by contemplating what the students are supposed to *learn* from the lesson. In other words, ask yourself why they are doing the tasks or activities that you plan to assign. If you cannot think of a cogent reason for its inclusion, you should carefully reconsider including the activity or task in your lesson. After you have decided on what it is that you want students to learn, start to imagine what they will be physically doing during your lesson that will demonstrate for you that they have met the objectives.

The procedure for turning standards into objectives is roughly as follows: (1) Look for the relevant skill, grammatical form or function in the materials and activities that you plan to use. (2) Find the relevant standard in the curriculum document that connects to the skill or language that you want to teach (3) Write an observable and measurable objective that includes the condition, performance and criterion based on your materials that meets the curriculum standard.

When developing your objectives, it is important to consider the target language structures that your lesson will focus on. Depending on the aims of your lesson, you will want to include objectives that focus on grammar, lexis and skills. Grammar objectives will need to ensure that learners can comprehend and produce a target structure accurately and in appropriate contexts. For example, students learning the structure "can + main verb" should know how it is formed in a sentence, that it denotes ability or possibility and that it is often used to express ability or give permission. Lexical objectives address the vocabulary or multi-word expressions to be learned in the lesson. Skills objectives relate to the language skills that will be practiced in the lesson including listening, speaking, reading and writing.

Realize also that the development of your lesson objectives involves some recursive negotiation between the materials that you have access to, your students' proficiency and what you intend to accomplish. So, you will have to navigate between the curriculum documents and the course materials (e.g., textbook) to devise objectives that you believe will address the unique constraints imposed by the particular curriculum, materials and students that you work with.

2.7 Lesson activities

After you have decided on your objectives for the lesson, you will need to select the lesson activities you will use to achieve your objectives. The remainder of the book will offer activity ideas that you may want to consider when planning lessons for each of the four skills as well as integrating skills. The following example lesson format is the same kind that is commonly used in many EFL contexts. It is widely known as the present-practice-produce (PPP) format that is used to structure speaking lessons. While the PPP format has endured several criticisms over the years, it has been included here because of its wide use as well as the fact that it offers a manageable structure for beginning teachers and lower-level learners (Carless, 2009; Thornbury, 1999). This format is typically used to introduce new lexis and grammar as well as practice speaking.

It should be noted that PPP is only one way among many of structuring speaking lessons. Interested readers should consult Aslan (2016) for an extended discussion of alternatives to the PPP lesson structure. As well, lesson structures for teaching the other language skills differ considerably from the PPP format. A listening lesson, for example, is structured as before, during and after listening rather than being present, practice and produce (Underwood, 1989).The following chapters are organized according to lesson structures that are widely agreed to be effective for teaching each of the particular language skill presented in the chapter. Some lesson structures are quite similar (i.e., listening and reading) while others are quite different (e.g., reading and writing). More comprehensive suggestions for lesson activity ideas to practice each of the four main language skills will be discussed in greater depth in the rest of this volume.

Lesson plans should typically contain the following elements:

Teacher: The name of the person who will be teaching the lesson.

Date: When the lesson will take place.

Class: A concise description of the learners who the lesson is designed for that includes their age, proficiency level and grade.

Curriculum standards: include the curriculum standards from which your lesson objectives were developed.

Lesson objectives: write out the two or three cognitive, psychomotor and/ or affective objectives that you want the learners to achieve by the end of the lesson.

Subject matter: Identify the theme of the lesson such as "sports" or "travel."

Language: identify the target lexis, key expressions, grammar structures or language functions that are the focus of the lesson.

Materials and media: list all of the materials and media that you and the learners will need to complete the lesson.

Anticipatory set: help students connect information from the previous lesson to this new lesson with a review. Grab students' interest with a surprising quote or image and explain what they will learn in the lesson.

Procedures: Identify the main stages of the lesson and the activities that you will include in each stage. Outline each sequence of steps you will follow to conduct each of the activities in the lesson. Note the approximate time each activity will take as well as the roles of the teacher and students during each activity. Procedures should be written so that someone else like a substitute teacher could take your plan and be able to follow it to generally reproduce your lesson.

Closure: Conclude the lesson. Review the lesson objectives and summarize the key points of the lesson. Ask students what the main idea was or to summarize the lesson.

Remedial/ enrichment: mention scaffolds for challenging parts of the lesson and activities for those who quickly meet the objectives.

Assessment: include the formative classroom assessments that you will use to assess whether students met the objectives.

2.8 An example of a speaking lesson

A PPP lesson ordinarily begins with an introduction that includes the presentation of new vocabulary and grammatical structures. During the presentation phase of the lesson, the teacher will introduce the topic, activate learners' background knowledge. The teacher will also present the target vocabulary and grammar structures. The teacher should also attempt to motivate the learners and make them feel at ease with some small talk such as asking about their day so far.

From there, the teacher could have the learners review what they learned about in the previous class. Once the review is completed, the teacher introduces the topic for the current lesson by saying something like "Today we are going to learn about sports." When presenting the new topic, the teacher will want to connect the topic to learners' experiences by asking questions like "What are your favorite sports?" These questions personalize the topic for the learners which in turn increases their engagement, curiosity and interest. An additional benefit of personalized questions is that they help to activate learners' background knowledge. Equally, learners' relevant knowledge can also be stimulated through discussing the contents of pictures or short video clips related to the topic. Another particular effective and versatile presentation technique is to have learners brainstorm about the topic such as through naming all the sports that they can think of and then placing them into categories.

Once the main topic of the lesson has been introduced and discussed, it is time for the teacher to introduce the target language. There are a variety of techniques that can be used for presenting new language such as using a text, a situation, a dialogue, a picture or any other creative ideas that help students connect the form, meaning and function of the target vocabulary and structures. Many of these techniques will receive more attention in future skill chapters. For now, by way of providing a brief introduction to a speaking lesson, a more in-depth example of one way of presenting new language will be provided.

One effective way of introducing new vocabulary or lexis (i.e., multi-word units) is to try to elicit the target language from the learners before present it. Eliciting new words is good practice because it allows you to assess what students already know at the same time as activating their background knowledge about the topic. You can elicit vocabulary by showing them realia (authentic materials and items) or pictures and asking "what's this?" You could also brainstorm with learners about the topic as a way of drawing out the words they already know from them.

With regard to presenting new grammar, it is a good idea to decide upon the minimum amount of information that learners will need to understand how the grammar structure works. Before you attempt to teach a grammar point, you will probably need to learn more about its structure, meaning and function. You can do this by finding several clear and succinct reference books that have been written for English teachers. Read the explanations and do some internet searching for additional clarification and helpful instructional videos. This study should give you a clearer sense of the how the language is structured, what it means and when it is used appropriately. One of the obvious advantages of a PPP lesson structure over task-based approaches is that you can take it day by day and slowly build up your knowledge of English grammar with each lesson as you go.

One word of caution. Once you have worked out how the grammar point functions, do not be tempted to share all of your hard-earned new knowledge with your learners. In general, you will want to avoid too much grammar explanation because it can be off-putting for many learners and it is often unnecessary for them to be able to learn to use the structure in their L2 communication. As a general rule, the younger the learner, the less grammar explanation they should get. With that said, even older learners usually benefit more from actually seeing lots of examples of the target language in input and output activities rather than hearing lengthy grammar explanations.

One helpful suggestion for presenting a new grammar structure is called a situational presentation of a grammar point. An example of using a situational approach to teach the future conditional structure "If I …, I would …" is as follows: You could show a picture of someone holding a lottery ticket waiting to hear the numbers. Explain that this is your friend John. Ask "what is he doing? Students will answer "trying to win the lottery." Write the structure "_______ I had a lot of money, I _______ buy a sports car and a big house" on the board. Try to get the class to fill in the blanks.

The point of this exercise is not necessarily to elicit the target structure. Instead, it is to push students to wonder "Hmm, how would I say that in English?" Their asking themselves this question creates a communicative need where they want to fill in this gap in their knowledge. When they are told the correct structure, they can feel a powerful sense of realization or a kind of "a-ha" moment. This moment of insight may cause the structure to stay in their memory. Once students have been introduced to the grammar concept, it can be helpful to ask them several comprehension check questions (CCQ) to ensure that they understand the important elements of the new grammar structure. Comprehension check questions are explained in greater depth in chapter three.

After learners have become acquainted with the basic form, meaning and use of the newly introduced structure, it is important to provide them with opportunities to practice the new language through various activities. Practice allows learners to begin using the new language in controlled circumstances with a focus on producing the new language accurately. Practice activities also provide the repetition of the new structures necessary from them to be remembered. Some examples of the wide assortment of activity types available for practice is gap-fill or finding errors in written sentences among many others. The unique advantage of written exercises is that they allow learners to work at their own pace and really take their time to ponder some of the finer points of the new structure.

Others types of practice activities rely more on oral production. These oral activities include pairs reciting scripted dialogues or classroom oral drills such as repetition, backward buildup, substitution, transformation and question and answer drills. When learners seems to have gained a firm grasp on the new structure through drilling, you may move on to less controlled activities like information gap.

Basically, an information gap is an activity where one learner has some information and her partner has other information. The aim of the activity is for the learners to use the new target language to exchange this information with each other while also practicing the new structures. An example of an information gap can be seen in table 2.1 below. In this example, student A and B have to ask and answer questions like "What is Rick's favorite sport?" to find out the information missing from their table that their partner has. Information gaps have been found to be particularly helpful for encouraging all learners to talk while also scaffolding the language they will need to talk (Kayi, 2006).

Table 2.2 Example of an information gap activity

Example dialog:
Student A: What is Lee's favorite sport?
Student B: Rick likes karate.

	Favorite sport	Favorite food	Favorite pet
Rick	Hockey		Lizard
Lee		Fried chicken	
Diane	Soccer		Cat

Student B: What is Rick's favorite sport?
Student A: Rick likes hockey.

	Favorite sport	Favorite food	Favorite pet
Rick		Pizza	
Lee	Karate		Dog
Diane		Hamburgers	

Another example of a practice activity is games. These can include games like "20 Questions," "Jeopardy," "Find Someone Who" among literally hundreds of others. There are a number of unique benefit of games. For one thing, games encourage meaningful communication among learners (A. Wright, Betteridge, & Buckby, 1984) that offers them chances to integrate the four language skills (Lee, 1995). As they interact during the game, learners also practice important language functions like disagreeing politely while simultaneously learning how to cooperate with peers (Jacobs & Liu, 1996). In addition to these linguistic benefits, games promote student enjoyment (Bransford, Brown, & Cocking, 1999), team spirit, and foster healthy competition (Orlick, 2006). All of these emotional benefits in turn appear to help lessen students' language learning anxiety (Richard-Amato, 1988).

The final stage of a PPP lesson is the production stage. This is when learners have the opportunity to use all the L2 language resources they have at their disposal to communicate to the best of their ability. This stage was missing from traditional language teaching methods like audiolingualism and teachers soon realized that while students were able to use language structures in the classroom, when they attempt to actually use the target language, they had significant difficulty communicating effectively (Xia, 2016). Their inability to communicate in real contexts was likely due to their not having a script that they could follow as they did in their language classes. Therefore, we now realize that students need chances to use the target language in the language lesson in less structured activities.

The production stage of the lesson could be compared to scrimmage in basketball or soccer. While it is not a competitive game, it gives the players the chance to try out some of the skills they have been practicing in their drills in a less predictable environment that more closely matches the situation they will face in a competitive match. The same is true for language learners who eventually have to face the hurly-burly of real conversation. Production activities can help them to prepare for the L2 communication situations that they will eventually have to face beyond the classroom.

Another considerable benefit of language production activities is that they push students to use the new language for their own authentic reasons to express their own meanings. These activities often relate to students' own real lives which personalizes the lesson for learners and thus makes it more comprehensible and engaging. As mentioned above, these activities are usually unscripted or semi-scripted and the focus is on fluency rather than accuracy. As a result, the language learners produce during these activities oftentimes won't be as articulate as we would like. However, giving learners changes to participate in production activities is vital in order for them to automatize their language (Ur, 2018) in addition to developing their psycholinguistic capabilities such as noticing, linguistic hypothesis testing and reformulation as well as the discourse competence required to successfully navigate real target language use situations (Criado, 2013).

Information gaps are a classic example of the kinds of activities that learners should do at the production stage of the lesson. However, these kinds of information gaps differ from those used at the practice stage in that they should be somewhat less structured and controlled. These information gaps should allow learners to have more flexibility to produce their own language rather than using language supplied by the teacher or materials. An example of a less-controlled information gap activity is one where pairs of learners have two different versions of a grid with general information about people such as their job, hobbies, where they live etc. They would each have information that their partner does not. Their task is to make up their own questions and answers to find out the information that they do not have.

Table 2.3 Example of a less-controlled information gap activity

Student A			
	Lives	**Job**	**Hobbies**
Rick	San Diego		Karate
Lee		Photographer	
Diane	Toronto		Reading

Student B			
	Lives	**Job**	**Hobbies**
Rick		Teacher	
Lee	Vancouver		Play hockey
Diane		Nurse	

Role plays are another useful activity at this stage. They are in some ways more challenging than an information gap because the learners have less guidance on what language they have to produce while also having considerably more freedom to talk about whatever they want. Role play has the additional advantage that it offers a wide (almost limitless) number of scenarios that you could devise that will allow learners to practice a variety of speech events language such as interviews, discussions or debates (J. C. Richards, 1985) that they may otherwise not have the chance to use during regular classroom activities. However, some learners may struggle to engage in this activity if they have not been prepared for it beforehand. By way of preparation, providing learners with role cards can give them a clearer sense of how they can plan and structure what they want to say.

Cooperative learning tasks are also commonly used production activities. One illustration of these sorts of tasks is a jigsaw activity. For this task, learners are first placed into a home group where they are given a section of a longer text.

The group has to read, discuss and agree on the main ideas of that section as well as the meaning of any unknown vocabulary. Once all of the home groups have done this, they groups are reorganized into jigsaw groups that each contain one member from each of the home groups. When the new groups are formed, the members must each take turns explaining the section of the text that their home group was responsible for. A distinctive advantage of cooperative learning activities is that in addition to developing their L2 proficiency and content knowledge (Liang, Mohan, & Early, 1998), they also cause "increased self-esteem, greater liking for school, enhanced inter-ethnic ties, and improved complex thinking" (Jacobs, 2004, p. 8).

A final example of a production activity is a group decision-making task. These kinds of tasks include those where learners have to discuss and agree on items to use on a desert island. They tend to elicit a variety of important language functions such as explaining one's ideas, arguing one's point with evidence, and disagreeing politely among others. A unique benefit of using decision-making tasks is that while learners develop their L2 ability, they can also improve their higher order thinking skills (Chinnery, 2014).

The concluding stage of the lesson is the consolidation. This is where learners will review the content of the class and connect it to what will come in the following class. As you review the class through a brief quiz or class discussion, you will also want to assess whether you were able to meet all of your objectives. Those objectives that were not met will need to be re-presented or practiced more. The consolidation phase will also include assigning any homework planned to reinforce new skills. After quickly reviewing the lesson, you should connect it to the next class with a brief preview of what is to come. Lastly, you might want to wrap-up the lesson with a fun activity such as a puzzle or a brief game to keep motivation high and have learners looking forward to the next class.

2.9 Enrichment and remediation

In addition to the lesson procedures, you will also want to keep in mind the need for student enrichment and remediation. Some students will probably need extra input to bring their prerequisite knowledge up to where the majority of the other students in the class are. In this case, the learner may simply be less familiar with the subject matter being discussed in the lesson. For example, if the class is talking about animals on a farm and a learner has never been on a farm they may need a bit of extra attention. Activities that could facilitate this would include providing direct experiences (e.g., field trips) or access to comprehensible resource books, websites or online videos that the learner can access to build his background knowledge related to the content of the lesson (Fisher, Frey, & Lapp, 2012).

Instead of building their background knowledge, others will need more practice with the language and/or skills presented in the lesson to ensure that they can achieve the lesson objectives. Additional practice opportunities can be incorporated into the lesson through including extra grammar or pronunciation items or exercises. Likewise, simplified materials that may also include some brief L1 explanations or glosses can offer learners the extra little bit of information that they need to better follow the lesson. Some learners may even benefit from teacher or peer assistance as they begin to come to grips with unfamiliar or challenging concepts.

Other learners may progress through the lesson and meet objectives much faster than anticipated. In this case, the teacher will need follow up enrichment activities that allow the learner to further develop and expand upon what she learned in the lesson. Examples of such exercises, activities or tasks include logic puzzles, guessing the ending of a story with a twist or creative expression projects such as writing and illustrating an acrostic poem. Enrichment work should be slightly more challenging than the content of the regular lesson and not just more of the same work. It should also be engaging because if it is not students may come to see this as a punishment for finishing quickly and they may not want to strive for their best in future lessons.

2.10 Lesson assessment

Assessment is another import element that you should attempt to infuse into your entire lesson. The primary purposes of your assessment is to ensure that the students accomplish the lesson learning objectives (Chappuis & Stiggins, 2002), offer students feedback, diagnose their specific needs and provide information on whether and how you may need to adapt your materials and methods (R. J. Wilson, 1996). When you evaluate learners, you will usually want to assess their knowledge of all of the four skills (i.e., listening, reading, speaking, and writing) although, if the focus of your class is only on one or two skills (e.g., a reading and writing class) your assessments should mainly relate to those two skills.

Contrary to what many believe, the main function of learning objectives is for assessment purposes. That is, the objectives not only direct the activities of the class, they also serve as the standard that is used to ascertain whether those aims were achieved. Therefore, in the process of assigning classroom tasks, you will want to build classroom assessment into those tasks as much as possible. For example, when assigning a speaking information gap activity, you could devise a brief observational checklist that allows you to circulate and quickly determine whether the learners were able to perform the task and identify what problems they had to address those difficulties after the completion of the task or in a future lesson.

Another issue to bear in mind with regard to assessment is how to conduct integrated assessment. Integrated assessments allows you to evaluate student use of a combination of several L2 skills simultaneously. For example, using story retelling as an assessment of reading comprehension and speaking ability. These kinds of assessments are advantageous because they more closely reflect how the target language is used in authentic contexts.

As well, as mentioned above, the purpose of assessment is not solely to evaluate students. It also should be used as a tool to assess ourselves. That is, we should use assessment results when we reflect on and plan our lessons to increase their effectiveness. Ordinarily, when learners failed to perform well on a test, we blamed them. However, we need to realize that flaws in our instruction may better account for their performance. Thus, when we plan, we should review assessment data and use it to consider how we might present content more clearly or organize classroom activities that help learners to practice language skills more efficiently.

2.11 Informal classroom assessments

Informal classroom assessments have been characterized as assessment for learning rather than assessment of learning (Black, 1993). Stiggins (2002) clarifies the distinction as stating "If assessments of learning provide evidence of achievement for public reporting, then assessments for learning serve to help students learn more" (p. 61).Formative assessment can improve student learning because it occurs during instruction thus facilitating feedback and learning

(Shepard, 2003). In general, the purpose of informal assessment is to decide whether students are ready to move on to the next lesson. In contrast, the purpose of formal assessment (i.e., assessment for learning) is to make decisions about learners such as whether or not they should be admitted into a program, progress to the next level or be classified as an intermediate level of language proficiency (Bachman & Palmer, 1996).

A substantial amount of classroom assessment should be informal because these assessments provide you with immediate and ongoing and feedback on how learners have met your lesson objectives. Frequently, the best assessment tools you have are your eyes and ears as you closely observe learners performing tasks and determine whether they are accomplishing the lesson objectives. In addition to your own observations, there are a variety of more structured informal assessment tools that you can use to aid you in your decision making. There are a number of informal assessment tools that can be used to help you evaluate learner performance on each of the four language skills.

Oral proficiency development is a fundamental part of L2 learning. In the case of listening, one relatively straightforward assessment relies on learners' ability to physically demonstrate their comprehension through total physical response (TPR). A second possibility could be gap-fill or cloze where learners have to listen intensively and fill in the blank. These assessments allow us to evaluate learners' bottom up listening skills. A third more intensive option is dictation that encourages learners to activate bottom up listening skills as well noticing of target language features. Speaking can similarly be evaluated through a variety of methods. For instance, learners could do activities such as interviews, group discussions, debates, skits or presentations that can be recorded. These activities can be assessed through rubrics, observational checklists or even anecdotal records.

As with oral language, literacy is also necessary to ensure a well-rounded target language user. We can informally evaluate our learners' L2 reading proficiency using numerous tools that include running records, informal reading inventories, and response journals. Artwork, drama, and reading response journals can be other formative evaluation tools that we can use to provide us with a window into learners' comprehension of texts.

Feedback and guidance on writing can be provided in a number of ways as well. Dialogue journals between the teacher and student can reveal useful information to the teacher about the reading and writing strategies the student is more and less familiar with (Valdéz Pierce & O'Malley, 1992). She can then plan her future classes based on this information.

Portfolios that include samples of students' written work are other informal evaluation tools. These work samples can be collected and evaluated to provide feedback to the learners. Students should have some input into deciding what to include in a portfolio because the selection process can help them better internalize the criteria for quality work (Arter, 1995). Rubrics can also make writing more transparent so learners can feel less anxious about their planning and writing (Panadero & Jonsson, 2013). Conferences are another uniquely effective way to give feedback because they are a space where the students and teacher can discuss the writing and the teacher "responding in conferences is more effective than in writing because... the teacher, can interact dynamically with the students to understand the intent" (Sokmen, 1988, p. 5).

2.12 Formal tests

The second kind of assessment tool that teachers need to be familiar with is formal classroom tests. These tests are generally for the purposes of assessment of learning rather than assessment for learning. This difference is that their purpose is to make decisions about students such as their grade in a particular grading period or whether they can pass the course (Chappuis & Stiggins, 2002). These classroom tests generally break down into two types. The first is diagnostic whose purpose is to tell the teacher about the learner's relative strengths and areas of need (Brown, 2005). The second type measures learners' achievement on the four skills and language features such as vocabulary and grammatical knowledge. These tests include unit, midterm or final exams that are usually taken after a unit of study is complete.

Generally, formal tests are of two main types. Hughes (2007) explains that discrete point tests are the more traditional kind and are comprised of individual test items such as multiple choice. In contrast, integrative tests such as cloze or dictation ask test takers to blend several linguistic features to perform the task. It is beyond the scope of the present text to discuss the development of formal classroom tests in depth. However, texts by Brown (2005), Hughes (2007), and Fulcher (2013) can be helpful places to start for new teachers who are just beginning to learn about second and foreign language assessment.

2.13 Summary

Planning is a central element of successful language instruction. Without sufficient planning, lessons will be less purposeful, disordered, and wasteful of students' time. These chaotic lessons are sure to result in classroom management issues. On the other hand, effective lesson planning can help ensure that the teacher has a clear aim and path to get to it. Students can usually sense whether or not a teacher is prepared and not wasting their time. Often they respond accordingly.

This chapter provided an overview of some of the key issues associated with planning lessons in the ESL/ EFL classroom. To begin with, we looked at some of the reasons for planning such as the need for direction in the lesson. We then briefly touched on some important considerations in course planning such as giving thought to the syllabus, materials and methods that will be used. Following that, we then reviewed the lesson planning process which included creating lesson objectives and sequencing lesson activities. This process was then illustrated with an example speaking lesson. Some suggestions relating to lesson enrichment and remediation as well as informal and formal classroom assessment were also discussed.

SLA in Plain English

Chapter 3

Teaching Grammar and Vocabulary

Chapter 3

Teaching Grammar and Vocabulary

3.1 Introduction

This chapter covers vocabulary instruction which includes discussion of what it means to know a word, principles for teaching new vocabulary and lexis, the words we need to teach, and suggestions for activities to reinforce new vocabulary. Grammar pedagogy is also discussed beginning with a review of more established methods in teaching grammar which consist of explicit and deductive approaches as well as both implicit and inductive approaches. More recent developments in pedagogical grammar also receive some attention including corpus-informed grammar teaching, systemic functional linguistics and principled eclecticism.

The ability to present and reinforce new vocabulary and grammar structures is a foundational language teaching skill upon which other instructional competencies related to the teaching the four skills are built. It is exceedingly difficult to effectively facilitate the development of learners' listening, reading, speaking or writing proficiency if you struggle to teach them the actual language they must use to practice these skills. Thus, the following discussion of vocabulary instruction should prove useful when you have to decide what words you should teach as well as how to teach vocabulary in a variety of ways to keep learners engaged. It should also be helpful for deciding how to recycle and reinforce vocabulary that has been previously taught to students.

Likewise, the section on grammar instruction will acquaint you with the various options available for teaching grammar to many different types of learners so that you can adjust your instruction to better meet their specific needs. For example, if you are teaching learners who are younger and have less school experience, you will probably want to choose methods that rely more upon implicit and inductive learning rather than explicit and deductive learning which tends to be too abstract for young learners.

3.2 Knowing a word

Knowledge of a word includes many different aspects. Grabe (2009) points out that when we know a word, we have knowledge of its pronunciation, spelling, meaning, morphology, collocations, and linguistics register where it is most typically found. Given all of the various facets that are involved with learning a word, it makes sense that vocabulary knowledge is argued to follow along a continuum from knowing less about a word to knowing more about a word (Wesche & Paribakht, 1996). Knowledge of a word is therefore thought to be built up incrementally over time (Schmitt, 2008). This knowledge is obtained from exposure to the word across many different circumstances and seeing how the word functions in a variety of different texts (Fraser, 1999). Nevertheless, the fact that vocabulary knowledge is reinforced through exposure does not mean that some explicit instruction of vocabulary is not valuable. Indeed, explicit instruction of new vocabulary aids L2 learners' vocabulary acquisition (B. Laufer & Girsai, 2008).

3.3 Teaching new vocabulary

This section discusses how to teach new vocabulary words. An often recommended way to introduce new vocabulary is through attempting to elicit the word first. The benefits of eliciting are that in addition to activating the new vocabulary, learners' background knowledge related to the topic can also be stimulated in a learner-centered way (Darn, n.d.). Probably the most straightforward way to teach new vocabulary words especially if they are challenging is to simply to translate the new vocabulary word into the first language (Cook, 2002). A substantial amount of research shows that understanding the meaning in the first language is helpful for remembering new vocabulary (Jiang, 2004). Translation into the L1 is also particularly helpful when words are less central to the meaning of the text and it is difficult to convey their meaning through other means.

Visuals such as pictures, gifs, drawings, figures, and charts can be valuable resources for vocabulary instruction. Along with visuals, realia might more helpful because learners are able to see the actual object and physically handle it thus making their own mental connections as they interact with the object. As McGuire (2005) points out "realia, real objects and demonstrations used to augment or illustrate a lesson, can enliven a classroom, using the senses to involve the audience in what is being presented. The learning is natural and not forced" (p. 2).Related resources might also include the use of video games. As with realia, learners are able to interact with these resources and possibly make more mental connections in the process (Aghlara & Tamjid, 2011).

Miming and the use of body language and gestures can be helpful for conveying the meaning of new words as well. Body language can often be the most efficient way to show the meaning of the verbs or adverbs. As well, the teacher does not have to be the only one using body language to express meaning. The students can also reinforce the meaning themselves through the body language. For example activities such as total physical response (TPR) and games that illustrate the meaning of certain words such as playing the game the duck, duck goose to illustrate the meeting of the verb "chase."

As learners advance in their proficiency, other ways to teach vocabulary that is more suited to intermediate level learners and beyond become options. For example, explanation of the target vocabulary item in the second language becomes increasingly possible. Ideally, this explanation should be phrased in language that is simpler and easier to understand than the word being taught. This explanation can use synonyms or antonyms to help clarify the meaning. The greatest benefit of using the target language to explain the target language is that learners benefit from both learning the new vocabulary item as well as getting additional comprehensible input through the L2 explanation.

Listening to stories and reading can be powerful methods to acquire new vocabulary incidentally. Based on the results of their research, Mason, Vanata, Jander, Borsch and Krashen (2008) conclude that listening to stories is an efficient and enjoyable way to learn new vocabulary. Similarly, reading texts that contain comprehensible input can be a very effective way to learn new vocabulary as well. If the students know most of the words in a text (i.e., 95-98%), it is very likely that they will be able to guess the meaning of unknown words that they see in that text (Hu & Nation, 2000). Achieving this kind of high proportion of known words in a text for L2 readers is usually possible through using graded readers (Krashen, 2004). Thus, learners can begin with graded readers and as they acquire more target language vocabulary through reading they can gradually move on to more challenging texts (McQuillan, 2016).

Songs and chants are an enjoyable and memorable way that we can introduce new vocabulary to learners. Murphey (2013) points out a number of important advantages of using songs and music in our classes. Some of their main benefits are that it can teach rhythm and timing and pronunciation in a pleasurable way that is often easier for learners to remember. Songs allow for natural repetition that is much more enjoyable for learners than attempting the same amount of repetition with other kinds of listening texts (Purcell, 1992). It is also quite easy to integrate dance and gestures with songs to the benefit of kinesthetic learners.

Whatever method is selected to introduce and teach new vocabulary and lexis, it is also important to vocabulary instruction is followed by concept check questions (CCQs) that allow us to confirm students' understanding of the meaning of keywords that have been presented (Darn & White, n.d.). Briefly, concept check questions allow the teacher to ascertain whether and how well students grasped the central aspects of the meaning of a word or target structure. They will be discussed in greater depth in the grammar section below.

3.4 Words we need to teach

Traditionally, there has not been enough focus on teaching vocabulary (Laufer, 1986; Meara, 1980). However, this attitude has changed in recent years with teachers and scholars increasingly recognizing that words are central to text meaning. Indeed, Wilkins (1972) observed that "...while without grammar very little can be conveyed, without vocabulary nothing can be conveyed" (pp. 111–112). This is why it is so important to take time to focus on vocabulary instruction. However, when teaching vocabulary it is important not to spend too much time on low frequency vocabulary (Leech, Rayson, & Wilson, 2001). As language teachers, we need to decide what the most important words are to teach and how we can teach those words. As discussed above, one of the best tools for helping us to decide which words we should teach is word frequency lists taken from either spoken or written corpora (Nation, 2006). We can use these lists to tell us which words are the most common and that will lead to the most efficient learning when we teach them in the classroom.

According to Grabe (2009), there are three "tiers" of vocabulary that require our attention. First, we should not spend too much time teaching low-frequency non-essential vocabulary. That is, we ought not to use much class time teaching vocabulary that students will not encounter often in their listening or reading. Thus, Grabe contends that we should teach the most frequent 300 words first. These words act as a glue that holds the language together and can be touchstones that learners can use to make sense of text because they will be found in almost every text learners will encounter.

The second tier of words learners should be taught are the words from 300 to 1500 in terms of their frequency. The third tier of words we should teach run from the 1500 most frequent to the 2500 most frequent. Grabe (2009) claims that these should be taught "whenever opportunity arises and it is reasonable to do so" (p. 280). Thus, this third tier of words does not necessarily have to have the same amount of focus as the other two and may be taught a bit more opportunistically. Accordingly, the words we should focus on in teaching explicitly are essentially the 1500 most frequent words in English while devoting some time to the range of words from 1500 to 2500 in terms of frequency. Beyond this, we should give students multiple exposures to a wide variety of vocabulary through extensive reading, learning content through English, discussing words that they encounter, encouraging them to collect words that are interesting and relevant to them, and teaching them strategies such as memorizing flashcards that will help them to learn vocabulary on their own. Beyond that, based upon his review of relevant research, Grabe also recommends teaching the most frequent 6000 words in English from several word lists such as Coxhead's (2000) Academic Word List and Nation's (2004) British National Corpus Word List.

When selecting new vocabulary to teach, we also have to make the distinction between teaching the word and teaching the concept behind the word. If the students who are already understand the concept when they learn an unknown word then they are simply learning a new label for an idea they already have. However, if they do not know the concept behind the word they will have to be taught that as well. Thus, when considering the materials to use and vocabulary to teach to our learners, we should also bear in mind that some concepts may be beyond their intellectual level. For example, attempting to explain the concept of exploitation to third graders would a lost cause. A workable rough criterion is that if they do not know the word or concept in their first language, it may be too difficult for them.

3.5 Activities to reinforce new vocabulary

After vocabulary has been initially presented, learners still need opportunities to work with the new vocabulary and recycle it several more times until it becomes part of their repertoire. Some research has identified that learners typically need to meet many new words anywhere from 7 to 20 times before those words become part of their personal lexicon (Brown, Waring, & Donkaewbua, 2008; Pigada & Schmitt, 2006). Accordingly, what are some activities that learners can do to reinforce this new vocabulary?

One way they can begin to reinforce new vocabulary is through the use of games as vocabulary learning methods. Some examples of these sorts of methods include matching words with definitions, completing crossword puzzles, word searches, acrostics or gap-fill activities (Uberman, 1998). In addition to these vocabulary games, learners can choose activities that help them make connections and associations among words. Some examples of these activities include creating word webs, or brain storming word associations through the creation of semantic maps (Hippner-Page, 2002).

A third type of vocabulary reinforcing activities for learners is through paired-associate learning activities. These include doing spaced repetition practice with flash cards or flashcard apps (e.g., Anki). Flashcards are quite straightforward to make. Nation and Webb (2011) recommend that learners simply have the L2 word on one side of the card and an L1 translation on the other. With smartphone apps, learners can review the words at their leisure. The advantage of spaced repetition apps is that when the learner correctly recalls the word the interval until the next time she sees it gets increasingly longer and longer. In the classroom, learners can also play memory flash card games such as taboo or matching pairs of cards that are laid face down on the desk (Toma, Alexandru, Dascalu, Dessus, & Trausan-Matu, 2016).

Lastly, learners could do vocabulary reinforcement activities that are more personalized. One example of these types of activities could be extensive reading of self-selected material. Extensive reading has been demonstrated to benefit L2 learners in various ways including improved overall L2 proficiency and vocabulary learning (Krashen, 2011). Using journals that include personalized dictionaries of words that they would like to learn can be an effective tool for remembering vocabulary as well (Cobine, 1995). As all of these various activities that draw on games, word association, flashcards, and personalized tasks demonstrate, L2 teachers have a wealth of activities at their disposal to teach and reinforce new vocabulary in the second and foreign language classroom.

3.6 Teaching lexis

When teaching vocabulary, we also need to consider how to teach words beyond the word level. That is, how words associate with each other. For example, we should teach collocations which are frequently used two or more word combinations that sound right (Walter, 2008). We also need to teach lexical phrases which are "conventionalized structures that occur more frequently and have more idiomatically determined meaning than language that is put together each time" (Nattinger, 1986, p. 3). Besides these, we should spend some time talking with students about metaphors and idioms. As Hill (2000) points out, teaching lexis is important for many reasons with a primary reason being that "the way words combine in collocations is fundamental to all language use" (p. 53). She adds that a large proportion of authentic text is comprised of multiword units. Knowledge of collocations enables us to think and communicate more fluently in the target language.

A number of different methods have been suggested for raising learner awareness of lexis. Many of the activities for teaching vocabulary discussed in the previous section can also be used for teaching lexis. As well, some other activities that are more specific to the teaching of lexis can be added to these. Examples of these types of activities include matching words with collocates, completing grids or diagrams, or using lexical items to complete a task like writing an example sentence or drawing a related picture (Scrivener, 2011). Other helpful lexical practice activities include finding collocations in texts, paraphrasing collocations, finding collocates for synonyms, word sorts, and translating collocations (Hill, Lewis, & Lewis, 2000).

3.7 Principles of teaching vocabulary

To conclude the vocabulary section of this chapter, it is worthwhile to discuss some general principles of vocabulary instruction that teachers should bear in mind. First, we need to be aware of what vocabulary we should focus on teaching. We must remember to focus more on high frequency words so that students will be able to see the words they are learning more frequently in their input (Grabe, 2009). As a result, they will be able to effectively use those words when they tried to communicate themselves.

Language teachers should also have a firm understanding of how to students learn vocabulary and how it can be efficiently taught. Students learn both implicitly and explicitly so we should teach words both explicitly and implicitly (Ellis, 1995). This means that we should directly to teach the meaning of some words and expose students to a wide variety of comprehensible input activities like extensive reading to allow them to come into contact with a variety of other types of vocabulary that they can learn incidentally (Krashen, 2004). We should also teach new words before students will need them. For example, we can teach each key vocabulary item for a speaking lesson or prior to reading a particular text. Pre-teaching key vocabulary in this way will facilitate activation of learners' topic-related background knowledge and improve their text comprehension (Nation, 2001). When explaining new vocabulary we need to remember to keep it clear and simple using easy rather than difficult words (National Reading Panel, 2000). Relatedly, we should present new vocabulary through a wide variety of methods such as oral, written, translated, visually among others. Additionally, "...methods should be varied and combined according to the learner's individual needs and preferences" (Levine & Reves, 1990, p. 45). Thus, exposure to various forms of the target vocabulary will benefit both learners with many different learning styles.

After we have presented vocabulary to learners, they will also need many opportunities to use learning strategies to strengthen their vocabulary knowledge through engaging in activities that cause them to process vocabulary more deeply such as creating mental images. Memory strategies that draw upon deep semantic processing work better than rote repetition that only encourages shallow processing (O'malley & Chamot, 1990). To ensure that learners retain the new vocabulary, we should recycle previously taught lexis with spaced repetition. As mentioned previously, teachers do not recycle vocabulary enough to help learners retain it (Tomlinson, 2008). We need to remember that just because we have taught word once does not mean we should not revisit it multiple times to give students chances to gradually come to understand its meaning and recall it better (Nakata, 2008).

Lastly, we will want to foster learner autonomy by encouraging them to use dictionaries and collect in review vocabulary that is relevant to their lives and interests. We also need to teach learners to figure out the meaning of words in context (Nation, 2001). Giving learners access to these kinds of self-study tools can make them more independent and allow them to continue to learn vocabulary beyond our classroom (Wright, 1998).

3.8 Teaching grammar

Grammar instruction has traditionally been the primary focus of language teaching. Larsen-Freeman and Anderson (2013) point out that both the grammar translation and audiolingual methods had a strong focus on grammar although the grammar translation method included explicit instruction of grammar rules while the audiolingual method relied upon implicit learning of rules through pattern practice drills. They add that with the advent of communicative and task-based language teaching, there was a movement away from grammar instruction to focus more upon meaning.

More recently, there has been increasing acknowledgement of the vital role of grammar instruction in L2 teaching and learning. Even within communicative approaches that tend to placeless emphasis on grammar, grammar practice is finding its way back into their lessons (Azar, 2007).

Thus, as an English teacher, it is worthwhile to be aware of some of the options that are available to you for facilitating your learners' English grammar development. Several different approaches to grammar instruction have been developed over the years that you can choose from based on your beliefs and preferences for how you think English grammar is most effectively learned. The following section will review some of the more commonly used grammar instruction methods.

3.9 The deductive approach

The deductive approach is the more traditional method of teaching grammar. It is commonly associated with the grammar translation approach to language teaching (Larsen-Freeman & Anderson, 2013). Essentially, the deductive approach has the teacher explicitly explain the grammar rule. This rule explanation is commonly given in the learners' L1. After listening to the teacher's explanation of the rule, learners then practice the rules through activities such as fill in the blanks for various types of grammar drills like substitution or transformation drills (Norris & Ortega, 2000). Recently, deductive grammar teaching has come to be associated with the present-practice-produce (PPP) approach to language teaching (Ur, 2018). It is represented by the "present" part of the approach where learners our first taught the form, meaning and use of the target structure. In the

PPP approach, after students learn the rules, they then practice the rule through activities such as gap fills and drills.

There are a number of unique benefits for teachers and students when a deductive approach to teaching grammar is used. First, it allows teachers make their point quickly without having to waste time going through elaborate activities analyzing examples in an effort to lead students to work out the rule for themselves (Krashen, 1982). Secondly, because the teacher saves time explaining the rules up front rather than having learners try to decipher it themselves, they can have more time to do exercises, activities or tasks that practice the rules (Widodo, 2006).

Thornbury (1999) points out several other advantages of a deductive approach to grammar instruction. The deductive approach to grammar instruction respects students' intelligence. It sends the message to learners that while the teacher knows the grammar complex and abstract, the teacher believes the learners can handle it. This approach also aligns with many learners' expectations about what should be happening in the classroom. They believe that their English teacher should know about English grammar and to be able to explain what she knows clearly. Thus, when we explain a grammar point clearly, we meet their expectations and demonstrate our competence as an English teacher. If the prospect of this requiring grammar knowledge intimidates you take heart. Another considerable benefit of a deductive approach is that you only need to know the grammar point you will explain in the lesson. Therefore, you can build your grammar knowledge piece by piece as you learn about each grammar structure before teaching it to your learners (Scrivener, 2011).

Although the deductive approach has some clear benefits, it also has several drawbacks that you should take into consideration. For one, it can feel more mechanical to learners because the meaning of the language may receive less emphasis. As a result, learners may find deductive practice to be uninteresting (Spratt, 1999). Likewise, the grammar presented during deductive lessons can be somewhat isolated and decontextualized. Work with such decontextualized language may cause learners to fail to learn appropriate sociolinguistic uses of the target structures (Larsen-Freeman, 2015). Thornbury (1999) mentions some other bothersome features of deductive explanations are that they may contain technical terminology and concepts that make them difficult to understand and remember. They also tend to be quite teacher centered and thus restrict learner participation. Both of these shortcomings may contribute to learner frustration in the grammar classroom.

3.10 Implicit and inductive approaches to grammar instruction

In contrast to deductive approaches to grammar instruction where the teacher explains the grammar rules to the learners is the inductive or implicit approaches to teaching L2 grammar. In implicit approaches, the teacher exposes learners to plenty of comprehensible input and they acquire the rule (Krashen, 1982). In this instance, acquisition is claimed to occur naturally without any reflection on the grammar rule. Implicit learning is based on the notion that we acquire our second language in a similar way as we acquire our first language. That is without learning explicit rules. It is thought that exposure to complete texts such as stories and songs learners will enable learners to naturally acquire the language in the texts that is at their next stage of development provided that these texts are comprehensible (Krashen & Terrell, 1983).

Implicit approaches differs somewhat from inductive approaches. Inductive approaches end up with learners having conscious knowledge of the grammar rule (Gollin, 1998). They gain this conscious knowledge from analyzing and discussing with other students examples of the grammar rule. That is, the teacher gives the learners several example sentences for the rule and the students have to work out what the rule is for themselves rather than be told by the teacher as with deductive approaches (Norris & Ortega, 2000). Inductive approaches are argued to be more effective because proponents claim that when the learner has to work out the rule for herself, she will be better able to understand and remember it (Thornbury, 1999). Some research shows that inductive approaches benefit learners in terms of exposing them to meaningful language in context and gradually guiding their understanding of the new structures (Haight, Herron, & Cole, 2007).

A number of advantages have been identified for inductive grammar instruction. First, the cognitive processing required to extrapolate grammar rules forces the learner to process the language on a deeper level that helps the new grammar knowledge enter their long term memory (Thornbury, 1999). Secondly, having learners develop their own grammar rules from examples allows them participate in the class more actively (Widodo, 2006). This active participation can improve their motivation because instead of their having to passively listen to a lecture, they can actively work to make sense of the new language themselves. A final advantage of inductive grammar instruction is that it can make learners more autonomous and self-reliant (Thornbury, 1999). This self-reliance is possible because giving learners opportunities to discover grammar rules for themselves helps them to realize they can decipher target language grammar with minimal teacher input. Thus, they also obtain the additional benefit of realizing that they can learn the target language independently.

In addition to the advantages of inductive grammar instruction, there are several shortcomings that should be noted. Thornbury (1999) identifies some possible limitations of an inductive approach. First, inductive grammar activities can be considerably more time consuming then a brief explanation of the grammar rule with a few examples. Second, learners may erroneously interpret example sentences they are given and arrive at an incorrect understanding of the grammar rule. Without appropriate input from the teacher, they may persist in their misunderstanding. Widodo (2006) adds a few more limitations with this approach. A third disadvantage is that a technique that asks learners to figure out grammar rules for themselves maybe quite frustrating for some learners. That is, learners who are younger or have limited academic language learning experience may struggle to do these tasks and express considerable displeasure with having to do them. A final disadvantage of the method is that it can be quite time consuming to create the necessary scaffolding task materials. At present, there are not many course books that use an inductive approach to teach grammar so teachers who would like to use this approach would have to design and create a lot of the associated classroom materials themselves. Creating these materials from scratch would put additional strain on many teachers' already demanding schedules.

3.11 Recent developments in pedagogical grammar

In addition to the deductive and inductive approaches to grammar instruction, there are a number of newer developments in L2 grammar pedagogy that warrant some discussion. For instance, the notion of noticing is a somewhat more recently developed concept related to grammar instruction. It is based on the claim that in order for second language input to become intake and enter the learner's interlanguage system some feature of the input must be noticed (Schmidt, 1990).

That is, the features of the input that get noticed are those that get learned or acquired. Jones and Lock (2011) point out that teachers' primary aim in promoting noticing involves drawing students' attention to key features of the target language to "raise learners' awareness of how differences in grammatical forms express differences in meaning"(p. 3). They argue that the target language should be challenging for students, but they also need scaffolds to support their noticing. Teachers can accomplish this aim by having learners engage in activities such as comparing, sequencing, gap filling, restructuring, elaborating and transforming sample texts.

Consciousness raising (CR) is another approach to grammar instruction that is similar noticing. In essence, CR consists of activities that the teacher can use to promote the noticing of particular second language features like grammatical morphemes. The main difference between CR and noticing is consciousness raising aims to develop learners' explicit knowledge of target structures but not necessarily their ability to use the target structure in their communication. However, after doing consciousness raising activities, it is hoped that learners will be able to notice a target feature in input (Ellis, 1997). Cross (2002) also points out that "...a key difference between noticing and consciousness raising is that noticing has supposed implications for language processing and the actual acquisition of linguistic features" (para. 2). Thus, while consciousness raising does not assume learners will necessarily have acquired the target grammar structure noticing assumes that they will have.

Ellis (2002) argues that "consciousness-raising ...involves an attempt to equip the learner with an understanding of a specific grammatical feature - to develop declarative rather than procedural knowledge of it" (p. 167). He states that the main features of CR activities are that (1) a specific linguistic feature receives focused attention. (2) Learners analyze a language sample containing the target structure that may be accompanied by an explanation of the relevant grammar rule. (3) Learners reflect on the information supplied to comprehend the target structure. (4) Any points of confusion are clarified with additional examples or explanation. (5) Learners may also try to summarize their understanding of the new grammar rule. An example of consciousness raising task would be having learners read a text that contains a particular English tense structure and decide what the form of the tense is, what it means and why it is used in the text.

CR is generally assumed to be a part of a lesson structure that is somewhat different than the traditional present-practice-produce (PPP) lesson format. While the PPP format decides what structures to teach in advance, the CR approach is more responsive to issues that arise during task-based lessons (Ellis, 2002). Thus, CR is typically based upon a task based lesson format. While learners are completing a task, they may experience some difficulties expressing themselves due to grammatical errors. The teacher can select a commonly-occurring error. The teacher can then do a consciousness raising activity in a future lesson that helps learners to better understand the problematic structure.

Processing instruction is another recently developed approach to grammar instruction Based upon the work of Bill VanPatten. Input processing asks how we mentally transform the flow of language input that we receive into knowledge of the target language or intake. Intake is defined as input that learners pay attention to and from which form-meaning connections have been made (VanPatten, 1996a). Thus, we seek to know "...under what conditions learners may or may not make connections between a form in the input and a meaning, and the processes they initially bring to the task of acquisition" (VanPatten, 2004, p. 6). However, this model does not describe how these connections are permanently integrated via restructuring into the learner's interlanguage for future output.

Input processing researchers contend that we turn input into intake through input processing which uses classroom activities that encourage learners make form-meaning connections between target structures in the input and their meaning. Input processing activities are necessary because forging form-meaning connections is difficult. L2 learners tend to remember the meaning of input but not the form so the form is typically not processed. Therefore, teachers need to find ways to help the learners focus on the form and meaning at the same time (VanPatten, 1996a).

Input becomes intake through input processing and input processing is argued to happen as a result of processing instruction. Processing instruction uses structured input activities to draw learners' attention to grammar structural forms in reading or listening texts that they would ordinarily not pay attention to (VanPatten, 2004). That is, processing instruction pushes the learner to make form-meaning connections in interactions with input that would not otherwise be made.

Lee and VanPatten (2003) define structured input as "input that is manipulated in particular ways to push learners to become dependent on form and structure to get meaning" (p. 142). For example, learners might be presented with a sentence like "Susan played hockey" and they would have to indicate whether the activity occurred now or in the past. Since there are no other linguistic clues that the event is happening in the past like adverbs of time (e.g., yesterday), the learner is pushed to pay attention to the –ed morpheme and process it as indicating that the event happened in the past.

In this way, structured input activities use example sentences with language in them is organized so that the learner is forced to notice target grammar structure (in this case the past tense morpheme) and reflect on its meaning. This pushing of form-meaning connections can be achieved through a number of tasks such as matching, binary options (e.g., True/False), ranking etc.

3.12 Corpus-informed grammar teaching

Corpora is becoming an increasingly popular and effective tool for teaching vocabulary. In his review of relevant research literature, Smart (2012) enumerates the many specific benefits that teachers can gain from using corpora in their classes. For example, corpora can provide more accurate descriptions of grammatical patterns than the intuitions that grammar "rules" in textbooks are often based upon. Corpus data likewise puts learners in touch with contextualized authentic language from a variety of genres or registers. As well, once learners have a clear sense of how to analyze corpus data, they can then begin to identify linguistic patterns themselves and learn autonomously. We can use corpora to learn about linguistic patterns such as word frequency, chunks (e.g., lexical phrases or idioms), collocations and concordances that show instances of a target lexical item in context (Reppen, 2010). In particular, the use of corpora has been found to be helpful in supporting English for specific purposes (ESP) instruction. Thomas and Short (1996) have noted that corpus data can be more informative than textbooks or field specialists in terms of providing accurate information about how the target language is actually used in a particular context or knowledge domain.

To aid in the analysis of these corpora, numerous corpus-based digital tools have been developed. Some examples of popular corpus-based tools include Lextutor, Backbone, Webcorp, AntConc, UAM Corpus Tool and Ludwig Guru. Many of these tools have a variety of functions which include the ability to generate word frequency counts that can tell the user whether the texts analyzed represent natural language samples in terms of how well they reflect the authentic usage of common words (Elorza & García-Riaza, 2010).

Most corpora also provide information about word collocations found in the corpus so users can search a corpus to find what other words collocate with a word they are interested in. Similarly, corpora typically provide a concordance with examples of a key word in context (KWIC). The KWIC feature allows the user to examine and compare many instances of the key word they are interested in within the context of many example sentences. N-Gram extractors are another tool that allow the user to search a corpus fora contiguous arrangement of words. This function can facilitate determining the acceptability of particular phrases that learners might be unsure of.

Classroom activities based on corpus data can help learners to analyze examples of a word or grammatical structure in the context of numerous sentences with a concordance (Donley & Reppen, 2001). Reppen (2010) mentions that students can search corpora to find word collocates that offer them a more refined sense of what other words a vocabulary item tends to appear with. She also points out that another powerful tool is the ability of most corpus software to allow learners to build a "self-made" corpus created from texts that the learner has chosen and uploaded to the corpus. The unique advantage of such a tool is that learners can collect texts for analysis that relate to one specific domain of knowledge and its associated language register.

Systemic functional linguistics (SFL) is an approach to second language grammar instruction that differs substantially from the approaches discussed above.I n this perspective, language is viewed as a social meaning making resource that we use to accomplish communicative purposes such as describing a scene, arguing a viewpoint or narrating a story (Knapp & Watkins, 2005). SFL promises certain unique advantages to learners over other views of grammar. Its advocates claim that SFL helps students determine the structure of various genres of speech and writing which in turn enables them to reproduce those genres (Hyland, 2004). This ability can be particularly helpful for learners who have had limited exposure to the genres of school and consequently struggle to produce academic spoken and written genres (Martin, 1992).

Several key principles of SFL distinguish it from other perspectives on language and grammar. For one, its proponents contend that language and grammar is shaped by the uses to which it has been put. As Halliday (1970) explains "the nature of language is closely related to the demands that we make on it, the functions it needs to serve" (p. 141). Secondly, SFL theorists claim that grammar is a system of interrelated choices from among structural alternatives that encode experiential, interpersonal, and textual meanings differently in users' utterances (Halliday & Matthiessen, 2004). Accordingly, less emphasis is placed on formal accuracy and more on how various linguistic forms can be employed to different effect depending on the social relationships, subject matter and medium used in the communication event. A third revealing insight of SFL is that grammar operates beyond the sentence level so unlike traditional grammars that tend to focus on clauses and sentences, SFL gives more serious consideration to issues like how coherence and cohesion are achieved in diverse text genres (Liamkina & Ryshina-Pankova, 2012).

In his discussion of using a genre-based pedagogy in second language writing, Hyland (2004) identified several classroom activities and techniques that are commonly associated with this approach. For instance, modelling text analysis and construction is recommended as an effective means to help learners distinguish various types of genres and identify the genre of an example text. Joint text analysis and construction of the unique linguistic features of a particular genre can provide learners with tools to reverse engineer sample texts into their component parts. Learners can then independently construct target language genres with the aid of scaffolds like graphic organizers that enable them to compare genres, name genre stages, and arrange genre stages in order.

3.13 Informed or principled eclecticism

The good news is that because teachers are not theoretical linguists we do not have to worry about being theoretically consistent in our teaching. We are able to experiment with a mix of methods, techniques and approaches and see what works best with our learners depending on their age, the structures being taught and other factors relevant to our teaching context (Larsen-Freeman & Celce-Murcia, 2015). Indeed, Azar (2007) reminds us that grammar instruction in the real world does not have to favor any particular method. She contends that it is preferable to be able to choose from traditionally conflicting approaches (e.g., deductive and inductive) depending on the grammar structure being taught. Spolsky (1989) adds that teachers should develop their own techniques through experimentation in their own classrooms rather than having methods forced upon them by outside "experts". This kind of approach allows them to better ensure that their classroom practices more closely connect to their learners' unique strengths and needs. Brown (1994) states that a growing number of language educators now "… recognize that the complexity of language learners in multiple worldwide contexts demands an eclectic blend of tasks each tailored for a particular group of learners in a particular place, studying for particular purposes in a given amount of time" (p. 74).

3.14 Summary

In this chapter, we reviewed some ideas for teaching vocabulary and grammar in the L2 classroom. Our discussion of vocabulary covered what it means to know a word, words we need to teach, as well as how to teach and reinforce new vocabulary and lexis. The section on grammar compared implicit and inductive approaches to teaching grammar with explicit and deductive approaches. Some newer approaches to teaching grammar were briefly introduced including processing instruction, corpus-based and systemic functional linguistics. The chapter concluded with a brief reflection on the value of an informed eclectic stance in grammar instruction.

Knowledge of how to teach grammar and vocabulary should help you in a number of ways. First, as an English teacher, you need to present the new lexis and grammar structures in a lesson because they are usually the focus of the lesson. Many teaching approaches (e.g., PPP or Task based) expect that you will be teaching grammar at some point in the lesson. As well, unlike in the CLT of days past, it is increasingly expected that you will be able to teach grammar confidently. Your employer may ask you to teach a grammar class or one with a large grammar component. You will need to be ready. Learners may also expect to be explicitly taught grammar. At least, they will presume that their English teacher can explain vocabulary and grammar in a way that makes sense to them. To accomplish this aim, you need to know a variety of techniques so that you can meet the diverse needs of your learners in helping them become more accurate and fluent speakers of the L2.

SLA in Plain English

Chapter 4

Teaching Listening and Speaking

Chapter 4
Teaching Listening and Speaking

4.1 Introduction

If you have not had much experience teaching English as a second or foreign language, it may seem daunting when you start thinking about how to organize your listening and speaking lessons. Fear not, this chapter will guide you through a series of well-defined steps that you can follow to help facilitate the planning process. The following paragraphs will outline the elements that you should include in your listening and speaking lessons as well as the sequence of steps you should follow when you teach a listening or speaking lesson. The chapter will also include a few activity suggestions that you might use for each part of the lesson. For listening lessons, we will look at what kinds of activities we should do before, during and after listening to a text. As for speaking lessons, we will consider activities that we can use to present, practice, and produce the target language of the lesson.

Effective listening and speaking lessons can help learners to internalize the L2 while enjoying the process. Listening and speaking are increasingly valued as the most sought-after skills of the modern language learner for compelling reasons. First, as rapid transit and online interconnection continues to shrink the world, face-to-face contact with speakers of English as a lingua franca becomes the norm. Oral English skills also allow learners to participate in these growing transnational and online communities. As well, more and more higher education instruction is happening in English so learners' oral ability becomes increasingly related to their future educational and employment opportunities.

You will be able to use the information presented in this chapter to more clearly structure your listening and speaking lessons. The chapter content should also help you to more accurately distinguish which activities are suitable for each of the stages of your listening and speaking lessons. As well, this information will enable you to reflect on and evaluate your listening and speaking lessons to decide what worked and what might need to be revisited.

4.2 Teaching listening

Listening is fundamental for communication in the L2 both in the L2 classroom and beyond. If the learner can speak with some degree of confidence in the L2 but is unable to understand what is being said to him communication simply cannot proceed. However, if he understands but has some difficulty speaking, limited communication can still take place because the learner understands what his interlocutor is saying and can probably find basic words and expressions to make himself understood. A second reason for the importance of listening comprehension is that oral language is a valuable source of comprehensible input through which learners can acquire more of the target language (Krashen, 1982). However, in order for them to use this input, learners need to understand most of the language in the messages that they are hearing (Renandya & Farrell, 2010). Improving listening ability can only facilitate learner access to comprehensible input. This understood input begins the virtuous cycle of comprehending input and using that input to further strengthen L2 ability.

4.3 Types of listening

Learners listen for a variety of different purposes in their daily life and when they learn another language. Brown (2000) divides listening into several different types. The first of these is reactive listening. Reactive listening is characterized by its focus on form over meaning. Examples of classroom activities that practice reactive listening include choral repetition and pronunciation drills. Reactive listening could be helpful for developing learners' ability to notice particular features of the L2. Another category of listening activity is intensive listening. These activities involve the learner listening to short texts in order to understand their content very well. In this type of activity the text would typically have a higher proportion of unknown language. Intensive listening is commonly done to introduce new language for a lesson. Examples of intensive listening classroom activities include dictation and oral drills.

A third kind of listening is known as responsive listening (Brown, 2000). In the case of responsive listening, the learner must listen and then provide some type of appropriate response. For example, the student listens to the teacher's command to walk to the front of the room and gives a brief response by following it. Responsive listening can be helpful for developing learners' ability to appropriately respond with short gambits in a conversation.

Selective listening guides the learner to process the listening passage to pick out key pieces of information that she needs to achieve her listening purpose. For instance, the teacher may play a text of airport flight announcement and the learner would have to listen and record key information such as flight and gate number. Another selective listening task would have leaners extract key information from the headlines of a news broadcast. This sort of listening work facilitates the learner's ability scan for and to pick out important information from longer stretches of text.

Extensive listing involves listening to longer passages such as stories. It is usually self-selected (e.g., self-access) and learners do it for pleasure. The aim is to understand the general gist of the story rather than the details. Therefore, comprehension questions typically do not accompany the passage. When choosing a text, it is best if the teacher tries to limit the number of unknown words to only less than 5% of the text by using adapted or simplified texts.

Brown's (2000) final form of listening is interactive. For interactive listening, the learner has to integrate all of the listening skills used in the other listening types. Some classroom activities that practice this skill include conversations or debates. These sorts of activities develop the learner's ability to integrate listening with the other language skills as well as become accustomed to more authentic listening interactions.

4.4 Listening strategies

In addition to exposing learners to different types of listening activities, it can also be helpful to acquaint them with a variety of listening strategies that they can use to perform better when they listen in authentic situations outside the classroom. Listening strategies are techniques learners can use that will help them to understand and recall listing content more effectively (Rost, 2013). Listening strategies have been classified in a number of ways but one categorization that draws on the work of Oxford (1990) as well as O'malley and Chamot (1990) may be helpful for those who had are trying to understand how the various strategies fit together. Under this configuration, there are three types of strategies that include metacognitive, cognitive and socio-affective.

Metacognitive strategies involve learners thinking about their thinking. Metacognitive strategies are defined as "...skills such as planning, monitoring, evaluating, and problem solving are used by learners to manage, regulate, and guide their learning" (Vandergrift, 2005, p. 74). Planning is a representative example of a metacognitive strategy because it demonstrates these strategies primary function of directing one's thought process. A related strategy is directed attention whereby learners consciously direct their attention to specific elements of a listening task such as listening for key words. Self-monitoring and self-evaluation are two more related meta-cognitive strategies. In this case, as learners perform the language task, they pay attention to how well they are doing and identify possible areas of difficulty.

O'Malley, Chamot, and Küpper (1989) point out that cognitive strategies are thinking strategies used during specific learning tasks whose purpose is to help the learner better manage the learning task. Examples of cognitive strategies are repeating, translating, taking notes, making inferences, and elaborating on information students are learning. Cognitive strategies benefit L2 learners because they involve rehearsal which promotes practice, organization which enriches understanding and remembering, as well as elaboration which connects the known with the new (O'Malley et al., 1989).

In addition to cognitive language learning strategies, there are also socio-affective strategies. These social strategies rely on tactics that encourage the learner to cooperate with her interlocutor like asking questions when the message becomes unclear to maximize mutual comprehensibility (Vandergrift, 1999). Socio-affective strategies also entail the learner attempting to control their emotions when anxiety levels raise during language learning or use situations. They do this through positive self-talk, and relaxation techniques (Rubin, 2001).

4.5 Approaches to teaching listening

Traditional approaches

Historically, listening instruction and practice did not receive much emphasis in the language classroom (Nunan, 2002). Previous approaches to conducting a listening lesson often left much to be desired. A typical approach to listening instruction in many contexts is one that resembles the testing of listening much more than the teaching of it (Nemtchinova, 2013). In essence, the teacher plays the tape, then present learners with comprehension questions that they answer individually after listening to the passage only once. When they were finished, the answers are checked by them being told if they were right or wrong. This approach to listening instruction is problematic for a number of reasons. First, it resembles testing more than teaching. At no point are learners actually taught skills and strategies for how to listen more effectively during that process. Furthermore, they receive no substantial feedback on how they could improve their listening based on their performance on the listening passage. That is, they are not encouraged to reflect upon their listening performance.

A suggested listening lesson structure

Over the years, insights from SLA and TESOL research have given us more insight into effective ways that L2 listening can be taught rather than only tested in the language classroom. Effective listening typically consist of before, during and after phases of the lesson. This lesson structure can also be used with a wide variety of during listening task types including listen and draw a picture, listen to a riddle and solve it among others. Now, let's have a closer look at each of the phases in the listening lesson sequence.

An important decision to be made in preparation for a listening lesson is the choice of the listening materials to be used. Indeed, selecting inappropriate materials can make all of our careful preparation for the listening lesson itself pointless. With regard to choosing suitable listening materials for our learners, Wilson (2008) discusses a number of factors that we need to keep in mind. Some of these factors directly relate to the language used in the text including its level, accent, and speed. Other text relevant text elements include its length, density and number of speakers in it. Still other concerns are less directly related to the language of the text such as learner interest and recording quality. You may also consider the authenticity of the materials in terms of whether they contain features of speech that we would expect in real communicative situations such as overlapping talk or background noise. Bear in mind that the lower the listening proficiency of the learner, the more likely they are to find these features to be a distraction.

Pre-listening

Preparation to listen begins prior to the teacher playing the listening passage. Before students actually listen to the passage, there are several things that the teacher should do to set them up for success when they actually start listening. First, you should activate learners' relevant background knowledge and fill in any gaps in their knowledge. You will want to activate their relevant background knowledge about the topic because it helps them to listen better when they connect the content of the listening passage to what they already know. An effective way to activate background knowledge is to have them predict what they think the text will be about based on the title or related pictures.

As well, often it's not enough just to activate what learners already know. You may also need to build up some of their background knowledge or knowledge of key vocabulary that they will need in order to understand the text well enough. They may also need to be pre-taught some important information or vocabulary before they listen to make sure that they have all the information they need to make as much sense of the texts as possible. This pre-teaching can be accomplished through class discussion about the topic and eliciting key vocabulary that they already know about the topic through activities such as brainstorms.

Hopefully, these class discussions and brainstorms will also achieve the second aim of pre-listening which is to motivate the students motivated to want to listen to the passage. That is, you want to find some way to pique their curiosity and lead them to want to know more about the content of the listening passage. Some other pre-listening activities that can help to motivate students by piquing their curiosity include showing them pictures that relate to the passage and having them do tasks like talk about what is happening in the picture or put pictures in order to guess the sequence of the content in the text that they are about to hear.

A third aim of most pre-listening activities should be to make sure that learners are clear about the purpose of the listening. The last thing you will need to do before hitting the play button is to make sure that learners know what they are supposed to be doing as they listen to the text. When you think about it, when we listen to something outside of the classroom, we always do it for a reason. Likewise, we want to give or students a reason to listen. This can be as simple as telling them what to listen for first such as: listen to the dialog and count how many speakers there are and the main topic of the dialog.

Learners can remain confused about what to do when the instructions are limited to telling them to "listening to this and answer the questions." Therefore, a pre-listening activity that can be particularly helpful in this regard is to have students discuss possible answers to the listening task. That is, they can preview the listening task(s) and guess what they think the answers to them will be. This listening task preview will allow them to get a clearer sense of what they have to do as they listen as well as increasing their curiosity as they wonder whether their guesses will be correct. Pre-listening activities could also give learners the chance to reflect on strategies that they could use to complete the listening task more efficiently. Activities that allow learners to reflect on listening strategies include making predictions or inferences about the listening text based upon pictures that accompany the text.

During-listening

After learners have been prepared to listen through pre-listening activities, they are ready to begin the listening tasks. During listening, it is best for learners to actually work through a listening text several times rather than only listening once. Additionally, the learner should have the chance to go through the listening text moving from listening with more of a focus on getting the meaning and gist to increasingly focusing more on hearing details and the exact language being used (Field, 2002). That is, the tasks or activities that you assign for the first listening will be activities that guide the learner to focus more on the meaning of the text. For example, these tasks could ask them to match the dialogue that they hear with a picture of where they think the dialogue is taking place (e.g., at the bank or the supermarket). By the time they are ready to listen a third time, the task should be more focused on the actual language from the dialogue. The third listening task might be something like doing a dictation or verbally repeating parts of the text.

Learners should listen to any text at least two times. The first time they listen will be for them to get the overall gist or main idea of the text. Tasks you could assign here would include choosing the best title or the picture that matches the text. You might also have them identify the speakers' emotions or the general topic of conversation. Any task you assign should be able to be accomplished with a rough understanding of the text (Underwood, 1989).

After students have listened to the text and decided on their task answers, you should let them compare their answers in pairs or small groups. This step is important because it allows them to get feedback about their ideas as well as to hear others' thinking processes about the text while they try out communication strategies such as asking for repetition or clarification (Field, 2002). After they have listened and decided on their answers, you could discuss their ideas as a class. You will want to discuss their answers before they listen again because it will fill in even more gaps in their background knowledge and prepare them better for a second listening task.

When you are satisfied that most students have a general understanding of the text, you can have them listen again for more detail. The second listening roughly corresponds to the kind of listening that is done in more traditional types of listening tasks in the second language classroom. At this stage, learners could answer standard comprehension questions about the text. Other tasks you might assign include short answer, true or false, checking the boxes etc. This is the phase of the lesson where you would expect learners to have a reasonable understanding of the key details of the text. If they don't, you may have chosen a text that is too difficult.

After learners have had another chance to discuss their answers to the comprehension questions in pairs, they can listen to the text a third time. Activities used for this third listening should focus on the specific language used in the text such as fill-in-the-blanks and dictation of a transcript or identify key linguistic features of the text. You might then have learners practice pronouncing key words or phrases from the passage or even ask more advanced learners to shadow the text.

When selecting during listening tasks, it is also important to give learners the chance to practice additional listening strategies that they will be able to use outside of the language classroom. Some of the strategies that we want them to be able to comfortably use include by recognizing key words, finding main ideas, making sense of non-verbal cues, making inferences, and seeking clarification among others (Richards, 2008). Thus, when we choose the listening tasks and activities, we should bear in mind the kinds of listening strategies these activities will improve.

Post-listening

The final stage of a listening lesson is the post or after listening stage. This is the part of the lesson where you want to connect the content of the listening passage to other skills and reinforce the new vocabulary and structures presented in the listening text. This is also the least restrictive and most creative part of the lesson. At this phase of the lesson, learners can connect the content of the listening or work with the language of the listening through activities such as giving their reactions to what they just heard through speaking, writing or artwork (Underwood, 1989). For instance, if they listened to a story, they might say why they did or did not like it. They could also talk about their impressions of the characters in the story and whether they agreed with some of the decisions that the characters made.

As a way of exploring the content, the teacher could bring in the other language skills for more practice including speaking, reading and writing. If the teacher wanted to give the learners more speaking practice, she could talk about the content of what they heard for less controlled speaking practice. Alternatively, they might try to do grammar substitution drills based on key structures from the listening text or have a dialogue that is structured similarly to the one that they heard in the listening passage.

One way of integrating a literacy skill like reading that is relatively straightforward as the teacher can ask students to read a related text and try to find the differences from it and the listening passage (Richards, 2008). Likewise, writing can quite easily be connected to post listening through tasks such as having students write a journal response to a story that they heard. They could also produce an alternate version of the ending of the dialog or story or try out some of the new language that they heard in the listening passage by doing classroom grammar practice exercises.

A final way for learners to connect with the content of a listening passage is through the creation of their own artwork which could be integrated into the lesson in an endless number of ways. It could involve learners acting out a dialogue or rewriting a script and presenting their performance to another class. Other ways of integrating art include drawing a picture that represents their reaction the listening text. An example of this could be a picture dictation type of activity. Learners could also use their smartphones to create their own videos as a listening response. They might, for instance, make a "movie trailer" or a review of a story that they heard. Post listening activities are really only limited by the teacher's imagination.

4.6 Extensive listening

This type of listening is another listening experience that your learners should have both inside and outside the L2 classroom. Although it falls outside of the typical lesson format described above, it is a vital component of learners' listening skill practice. To begin with, it is necessary to briefly explain what extensive listening is and how it differs from the kind of intensive listening that learners do in a typical lesson. A helpful analogy is to compare extensive listening to extensive reading because both follow the same principles. That is, both extensive reading and listening are aimed at listening to a lot of self-selected, relatively easy material for a more global understanding or gist. As well, the key aim of learners listening to these materials is for them to gain pleasure from the experience. Indeed, other research demonstrates that extensive reading and listening may be most effective when they are combined (Chang & Millett, 2013).

Learners need to do extensive listening because it can facilitate their language learning on a number of levels. First, extensive listening activities provide them with comprehensible input that scholars agree is a crucial element of L2 acquisition (Renandya & Farrell, 2010). Secondly, having these chances to try listening to the L2 using materials that they have chosen for their own purposes can help learners become more independent and autonomous L2 learners (Robin, 2011). Third, listening to these materials without the same careful teacher guidance as intensive listening helps learners to develop their tolerance for ambiguity as they try to make sense of the materials without the aid of the teacher. This tolerance for ambiguity with be useful beyond the classroom when learners try to communicate in the L2 and encounter language they do not know. Their confidence that they can still get the gist with allow them to not give up in their efforts to communicate. Finally, extensive listening chances enable learners to experience the enjoyment of listening to an interesting story that they have chosen and that they understand. This pleasurable experience will in turn increase their motivation to learn the L2 (Krashen, Renandya, Mason, & Bose, 2018).

4.7 Learners benefits from extensive listening

Comprehensible input that learners receive promotes their L2 learning which is a key driver of their ability to learn more target language from the experience of doing extensive listening (Kiany & Shiramiry, 2002; Renandya & Farrell, 2010). Besides their gaining access to input that prompts their L2 learning, they also develop their listening ability because they can get plenty of practice listening to material that is appropriate to their level and thus slowly come to build up their ability to listen naturally. The access to input that they get and the improvement that they begin to see in their own listening ability over time is also sure to bolster their confidence because they can see not only that they are getting better but also that they can actually listen to and understand a lot of what they hear. Lastly, and arguably most importantly, learners are able to enjoy the process and not see listening as the drudgery that it often perceived to be in many language classrooms.

4.8 Effective tools to promote extensive listening

Classroom read aloud is one effective tool that we can use to promote extensive listening on a regular basis (Trelease, 2013). We can simply look around for books that are at our learners' level and that they would probably enjoy listening to and then share those books with the learners. A helpful resource for finding such books is Jim Trelease's "Read Aloud Handbook" because it provides an overview of the many enjoyable books that are available for reading aloud. He has removed the guesswork for teachers in compiling what are more likely to be engaging books to read aloud to your students.

In addition to reading aloud, we can also find pre-recorded books. These days there is such a rapidly growing selection of these types of books that we can find and then introduce to our learners. The real benefit of pre-recorded books is that they can be particularly helpful for bilingual non-native speaking teachers. Allowing learners to listen to recorded books puts them in touch with a wide variety of accents of speakers who may have greater L2 proficiency than the teacher. Pre-recorded books can also be used by learners in a self-access way that allows them to choose the books that they want to listen to rather than having to always listen to stories that the teacher has selected. They are also able to listen at their own pace and listen to the same text multiple times. Learner choice in materials has been found to be vital for build student confidence and effective L2 learning (Dupuy, 1999). Students should also be encouraged to do repeated listening to the stories or recordings that they particularly enjoyed. Not only will they have a sense of pleasure in re-listening (Krashen, 1996) but they will acquire additional language the second time around and more importantly they will feel as though they understood more and get the sense of growth that is often hard to feel in many language learning situations.

4.9 Suitable materials for extensive listening

Guidelines for choosing the best materials for using with extensive listening can help to keep the process manageable and enjoyable for learners. With this in mind, longer texts are more suitable for extensive listening. That is, rather than the short texts that are ordinarily used in the classroom for intensive listening, learners need the chance to listen to a text for longer. Examples of a more extended text could be a story or an interview. In this sense, for extensive listening to work most effectively, the learners need to have access to more listening material than for intensive listening. Another important consideration to keep in mind that is that if possible the materials should be self-selected. As with ER, the engine that makes extensive listening work best is when the learner can listen to whatever they want. Having this choice is what will compel them to listen longer than they normally might because they are genuinely interested in the content of the listening passage.

The language of the text they are listening to is also important. For most learners, until they reach a high intermediate level, they will probably have to listen to materials that are graded in some way (Hammerly, 1982). They can be graded by the publisher such as when learners listen to stories designed for L2 learners or the recordings that accompany graded readers. They are also graded when the teacher previews the materials and simplifies them in a way that she believes will allow the students to better understand and enjoy them.

Examples of the materials that you might try with your learners include regular reading materials such as picture books or novels that are read aloud in one sitting or over time. Similarly, the teacher might tell a story that he believes that students would like. Another option could be interviewing someone that the students would be interested in hearing from and letting them listen to the video or audio recorded interview. Indeed, any recorded conversations that might appeal to students' interests should be brought into class. More advanced learners (i.e., high intermediate and above) could be encouraged to listen to podcasts and recorded TV shows in their spare time. They could also be encouraged to seek out materials on various topics that interest them ideally with an L2 transcript or subtitles that they could use to help them learn new vocabulary.

4.10 Suggested responses to extensive listening

"Nothing" is a reasonable response to this question. When you think about the kind of real life listening that we hope extensive listening will most closely emulate, we usually do not do anything in response. For example, when we watch a TV show or listen to a podcast, our typical response is to do or say nothing. If that is what we do in our daily life, then we should be able to ask our students (who we are preparing to communicate outside our classroom) to do the same thing. If we must give them a task before listening, we might just prompt them to simply listen and enjoy the story with no other directions. Imagine their surprise when, for possibly the first time, they listen to something in the language classroom and not have to be accountable in any way for what they heard.

If you feel leery about not assigning learners anything to do while or after they listen, you could ask them to react to the content of what they are hearing or discuss it with someone else. These reactions could happen as they are listening when they spontaneously speak out or say something to themselves. You do not have to discourage these unprompted reactions because we usually have them outside the classroom and it will probably give learners pleasure to react naturally (possibly for the first time) as they get caught up in the story. You might also pause throughout the read-aloud or story to give the learners the chance to talk to a partner about what they just heard and what might happen next.

Whatever you ultimately decide to do, try to choose extensive listening activities that are as authentic as possible. That is, try to choose something that a learner would probably do outside the classroom if they listened to the same type of text. As well, do your best to incorporate enjoyable activities like art or games that do not require learners to recall the details of what they just heard. That being said, you should not treat extensive listening as a fun optional activity but rather as a vital component of your learners' L2 learning experience. After all, what is the point of their doing often stressful intensive listening practice if they never get the chance to just listen and enjoy as they do in the L1?

4.11 Teaching speaking

Speaking is usually the most sought-after skill in the second language classroom for good reasons. The world is rapidly shrinking and as the global village becomes increasingly smaller we inevitably come into contact with speakers of other languages that we increasingly need to communicate with. This necessary communication may be because they are our trade partners, our clients, members of our community or even our family. Therefore, we must take seriously our need to communicate with speakers of other languages face to face which may require us to speak their language. As well, fairly or unfairly, when we say that we know another language, others will often assume that means we can speak it. This is because the standard that we often use to judge whether someone "really" knows another language is that they are able to speak it. For that reason, if we are serious about becoming a bilingual then we have to learn to speak our target language.

With respect to the L2 classroom, we must teach speaking because our classroom is in a sense the laboratory or practice space where learners can experiment and test out their growing knowledge of the L2. Our classroom provides them with a somewhat controlled and safe environment where they can attempt to use the target language, get feedback on their performance and gradually develop their ability to the point where they can engage in meaningful conversations beyond the classroom (Hatch, 1978).

4.12 Obstacles to speaking well in another language

Having a limited vocabulary makes it difficult for learners to engage in speaking beyond everyday pleasantries. They may find it challenging to initiate and maintain an extended conversation. When they try to speak, they may find themselves tongue tied. That is, they may have trouble finding the words that they want to say causing a negative spiral of self-doubt and poor speaking performance that eventually makes the learner give up on trying to express themselves in the second language.

Learners may also find that they have difficulty keeping up with the flow of a conversation. This is especially true if there is more than one other speaker and they are native speakers. Many foreign language learners have been in an exchange where they had just grasped the thread of the conversation and formulated something that they want to contribute only to realize that the other members had already moved on to a new topic. In a similar vein, many learners have also had the experience of finally getting an opportunity to contribute to the conversation, as they are trying to formulate what they want to say, a less patient interlocutors may interrupt and the conversation moves on without them. Thus, they experience how difficult it can be to hold the conversational floor in another language and that can be disheartening.

As a result of these kinds of experiences, the learner can gradually come to lose his self-confidence. They may become increasingly self-conscious which may in turn cause them to avoid the very opportunities that they need to speak and continue to develop their speaking ability and self-assurance. Therefore, language teachers need to strive to ensure that learners get opportunities to use the target language and learn to effectively face these obstacles.

4.13 Types of speaking

Brown (2000) discusses a number of different types of speaking that we all do in the language learning classroom. The first is known as imitative speaking which is when the learner simply follows the teacher's model as when they do listen and repeat or other type of grammar practice drills such as slot-fill or transformation drills. The main benefit of this kind of speaking practice is that the learner does not have to formulate what they want to say themselves so they can focus all of their mental energy on familiarizing themselves with the new language structures. The downside is that it is a somewhat mindless activity that does not require learners to come up with their own language so it has limited value for preparing them to actually communicate spontaneously beyond the classroom.

Intensive speaking involves learners speaking for short stretches using some language that is given to them in addition to formulating some of their own (Brown, 2000). An activity that represents this type of speaking is a dialog completion task where learners are given part of a dialog and they need to come up with the rest themselves. The benefit of this task is that learners get the best of both worlds in the sense that they have some support for what they want to say from having access to the first part of the dialog. This type of sentence frame can prompt them and help them to formulate their own language more efficiently. The downside of this activity is that the learner is still forced to come up with their own language which may be a challenge for limited proficiency learners. This type of exercise could be effective for beginners but it may be frustrating for intermediate-level learners and beyond because it unnecessarily constrains them and forces them to follow a certain pattern.

Responsive speaking places slightly more demand on the learner than imitative or intensive speaking because learners have to produce all of their own language (Brown, 2000). The unique difference is that while they have to come up with all of their own language they only do it for short exchanges such as standard greetings or engaging in limited small talk about topics like the weather. The main advantage of responsive speaking is that unlike other kinds of more controlled speaking, it pushes the learner to go beyond a script so that they learn to express their own thoughts in the L2. Thus, they have to use the L2 resources that they have to communicate to the best of their ability. Fortunately, the kinds of communication that learners engage in is still rather restricted so they only have to have conversations that they have probably already experienced in their L1 many times. As a result, they will feel familiar with these kinds of topics discussed and procedures that they need to follow. The limitation with this kind of task is that intermediate and advanced learners may find them to be boring because they have already probably had these same conversations in the L2 many times.

Interactive speaking includes the engagement in substantially longer and more complex kinds of dialogs that may involve multiple exchanges (Brown, 2000). For example, the learner may participate in a role play where they have to run errands that require them to visit several shops and have various conversations with the different shop owners. Another way that these kinds of dialogs are more complex is that they can begin to incorporate multiple partners. Anyone who has struggled in a foreign language to participate in a conversation with more than one native speaker understands how difficult that can be. Native speakers can use unfamiliar language and bring up unknown topics that are beyond your ability. This sort of speaking practice ensures that learners must navigate the more challenging kinds of communication that they will face outside of the classroom. As a result, they can be better prepared to handle these types of exchanges. Interactive speaking activities' main limitation is that lower proficiency learners may feel frustrated as they struggle to come up with the language that they need to effectively communicate in these exchanges.

Extensive speaking requires the learners to speak for a longer stretch of time than we ordinarily do in daily life (Brown, 2000). This kind of speaking is typically some kind of monologue that they have to present to a small audience or even a larger audience as in a public speaking situation. Some examples of extensive speaking are when a learner gives a sales pitch or a lecture about a topic that they are familiar with. Another example is if they tell a humorous story that they know. This could be a story about any topic they choose and unlike a lecture it could be only for one other listener. Still, successful story telling requires learners to carefully consider the structure and coherence of their language over a much longer stretch of text than the other types of speaking such as responsive or interactive speaking. Indeed, a long stretch of extensive speaking like a lecture can take hours.

The benefit of doing extensive speaking is that it gives learners practice speaking a lot which will help their speaking ability to improve. Extensive speaking also enables learners to consider how they can more precisely formulate their speech and put their ideas together in a way that is cohesive while also being informative or entertaining for the listener. A key advantage of extensive speaking is that, the learner usually has time to prepare in advance so they can reflect on and refine their language. The main disadvantage is that the learner should be more confident of his ability because public speaking is very anxiety producing for many people even in their mother tongue. Thus, learners may feel very uncomfortable with doing extensive speaking and not want to do it. One possible way of addressing this drawback while still giving them the chance to speak for longer stretches is to let them rehearse and then tell a story in pairs.

Knowledge of these various speaking styles helps us to realize that indeed all speaking processes are not the same. Knowing about different types of speaking gives us the tools to discuss L2 speaking with our colleagues in a more fine-grained way. This knowledge can likewise aid us in our lesson planning as we can be more aware of the different kinds of speaking that learners should be practicing in our lessons. We can then in turn make them aware of the wide range of possible speaking situations that they are likely to encounter as an L2 user.

We can also prepare a variety of more suitable activities for our learners depending on their stage of L2 development that will actually address the various kinds of speaking that they will do beyond the walls of the classroom. Many learners will appreciate our efforts to prepare them to handle various speaking situations and help them to become stronger L2 users. Finally, our ability to teach using various speaking activities will make our classes more engaging for learners because they will not feel bored always repeating the same limited repertoire of classroom speaking activities.

4.14 Communication strategies

Communication strategies are an invaluable addition to any second language user's repertoire of tricks that she can use to be able to get by in the L2. These strategies have been defined by Faerch and Kasper (1980) as "potentially conscious plans for solving what to an individual presents itself as a problem in reaching a particular communicative goal" (p. 81). In essence, they are the facilitative techniques that we can use to be able to more successfully communicate in an L2. The concept of communication strategies is commonly associated with Canale and Swain's (1980) notion of communicative competence and its insight that effective L2 use is about more than just knowing vocabulary and grammar. It also demands the ability to mobilize other linguistic, para-linguistic and non-linguistic resources appropriately to communicate a message effectively to interlocutors.

Oxford (1990) claims that we should teach communication strategies for a number of important reasons. First, when learners know communication strategies, they are better able to avoid communication breakdowns that could potentially derail a conversation. For example, if a learner is talking to someone and she forgot a key word but could not paraphrase what she wanted to say through circumlocution then the conversation would be at risk of ending prematurely. Another reason why we need to teach communication strategies is that they can allow us to repair communication breakdowns that have already occurred. To illustrate, if two learners are conversing and they realize that they no longer understand each other, then they must find a way to stop there, work out where they went wrong, back track and resolve their communication problem. A number of communication strategies such as back channeling and appealing for assistance can facilitate this process.

Another reason why language teachers should care about communication strategies is that they allow learners to keep a conversation going. In the process, the learner can gain more practice using the L2, building relationships with L2 speakers, and experiencing successful communication in the target language. Lastly, the effective use of communication strategies allows the learner to appear more fluent which serves a couple of other useful purposes. First, this apparent fluency will encourage their interlocutor to continue interacting with them in the L2 thus providing additional L2 input and practice. As well, it helps those are have a good command of their L2 to showcase their full abilities. We have all seen cases of L2 learners with extensive knowledge of the L2 vocabulary and grammar whose failure to use communication strategies effectively made them appear considerably less knowledgeable than they actually were.

Several different taxonomies have been proposed for organizing the various types of communication strategies that have been identified. However, the way that the strategies are presented below is a synthesis of several different taxonomies. The first category of communication strategy is paraphrasing. Tarone (1981) identifies a number of different tactics that learners can use to convey their message through paraphrase. For example, approximation relies on using an L1 word that shares some features of the L2 despite the learner being aware that the word cannot be used in the L2 in the same way. A variation on this tactic is word coinage. This is when the learner knows that the L2 does not have the word he is using but she believes that its meaning will be clear enough to convey her message.

A third paraphrase strategy is through "foreignizing" an L1 word when the learner takes an L1 word that he believes to be similar to the L2 and then says that word with and L2 accent. An instance of this from French would be saying the word "automobile" with a French accent in the hope that it is similar enough to the French word for car that the listener recognizes it. Circumlocution can be viewed as another type of paraphrasing strategy. With circumlocution the learner tries to "talk around" an unknown word by explaining, defining or giving examples of it in the hope that the interlocutor will understand what she means or supply the missing word. A final paraphrasing strategy is for the speaker to use a superordinate category of the word that is close to the unknown word she wants. For instance, if the learner does not know the specific breed of dog that he wants to refer to he might just say "dog" rather than Pit Bull Terrier.

A second category of communication strategies that learners often use is known as "transfer" strategies. These strategies refer to "the use of items from a second language, typically the mother tongue, particularly syntactic and lexical, to make good the deficiencies of the interlanguage" (Corder, 1983, p. 26). That is, relying on the L1 to overcome one's lack of knowledge of the L2. One example of these strategies is known as literal translation when the learner attempts to directly translate a word, phrase, or expression from the L1 in the hope that its meaning will be clear enough in the L2 to suit his purposes. A related form of transfer is when the learner switches from the L1 to the L2 which is a type of code switching (Paramasivam, 2009). Naturally, this form of strategy is most effective when both interlocutors are comfortable speakers of both of the two languages being used in the conversation.

A third grouping of communication strategies relies upon learner avoidance. These are somewhat more subtle and more difficult to observe because they are indicated by what we do not see (Tarone, Cohen, & Dumas, 1976). For example, if a learner believes that she does not have a firm grasp on a lot of the language in a particular domain of knowledge (e.g., a hobby of some sort) then she may simply try to avoid raising that topic or continuing dialogue about it. A second option for when the learner is struggling to express themselves is for them to abandon the message altogether. They could simply stop talking or say something like "I'm not sure how to express this." A final strategy that learners could use is message reduction. This tactic is probably the most subtle and difficult to notice. Message reduction entails the learner refraining from talking about certain parts of a topic or cutting what they intended to say short because the suddenly recognize that they do not have the language to fully express what they intended to say.

A number of other strategies exist that are more difficult to neatly categorize. One of these is restructuring which refers to developing an alternative way of structuring one's message. Restructuring might be used when a speaker realizes that she is struggling to find the right language to express a thought. Rather than abandoning that thought, she thinks of a way to reorganize what she wants to say that will save her from abandoning her intended message. To illustrate, a speaker may want to say "Next week, I will have been living here for five years." However, uncertainty about how to structure the utterance may prompt her to say "I have lived here for almost five years" instead.

Other strategies can help to facilitate the smooth progress of a conversation. Fillers can be effectively used as a way to buy time in a conversation. L2 speakers typically need more time than native speakers to formulate what they want to say in a conversation. However, a lot of silent pauses during a conversation can make interlocutors uncomfortable so these silences are best filled with words like "uhm" or "you know." These filler words can buy the L2 speaker thinking time to formulate their utterances without them having to relinquish their turn (Dörnyei & Scott, 1997). Backchanneling is another strategy that smooths the flow of conversation. Backchanneling allows the listener to give feedback to the speaker that indicates she is following what the speaker is saying. This strategy involves using phrases such as "uh huh", "oh, I see" or other expressions that signal to the speaker to continue (Yngve, 1970). Use of formulaic expressions is yet another tool that learners have at their disposal to enhance their performance in a conversation. So, if they know some fixed expressions such as "as a matter of fact" or "as you may already know" they use these conversational signposts to sound more fluent while also keeping the conversation flowing smoothly (Lewis, 1993).

Sometimes a learner may struggle to communicate an important message because she lacks the necessary language to do so effectively. In this case, there are still a number of strategies that she can use to express herself. For one, she can use gesture, body language and even mime to convey her message (Dörnyei & Scott, 1997; Faerch & Kasper, 1980). In addition to extra-linguistic communication tactics, she could also use paralinguistic communication devices such as tone of voice, intonation and pausing to aid meaning making (Corder, 1983).

If she continues to with difficulty relaying an important message she can always appeal for assistance by asking her interlocutor to help construct the utterance through expressions like "what is this word in English?" or "How can I say this in English?"

4.15 Teaching communication strategies

A number of methods exist by which communication strategies can be taught and promoted in the L2 classroom (Dörnyei, 1995). However, disagreement exists in the research literature regarding the value of trying to teach CS. Some scholars contend that it is not possible to teach CS so we should not even try. Instead, they insist that the time spent trying to teach CS that learners would have already developed in their L1 could be better used to improve their knowledge of the L2 itself (Kellerman, 1991). Besides, they argue, CS developed in the L1 can automatically transfer to the L2 (Kellerman, Ammerlaan, Bongaerts, & Poulisse, 1990). On the other hand, there are also those who contend that it is in fact beneficial to teach CS and that learners can improve their L2 communication ability as a result (Rost, 2013).

One suggestion for teaching CS relates to raising learner awareness about them and how they can be used to effectively communicate through activities such as "sensitizing [learners] to the appropriate situations where [CS] could be useful, and making them realize that these strategies could actually work" (Dörnyei, 1995, p. 63). Teachers also need to encourage students to use CSs by demonstrating to them that their use is acceptable in class then the learner will not suppress their natural urge to use them spontaneously during communicative classroom activities (Willems, 1987).

Likewise, teachers themselves should provide L2 models of the use of certain

CSs. One effective way of modeling these strategies suggested by Nolasco and Arthur (1987) is for the teacher to bring a video to class that demonstrates the use of a particular communication strategy. The teacher and students can view the video together and with the teacher's prompts the students can analyze the video to identify what the communication problem is and what strategy the learner in the video used to facilitate her communication. They can also discuss exactly what steps the speaker in the video is following to implement the strategy. In this way, learner awareness can be raised for how the strategy is used in real communication.

In addition to exposing learners to models of CS use, the suggestion has also been made for teachers to instruct CS use directly. Direct instruction can be accomplished through a short explanation of a strategy's purpose and when it can be used followed by a brief demonstration of how it works (Oxford, 2017). For example, teachers could teach particular sentences structures that students could use for circumlocution when they realize they do not know a needed word when speaking (Tarone & Yule, 1989).

Besides teaching learners about what communication strategies are available to them and how to use those strategies, learners also need chances to practice using those strategies through activities such as role plays based on scenarios of situations when use of the strategy could improve their communication. This classroom strategy practice may help learners effectively cope with any anxiety they experience from using CS to navigate communication in their L2 (Kellerman, 1991; Willems, 1987).

A final suggestion for guiding L2 users effective use of CS is the need to provide them with feedback on their strategy use (O'Malley, Chamot, Stewner-Manzanares, Russo, & Kupper, 1985). This feedback could occur while the teacher observes students talking in small groups to practice speaking through activities like information gaps or role plays. During these open-ended speaking activities, when the teacher sees students experiencing a communication difficulty, she can intervene to remind them about a particular strategy that might be helpful to resolve their problem. Alternatively, the teacher might take some time after a speaking activity to review useful language that she heard. The class could also review any communication problems they experienced and discuss what communication strategies might be helpful in resolving some of those problems.

4.16 What to teach in a speaking lesson

When we begin teaching speaking, we need to decide exactly what is it is that we are supposed to be teaching. A high priority is to make sure that learners speak accurately enough to be understood by their interlocutors. Spoken accuracy works on several different levels. Therefore, we will want to improve learners' pronunciation by focusing on key segmental and supra-segmental features of the sound system that maximize their intelligibility. Likewise, we will want learners to be reasonably accurate in their spoken grammar. For example, learners should know that they can use the modal verb "can" to express what they are able to do with statements like "I can jump." We will also want to guide learners to be able to make natural sounding vocabulary choices and organize their spoken discourse in a logical and coherent manner.

In addition to supporting learner accuracy, we will also want to encourage their fluency development. That is, we will want them to "[produce] language in real time without undue pausing or hesitation" (Ellis & Barkhuizen, 2005, p. 139). Along with their fluency development, we should also be concerned that learners are aware of the various types of speaking discussed above including intensive, responsive and interactive etc. This awareness is important because learners can realize that different speaking events will place differing demands upon them. We also need to be sure that learners actually know how to appropriately manage interaction itself. That is, they must know how to bid for a turn, hold the floor as they speak and relinquish their turn to another speaker among other conversational management skills (Bygate, 1987). Relatedly, learners need to understand how to properly negotiate meaning with their interlocutors to ensure mutual understanding so they need to be taught the appropriate communication strategies to achieve this vital aim.

4.17 How should we teach speaking?

When teaching speaking, various activities can be used that range from more to less controlled. An example of a speaking activity that is very controlled is a listen and repeat drill. While learners have to verbally produce the L2, itis controlled because the learner does not have to actually use their own language to do the activity. Another example of a controlled activity is a scripted dialogue. Although the learner would speak the dialogue, they would be taking all of the language that they use from the materials themselves.

A semi-controlled speaking activity draws on some of the learner's own language and some language from the teacher or the materials. An example of a semi-controlled activity could be an information gap. There is a structure to the dialog that learners must have with this kind of activity and some of the language they will use is also supplied in the materials. However, they also have to draw on their own language resources as well because information gap activities can be constructed in a way that includes some information and excludes other information. An example of a semi-controlled information gap activity can be seen in table 4.1 below. In this case, the learner would have to make up some information to supply to their partner as well as having to devise the language they would use in their dialog to share their information from the grid.

Table 4.1 Example of a semi-controlled information gap activity

Student A			
	Lives	**Job**	**Hobbies**
Rick	S-------		Karate
Lee		P---------	
Diane	Toronto		Reading

Picture description and drama-based activities are also considerably less controlled. Examples of such activities include role plays, problem solving or learner storytelling based on a picture or series of picture prompts. These activities are less controlled because the learner might have a role card prompt with some information about their character or a picture that they have to talk about. However, their limited control means that the learner needs to generate all of the language used to communicate during the activity.

The key elements of a speaking lesson

As with the listening lesson, there is also a sequence of steps to follow here that allows the teacher to effectively present new language and help learners to internalize it. Although there are other ways of teaching speaking (e.g., task-based), one approach that has been around for a long time and is widely recommended for new teachers is the present-practice-produce (PPP) approach. It is a relatively straightforward approach to master and it does not expect too much expertise in grammar from the beginning (J. Anderson, 2016; Ur, 2018). A novice teacher can expand on his own understanding of English grammar piece by piece with each lesson. As the name suggests, there are three main parts to this lesson that we will take some time to go through.

Present

The first stage of this type of lesson is the "present" stage. At this stage of the lesson, the teacher's main aim is to introduce the target vocabulary and structures for the lesson. There are a number of ways that the teacher can do this. Some ways that new vocabulary might be presented include through flashcards containing associated images (for words that are easily visualized) or the equivalent L1 word (for words that are less easily visualized). Other methods of presenting new vocabulary include using gestures, explaining them in comprehensible L2, and showing real items (i.e., realia). The most appropriate method chosen to present the word will often be suggested by the word itself. For example, a word like swim is more efficiently presented through gesture than through explanation. Of course, the choice of words to include in the lesson will also depend on the learner's stage of cognitive development and background knowledge. It is also important that vocabulary be recycled across lessons so that learners can encounter a word the many times necessary for it to be remembered (Schmitt & Schmitt, 1995).

Teachers should decide which grammar presentation technique is most suitable for their learners depending on the learners' age and ability level. A general rule is that younger ages and lower ability levels should receive less explicit or intensive focus on grammar. Grammar forms can be presented through stories, songs or chants that contain the new grammar structure. Often the most straightforward way to present a structure for younger learners is through pictures and examples. For instance, if the target grammar structure is "can/ can't + verb," the teacher can show a variety of pictures of activities like running, dancing, swimming etc. with accompanying sentences like "I can run" or "I can't fly." The teacher can then present these example sentences to the learner to ensure that the learner connects the form of "can/ can't + verb," with its meaning of being able to do an activity. Other aspects of the meaning such as possibility could be presented at a later time. Equally, the teacher could find or devise an inductive activity to help students discover the rule for themselves. Learners could be given examples of the grammar structure in context and students would have to work out the rule for themselves. See the example of an inductive exercise below.

When presenting a new structure to learners, the teacher will want to make sure that learners will take away from the lesson a strong sense of the form, the meaning, and the use of the structure. For instance, if teaching the regular past tense "-ed," the teacher will want students to understand that it is formed by adding "ed" to the end of the verb (form). They should also know that it is used when talking about the past (meaning). As well, they should be aware that it is used in situations such as when talking about the past (use). Remember, when it comes to teaching grammar, keep it simple. Less is more. More than 5-10 minutes explaining a grammar point is probably too much. Students should be using the bulk of the lesson practicing the grammar instead of hearing about it. Also, in preparing to teach the grammar point, reference resources should be consulted to determine exactly what the structure means, how it is formed and when it is used. Two particularly helpful references are "The Grammar book" by Marianne Celce-Murcia and Diane Larsen-Freeman and "Practice English Usage" by Michael Swan.

After presenting the grammar structure, the teacher should confirm that learners have understood it with some concept check questions. These are a series of simple questions that should have yes/ no, forced choice (e.g., big or small), or one-word answers. Students' correct answers to these questions demonstrate whether they understand the grammar concept being explained. Here is an example to help distinguish the main features of the present continuous.

Table 4.2 Example concept check questions

Target sentence: They are playing soccer.	
Concept check questions:	Have they started playing?
	Is the game finished?
	Is this the past, now or future?

Practice

After learners have had the opportunity to be exposed to new language, they then need the chance to internalize that language. They can do this through controlled use of the language through doing classroom activities that allow them to focus on manipulating the new forms without too many of the other pressures that can usually be found in a conversation. In this part of the lesson, the main focus should be on improving learners' accuracy (they can say it right) here rather than their fluency (they can say it quickly). The practice stage is where the learners can try out the new vocabulary and structures that they learned through controlled activities such as gap fills or drills. This stage of the lesson allows the learner to rehearse and familiarize themselves with the new language before having to use it during actual communication.

There are a variety of exercises that learners can do at this stage to help them begin to acquire the new target structures. For example, they could complete grammar exercises such as gap fills, finish sentence stems, choose the correct option, fix mistakes in a sentence, or sentence transformation (e.g., statement into a question). The main benefit of these types of exercises is that they allow the learner to have some time to process the language and think through how it works at their own pace. Of course, these kinds of exercises become boring quickly easily when too much of this kind of work is assigned.

Table 4.3 Examples of written practice items

The book is _______ the table. [gap fill]
The ball is through the chair. [fix the mistake]
The boy is... [finish the sentence]

Drills are a second type of practice activity that will allow learners to help them better acquire the new structures. Here as well, there are numerous types that learners can do. Drills essentially break down into two main kinds which are mechanical and meaningful. Mechanical drills only focus on allowing learners to manipulate the structure of the language without much emphasis on the meaning. These include repetition, backward buildup, substitution, question and answer, transformation and chain drills.

Repetition drills are used when the teacher says a target language utterance and the class has to repeat after the teacher. Backward buildup has the learner practice a target language sentence by saying the final word in the sentence loud. The learner then says the second-to-final word and the final word. She then repeats this process adding one word to her utterance until she says the entire sentence. An example of a backward buildup drill can be found in table 4.4.

Substitution drills work by the teacher saying a sentence that the learners have to repeat. Then the teacher says the sentence again with a prompt that the learners have to integrate into the sentence. An example can be found in table 4.5 below. Transformation drills are similar except that instead of learners changing one aspect of the grammar, they have to change the [mood] of the utterance. To illustrate, the teacher gives a prompt like "They are playing baseball" and the learners would have to transform it into a question like "Are they playing baseball?" Chain drill are a permutation of this [what?] where a prompt and response goes around the classroom one student at a time. For example, student 1 says "I like pizza but I don't like spinach." Student 2 say "I like strawberries but I don't like pears" etc.

Drills can be performed in a teacher-guided whole-class or student-centered small-group format. Ball-pass activities are often an enjoyable way to keep drills engaging through a fast-paced format. To do the ball-pass, one learner holding a ball says the prompt and passes the ball to another learner who has to answer the prompt, restate the prompt and pass the ball to someone else. Ball-pass drills can also be set up so that several groups are working at the same time.

Table 4.4 Example of a backward buildup sentence drill.

Ss: store
Ss: the store
Ss: go to the store
Ss: I go to the store

Table 4.5 Example of a substitution drill

Substitution drill
Ts: I am going to school. He.
Ss: He is going to school.
Ts: They.
Ss: They are going to school.

Table 4.6 Example of a chain drill

T: How are you?
S1: Fine, thanks. How are you?
S2: Fine thanks. [and so on around the class]

In addition to mechanical drills, meaningful drills are another more communicative way for students to practice new language. The main difference between these and mechanical drills is that meaningful drills encourage learners to practice the new grammar structure while actually trying to communicate a real message in English. A guessing game like 20 questions is a meaningful way to drill question formation. Another example could be to practice the use of prepositions to describe locations of places. Here, students would have a street map with various buildings identified in different locations. They are also given a list of prepositions such as across from, on the corner of, next to etc. They then have to answer questions such as "Where is the book store?" "It's next to the supermarket?" Etc. The practice is now meaningful because they have to respond according to the location of places on the map. Thus, they are actually conveying information to their partner in addition to practicing the target structures.

The key point with these types of information gap activities is that each of the learners will have information that their partner does not. They must then share that information with each other as they do the task. In the process of working together the information is equally distributed between partners. There are a wide variety of information gap activities that will push students to communicate using the new language. Some examples include picture dictation, asking and answering questionnaires, find someone who, grammar dictation and sharing information about schedules, hobbies, activities, likes/dislikes etc. A somewhat more complex type of information gap is a dictogloss where a group of learners must agree on the missing grammar elements in a text.

During and right after they finish practicing the new language, it is important to give learners explicit feedback because it can improve their performance (Li, 2010). The aim of the practice stage of the lesson is to promote learner accuracy so they need feedback on how accurate their production of the new target structure is. While they are practicing in pairs or small groups, the teacher should circulate to make sure that they know what they are supposed to be doing and they know the language they need to do the task. When correcting learners' errors, the teacher should not give recasts because learners will often not realize that they are being corrected. Instead, the teacher should give explicit correction with repetition of the correct form or use a prompt to elicit the correct form (if they seem to know it)(Lightbown & Spada, 2013). Another suggestion at the end of an activity is to put examples of common mistakes learners made on the board and have students correct them in pairs or as a class.

Produce

The final phase in the speaking lesson is the production stage. This is where learners should be given the chance to do less controlled practice that allows them to use all of the target language they have at their disposal to communicate to the best of their ability. The focus at this stage is on fluency rather than accuracy (Anderson, 2016). Learners will want to focus primarily on communicating their message. Therefore, the kinds of activities that learners do should be less controlled or open-ended that allow learners to generate their own language to do the activity.

There are a wide variety of activities that learners can do at this stage of the lesson. Some other examples of these activities include guided dialogs where they have to make up language for gaps in a dialog they have been given. They could also do a role play based on role play cards that tell them the basics of what their role is and what they have to talk about. Less controlled information gaps are another option that include a video information gap where one person hears the sound and the other sees the picture and they have to put the story together.

Opinion gap activities begin with the teacher dividing the class into several groups that will discuss or describe a topic from different perspectives. For example, "students might be given a social problem such as high unemployment and be asked to come up with a series of possible solutions" (Marzban & Hashemi, 2013, p. 944). After all groups finish, the teacher asks the groups to report to the rest of the class.

A reasoning gap is another type of activity that learners can do that is based more on communicating and problem solving. Shankar (2010) offers an example of a reasoning gap activity where learners could be given the following problem: A man is standing by a river with a wolf, a sheep, and some vegetables. He wants to get everything across the river, but he has a small boat that cannot carry all three things at one time. The wolf will eat the sheep if the man goes away, and the sheep will eat the vegetables if the man goes away. Learners then have to discuss how the man can get across the river without losing any of his belongings in small groups and agree on a solution.

At the conclusion of the production stage, the teacher should wrap up with a brief class discussion that allows volunteers to share their ideas and compare their answers with each other and the teacher. This step is important because it gives them a sense of closure to the activity and it lets them think that they did the activity for a clear purpose which was to arrive at a conclusion.

At this stage, the teacher will not want to provide too much feedback on learner performance. If you do want to give feedback, it would be best to collect examples of common errors that were made and discuss them with the class (Anderson, 2016).

4.18 Cooperative learning

An example of a student-centered teaching strategy that has been gaining popularity and that is an excellent fit for the L2 classroom is cooperative learning. Cooperative learning (CL) encourages students work together to complete a shared task. CL differs from more traditional forms of unstructured "group work" by its emphasis on learner accountability, full participation, positive environment, and productive interaction (McCafferty, Jacobs, & Iddings, 2006). CL fosters learner interdependence through its demand that for its associated task to be completed, all group members must contribute to achieving the final outcome. Group members have the opportunity to cultivate their social skills with guidance and coaching from the teacher as needed. They also have increasing accountability as they must answer to their team for their contribution to the task. Learners learn to self and peer-evaluate as they assess their own contribution as well as that of the other group members. Using cooperative learning into your lessons will enable learners to develop their oral communication, social skills, active learning, student responsibility and thinking skills (Jacobs, Power, & Inn, 2002)Power, & Inn, 2002.

Principles of cooperative learning

A basic principle of cooperative learning known as positive interdependence links students together so that they all must rely on each other for the group to succeed (Johnson, Johnson, & Holubec, 1998). Students can learn to collaborate to draw upon member's strengths while surmounting their weaknesses. Positive interdependence activities are characterized by how participation in them benefits each group member. They are facilitated by giving groups a common challenge to overcome, fostering a team identity, and assigning individuals unique roles that allow for their unique contributions. Students benefit most from positive interdependence by feeling supported by their peers while also realizing that team member's efforts are required for group success (Jacobs et al., 2002)2002.

Through simultaneous interaction, a positive classroom atmosphere is created where learners share knowledge and resources while supporting and encouraging one other. Johnson and Johnson (2011) explain that face-to-face interaction enables students to assist and encourage peers' learning attempts. They can do this by discussing task solutions, concepts, content or modeling learning strategies for each other. However, for this kind of interaction to work, learners need sufficient time, appropriate configuration of the learning space and teacher support. Opportunities for this kind of interaction can facilitate exposure to complex linguistic input, feedback from comprehensible output, and additional L2 practice (McGroarty, 1989).

Accountability is a third principle of cooperative learning. It urges group members to take personal responsibility for their role and task in the group and the group being accountable to the classroom learning community.

Accountability relates to the central aim of CL which is for students to improve their own individual proficiency through learning as a group. CL functions in a way that encourages learners to teach and share information with each other to complete the task (Smith, 1996). Group members learn to assist those who are struggling with the task and resist those who try not to do their fair share. Both formal and informal classroom assessments can be used to guide learners in their group functioning and provide them with feedback on their performance (Johnson & Johnson, 2011).

Unlike traditional approaches to group work, cooperative learning assumes learners may need social skills to be explicitly taught and modeled for them to interact effectively. Required skills to become a productive group include listening, sharing ideas, encouraging and respecting others and participating in the assigned activity or task. Effective implementation of these skills results in a democratic, collaborative class with prosocial skills and improved interpersonal relations that allows students to work in productive ways that build on their strengths (Kagan, 1986 as cited in McGroarty, 1989)

CL groups also need chances to continue to refine the functioning of the group to make sure that it works as smoothly as possible. This means members need to take time to step back and reflect on their work and interactions to learn how they can improve the process. With some teacher modelling and input, group processing allows CL groups to reconsider their dynamics to isolate those behaviors that most facilitated or hindered task completion. From there, the group can decide how to adjust workflow or interaction patterns to ensure improved functioning and productivity in the future (Johnson & Johnson, 2005).

Benefits of cooperative learning for students

Use of CL in the L2 classroom promises a variety of positive effects on the linguistic, intellectual, social and affective development of learners. McCafferty et al. (2006) draws attention to how regardless of the theory of L2 learning that one espouses, CL can be used to support second language learning. That is, CL provides the foundation of L2 learning regardless of whether it is comprehensible input (Krashen, 1982), opportunities for interaction and negotiation of meaning (Long, 1985) or noticing and hypothesis testing commonly associated with comprehensible output (Swain, 1985). Even other theories from developmental, cognitive and humanistic psychology can endorse CL. Thus, cooperative learning can be a tool in the belt of almost any teacher regardless of their beliefs about second language learning.

Along with linguistic growth, CL encourages students' ongoing intellectual development. It does so through pushing them to understand the content of the lesson more deeply through discussion and teaching it to each other (Cavanagh, 2011). These kinds of interactions in turn support the acquisition of high-level reasoning and critical thinking skills (Lie, 2002). As a result, use of CL has been linked to higher academic achievement (Slavin, 1991).

A third benefit of utilizing CL in the language learning classroom relates to the many positive effects that it has upon various aspects of learners' social skill development. One social gain from cooperative learning is that learners can become more able to cultivate the ability to see circumstances from another viewpoint. This other-perspective-taking can then lead to more positive and supportive relationships with peers (Slavin, Madden, & Leavey, 1984). From a pragmatic standpoint, these positive peer relationships promote greater time on task and fewer class disruptions. But more importantly, social skills transferred beyond the walls of the classroom make learners better workers, family members and friends (Johnson & Johnson, 1990).

A final advantage of CL is the constructive influence that learners' interactions with each another can have on their affective states. For example, these types of collaborative activities are student-centered and consequently support learner autonomy. The peer support that learners receive from CL has also been associated with lower levels of learner anxiety (Tsui, 1996) increased motivation (Long & Porter, 1985) and higher self-esteem (Slavin et al., 1984).

Student roles in cooperative learning

One of the cornerstones of cooperative learning is the assignment of student roles. These roles keep learners accountable to the group and ensure that each group member contributes to the completion of the task. A wide variety of possible roles can be created or altered to suit the requirements of a particular CL task. For example, group leaders manage the activities of other peers in the group by assigning roles, settling conflicts, and allowing others to share their thoughts. A secretary records the group's answers to the assigned task. A cheerleader encourages the rest of the team and might also occasionally remind them use English in their interactions. A supplier manages all of the materials necessary to complete the task. A presenter shares the groups' conclusions to the class. Of course, this list is not comprehensive and the teacher may have to devise other roles to give everyone a chance to contribute to the successful completion of a particular task.

Ensuring the smooth functioning of cooperative groups

Another important part of implementing CL in our lessons is the effective group management that urges learners remain on task and functioning cohesively as a group. This has to begin with the teacher always remembering that the fundamental purpose of cooperative learning is to offer students chances to do classroom tasks that guide them to practice and refine their L2 communicative competence as well as social and intellectual skills. Therefore, the teacher needs to constantly seek out and implement methods that facilitate learners' effective collaboration with minimal unnecessary conflict.

To achieve this aim, teachers should assign open-ended tasks without predetermined answers. Example tasks include deciding what items are needed on a desert island or agreeing on a grammar rule after analyzing example sentences. Littlejohn and Hicks (1998) enumerate several pros of open-ended tasks which include letting everyone in mixed-ability classes contribute by sharing their various ideas and supporting student self-direction while providing the teacher with a more direct window into their L2 proficiency. The teacher's scaffolding given throughout the completion of the task will usually guide learners toward wide-ranging and useful discussions and that result in thoughtful and creative task solutions. These scaffolds should take the form of a specific prompt like "Our top three main ideas are..." can aid group focus and communication rather than a vague prompt like "Our group's conclusion."

Classroom logistics is another important consideration when organizing CL tasks. Arrangement of the classroom space, presentation and demonstration of the classroom tasks, managing the noise level, student behavior and materials all need to be taken into account. To ensure the smooth functioning of CL groups, Jacobs (2004) recommends paying careful attention to task difficulty. As students are becoming familiar with CL, begin with less challenging activities and gradually build up to more complex work as they become accustomed to doing CL productively with their peers. Be prepared to explain and demonstrate task procedures so learners can have a clear idea of what they are supposed to do.

We should also circulate and monitor groups to intervene with necessary support whenever they appear to be struggling to complete the assigned task. We might sometimes see groups struggle to harmoniously work together due to the awkwardness of working with unfamiliar peers or personality conflicts. Some possible solutions for addressing these issues are as follows: Begin with explicit instruction and practice of social skills such as interrupting politely and encouraging peer participation that facilitate collaborative communication (Johnson & Johnson, 1990). Allow groups to experience success by making sure that their first few experiences convince them that CL tasks are both achievable and enjoyable. Besides this, we should have learners participate in teambuilding activities to develop peer rapport and trust.

Controlling classroom noise is another concern commonly associated with group work. We should expect that when students are working productively in their groups there will be a lot of talking which will generate a fair amount of noise. In that sense, some level of noise during CL activities is unavoidable. Naturally, the classroom will be noisier than when students are engaged in teacher-led instruction or individual seat work because everyone is talking at the same time. So, we have to accept some noise during CL activities because learners have to talk to accomplish the assigned task. However, we cannot allow our students to disturb other groups or those in neighboring classes so we must demonstrate an acceptable level of noise for them.

To reduce needless noise, one of the simplest and most effective techniques is to organize the classroom with students sitting close together and facing one another. That way they will not need to speak loudly just to be heard by other group members. Groups should also include a noise monitor who can prompt others when they are being too noisy. However, this role should change periodically so that no individual is forced to be the "minder" for too long. We can also combine these techniques with a warning signal such as flicking the lights when the noise level is too high. If the noise fails to be reduced after being warned two or three times, the activity could be shut down and followed up with something less engaging. Typically, students enjoy CL activities and they do not want to end them early so they will respond to these warnings.

Groups should also complete their tasks in English. The most important action that we can take to ensure that learners remain in the L2 is to carefully consider the difficulty of the task they have been assigned. Onerous tasks will cause learners to use the L1 more because they have to struggle with the two ambitious aims of using English to complete a task that is too difficult for them. That likely result is partial or total failure. Besides giving learners manageable tasks, we need to supply them with necessary linguistic scaffolds to perform the task in English. These can take the form of word banks and sample dialogues or dictionary access to confirm the meaning of unknown words.

Another way to avoid using the L1 is to include a skilled L2 user in each group who can help others when they are struggling to express themselves. Remember as well that learners may also need to occasionally be gently reminded to use as much English as possible but they do not have to be perfect. Also bear in mind that in addition to this gentle nudging, we should also give them liberal amounts of praise for all of their attempts to use the L2.

A final suggestion to help manage CL tasks is to be aware that some groups will finish earlier than others so you will need to be prepared with a follow up activity to keep them occupied – and not disrupting their peers – while the remaining groups are completing their task. These kinds of extra "sponge" activities occupy the remaining time for the early finishers while still promoting their English development. For example, we could allow them to work on homework, do extensive reading, help others complete their task, comparing their answers or a wide variety of other English enrichment activities. Just remember that sponge tasks should be engaging. They should also be able to fill the remaining time but easily cut short if necessary.

Examples of cooperative learning activities that promote the four skills

The following section contains some examples of more commonly used cooperative learning activities that focus on developing the four skills. Each of the following short summaries briefly introduces the CL activity and explains how to do it.

Jigsaw Reading

Groups have different sections of a text that they have to teach the main ideas from to each other. Groups then reform into new groups where everyone saw a different section of the text. Then they have to teach their section to the rest of their new group.

Send-A-Problem

Teams create practice problems based on the content of the lesson that other teams in the class then have to try to solve.

Match Mine

One partner dictates the content of a text, picture or describes an arrangement of objects (e.g., Lego Blocks) while another listener has to listen recreate the original design as closely as possible.

Snowball Fights

Students toss crumpled papers over imaginary volleyball net, pick up another student's "snowball" then mingle around asking and answering the question they have written on each snowball.

Numbered Heads Together

The teacher asks a question or gives a problem to the class. Groups discuss and agree on the answer. The teacher then calls a number and the student in each group with that number has to provide the answer for the group.

Inside/Outside Circle

Students form two concentric circles with pairs facing each other. Partners practice a dialogue, drill or discuss questions or those of the partner. After a time limit is reached, the outside circle rotates once to the left and they repeat the task. The same task can be done in two facing lines that rotate once after every turn.

Dictogloss

Learners write down key words from a text they hear. Then they get into small groups to add the grammar and reconstruct the text.

Teammates Consult

Students are given a series of questions to discuss. After they have discussed and answered all of the questions, they write a paraphrase of the group's answers in their own words.

Write a Jingle

Groups write a song, rap or chant based on the content of the lesson using a melody that they like. They can then incorporate karaoke music, clapping or finger snapping to the rhythm as they perform the song for the rest of the class.

Rotating Review

Teams discuss a topic, record their ideas, and then rotate to the next group's responses to read, discuss and add their thoughts and feedback.

4.19 Summary

This chapter is intended to provide a basic overview in how to plan a listening and speaking lesson. It has covered all of the key elements of each. With respect to teaching listening, teachers should prepare learners to listen by activating their background knowledge and spurring their interest with pre-listening activities. We should then gradually guide them through the listening process with a sequence of progressively easier tasks. These tasks should move from listening for gist and overall meaning to listening for details and focusing on the actual language of the passage. The listening lesson should be finished by connecting listening to other skills like speaking and writing to provide learners with additional practice interacting with the content and language of the listening passage.

The present, practice, produce (PPP) paradigm was suggested as a useful lesson structure for speaking instruction. We also discussed how key grammatical structures and vocabulary should first be presented through deductive or inductive methods. Next, we explored how practice activities such as exercises and drills should be integrated into the lesson. Finally, we touched on how learners need opportunities for production through activities like role plays or discussions so that they can become accustomed to using the target language while having to navigate actual communication.

This section on less-controlled speaking activities also incorporated some discussion of cooperative learning activities. This discussion reviewed some of the key principles of cooperative learning such as positive interdependence, accountability, social skills development, and continued refinement of group functioning. Some of the unique benefits of using CL were mentioned like its support of L2, intellectual and social skill development as well as positive affective states. A number of suggestions were made to ensure the smooth functioning of CL activities such as using student roles, open-ended tasks, noise reduction, and increased English use. Some well-known examples of CL activities were also introduced including: Jigsaw Reading, Numbered Heads Together and Dictogloss.

This chapter has provided the reader with a framework to organize listening and speaking lessons. The information presented in this chapter can enable you to prepare learners for listening as well as connect listening to other skills. This information can also facilitate the teaching of speaking in a structured manner that builds learners' skills rather than spending speaking lessons engaged in unstructured "free talk" that is of dubious value. As the world continues to become more and more interconnected, these L2 skills will only grow in value. Besides that, oral ability is typically the skill that the majority of learners desire most. It is also the skill that people typically use to judge a learners' L2 proficiency. Therefore, teachers have to make sure that they can prepare learners to develop these skills as much as possible in the limited time that we have with them.

SLA in Plain English

Chapter 5

Teaching Reading and Writing

Chapter 5
Teaching Reading and Writing

5.1 Introduction

This chapter introduces some key theories and concepts in L2 literacy education that can help guide novice L2 teachers as they seek resources to develop engaging and informative lessons for your learners. The chapter will cover the main differences between L1 and L2 reading and explain the distinction between intensive vs extensive approaches to L2 reading instruction. After that, some theories of the L2 reading process will be explained as well as how to plan a reading lesson. The second section of the chapter deals with L2 writing instruction. It begins with a brief history of L2 writing pedagogy and from there goes into produce, process and genre-based instructional approaches. The chapter finishes with a discussion of some ideas for connecting reading and writing through activities such as text mining, note-taking, and summarizing among others.

The information presented here should allow you to understand the main issues that we need to be aware of as a literacy teacher. It will also be helpful in giving you some guidance for how to structure your reading and writing lessons and integrating L2 reading and writing instruction. Few language teachers would deny the importance of English literacy in an EFL context and the many specific benefits of being literate in English offers. For instance, English literacy unlocks a vast amount of information for the learner. The fact is that English is the world's second language. It is the language of business, science, diplomacy, global cultural products, and international communication (The British Council, 1995). Thus, knowledge of English grants the learner access to cutting-edge information in these fields. It also allows the learner to connect with a vast global community of other first and second language English speakers.

A second important benefit of L2 literacy is the access that it can provide to comprehensible input for language acquisition. Indeed, Nuttall (2005) argues that "The best way to improve one's knowledge of a foreign language is to go and live among its speakers. The next best way is to read extensively in it" (p. 128). Likewise, writing can serve as a scaffolding device and memory aid for L2 learning that allows them to engage in additional private practice with the target language at their own pace. It is particularly helpful for haptic learners. Maybe best of all, writing also allows students to connect with people from around the world through the internet to share their interests and feel a community bond with likeminded people.

5.2 What should L2 literacy teachers teach?

A number of important concepts that have been found to have a substantial impact on learning to read in English as a second language (W. Grabe, 2009). These elemental components of reading are commonly known as the "Big Five". They include phonemic awareness, alphabet knowledge, vocabulary, fluency and comprehension.

Phonological awareness

Phonological awareness is "the ability to explicitly manipulate speech segments at the phoneme level" (Cunningham, 1990, p. 429). Phonological awareness includes the learner's ability to isolate, segment, recombine, blend, and compare sounds in a word (Anthony & Francis, 2005). This awareness underlies understanding the alphabetic principle upon which phonics instruction is built (Adams, 1990). Phonological awareness is widely believed to be the foundation of reading instruction because without phonological awareness learners are unable to make the sound-letter connections necessary to use phonics knowledge to decode text (Chard & Dickson, 1999). Indeed, phonological awareness in kindergarten predicts reading success throughout school (Shankweiler et al., 1995).

Phonics

English is an alphabetic language (unlike Mandarin Chinese, for example) so we can use the advantage of our alphabet letters and their associated sounds to "sound out" new words rather than just having to memorize the shapes of whole words. Phonics is the instructional method that teaches the relationship between phonemes (i.e., the sounds of English) and letters. Knowledge of phonics enables a reader to see the letters C-A-T and sound out the word cat.

It is important that we develop students' ability to use phonics so that they can decode newly encountered English words for themselves (Birch, 2014). Good phonics instruction shows clear sound/ letter relationships, does not confuse or overwhelm students with too many rules and gives chances for practice with real texts (not just decontextualized word lists) (Gunderson, D'Silva, & Murphy Odo, 2013). Bearing this in mind, an effective way to get children to improve their knowledge of letter-sound connections is through actually reading text that is at their level (Krashen, 2004).

Fluency

Pikulski and Chard (2005) define fluency as the "...accurate, rapid, expressive oral reading and is applied during, and makes possible, silent reading comprehension" (p. 511). Fluency is often called the bridge between decoding and comprehension because students have to be able to process words at a certain speed before they are able to put them together to comprehend text. It is thought to be comprised of accuracy, automatic word recognition, speed, and prosody/ expression (Rasinski, 2012). Fluency can be taught through teacher and peer modeling and regular practice, but it has often been overlooked in reading instruction (Rasinski, 2004). Timed reading, repetitive books and re-reading independent level texts are potentially helpful activities to build reading fluency (I. S. Nation, 2008).

Vocabulary and comprehension

According to Wilkins (1972), "...without grammar very little can be conveyed, without vocabulary nothing can be conveyed" (pp. 111–112). Indeed, vocabulary is fundamental to second language communication language and literacy instruction. Hu and Nation (2000) conclude that for learners to be able to read and comprehend a text at an acceptable level, they need to know anywhere from 95-98% of the words in that text. Therefore, we must teach vocabulary to enable students understand and communicate with others through English.

As students become more accurate and fluent readers, the texts they read become increasingly demanding in their assumed vocabulary knowledge. This vocabulary knowledge includes awareness of both individual words and lexical "chunks" (i.e., idioms). Nation (2001) points out that lexical knowledge includes knowing the form of a word (its pronunciation, spelling and parts), its meaning, its grammatical functions as well as level of formality.

Nation (2008) offers several useful suggestions for teaching vocabulary such as using word frequency lists to choose words to teach, pre-teaching key words before reading, simplifying texts or adding a glossary, using paraphrase and translation and other post reading exercises (e.g., fill in the blanks) as well as guiding students to guess new words in context and use dictionaries. A number of other researchers have argued that an effective way to acquiring new vocabulary is through extensive reading of graded readers (i.e., simplified texts) that are at an appropriate level for the learner (Krashen, 2011; Nakanishi, 2015). This is particularly true if extensive reading is combined with dictionary look up (Nation, 2015).

Some readers are good at decoding and may demonstrate acceptable fluency but still struggle with comprehension. There are two main reasons for this. One is that they may misunderstand that reading is sounding out words rather than getting meaning. That is, in their mind, reading is only sounding out the words on the page rather than trying to make sense of the text. This mindset may have been caused by previous instruction that focused heavily on phonics and decoding but left little space in the curriculum for making sense of the text (Lyle, 2014). Similarly, they may lack meaning vocabulary (they can decode the word but do not know what it means). This ability to read text without comprehending the meaning is sometimes referred to as "word calling" (Cartwright, 2011).

A second reason for learners' lack of comprehension could be that they have insufficient background knowledge about the content of the text (Langer, 2015). While building vocabulary knowledge is vital for text comprehension, it is not enough by itself. Equally as importantly, we need to be sure that the text relates to something that the student knows about. If a learner has to read a text about a topic that is completely unknown to her, even if she knows the vocabulary, she may still struggle to comprehend it. This is why Freire and Macedo (2005) point out that for learners to read the word, they must first read the world. That is, for a learner to successfully make sense of text, they must have some personal experience with the content of it. Langer (2015) referred to this kind of relevant world knowledge as envisionments which she defined as "worlds of knowledge in our minds that are made up of what we understand and what we don't about a particular topic or experience at any point in time" (p. 17).

We can foster greater student comprehension of the texts they read in our classes in a number of ways. First, we should ensure that learners have prerequisite knowledge and skills with regard to decoding (Perfetti & Hogaboam, 1975), fluency (Klauda & Guthrie, 2008) and vocabulary (Nation, 2008). Besides that, we need to facilitate their text comprehension by choosing texts that relate to their lives and interests and building background knowledge through exposing them to first-hand experiences such as field trips, as well as vicarious experiences like watching relevant video clips, having class discussions, doing theme-based teaching(Rupley, Logan, & Nichols, 1998).

5.3 Differences between L1 and L2 reading

Grabe and Stoller (2013) point out L1 readers differ from L2 readers in terms of the linguistic processing, individual experiential, and socio-cultural/ institutional dimensions of their experience. In general, linguistic and processing differences can be assumed for learners when they begin to learn to read in the L1 or L2. For instance, L1 readers will generally will have had more exposure to the oral language when they begin to learn to read. In contrast, L2 readers typically begin learning the oral and written language at around the same time (Grabe, 2009). Similarly, learners with varied L1 backgrounds will also cause different cross-linguistic influences on their L2 reading (Koda & Zehler, 2008). Lastly, L2 learners tend to have superior metalinguistic and metacognitive awareness due to their insights gained from having learned their L1 (Grabe & Stoller, 2013).

In addition to the influence of L1 variation, there are also individual and experiential differences that can result in varied outcomes for L1 and L2 readers. For example, differing levels of L1 reading abilities and motivations for reading in the L2can cause learners to have divergent experiences of the process of learning to read in an L2 (Takase, 2007; Yamashita, 2004). Likewise, differing exposure to L2 reading opportunities, genres of texts and language resources available in L2 contexts is sure to result in qualitatively different experiences for learners as well (Krashen, 2004).

Finally, socio-cultural and institutional differences also play a significant role in L1 versus L2 learners' experience of learning to read. The typically more varied socio-cultural backgrounds of L2 readers can lead to quite different expectations of the purpose and value of L2 literacy (Street, 1993).Cultural differences in ways of organizing discourse and texts may cause considerable challenges for learners reading comprehension if they approach texts with very different cultural schemata (Steffensen, Joag-Dev, & Anderson, 1979). Another important socio-cultural factor relates to the differing expectations of L2 educational institutions with respect to the emphasis placed on both L1 and L2 literacy. For instance, oddly, L1 literacy may be less of a priority in some educational contexts than L2 literacy(E. Williams, 1996).

5.4 Approaches to L2 reading instruction

L2 second language reading can be taught either through an intensive or extensive reading instructional approach. These two approaches to reading instruction can be distinguished from each other in a number of ways but one should not be considered to be superior or more important than the other. Indeed, effective L2 reading classrooms will include practice with a combination of both.

The materials used for intensive and extensive reading practice have some key differences. Intensive reading is typically characterized by using shorter texts to practice reading skills and strategies with a focus on accurate linguistic form. In contrast, extensive reading involves reading longer texts to understand the gist and experience pleasure while focusing on reading fluency and grasping the meaning of the text (Day & Bamford, 1998). Intensive reading materials are usually textbooks with passages that are relatively challenging for the learner because they contain more unknown language. As well, intensive reading passages are often accompanied with exercises that demonstrate learners' skill acquisition to the teacher. Extensive reading materials, by comparison, tend to be comprised of simplified books at the learners' level that are relatively easy with a large proportion of known words. These extensive reading materials also typically do not have accompanying exercises (Krashen, 2011).

The teacher's role tends to be more prominent in the generally teacher-centered intensive reading approach. The teacher-centeredness of this approach is demonstrated by the fact that intensive reading lessons occur more commonly in class following teacher selected materials (Renandya, 2007). Counter to this, extensive reading practice, while still requiring careful organization by the teacher, in practice tends to be considerably more self-directed on the part of the learner. This apparent learner autonomy is evidenced by the fact that learners rely more on self-selected materials that they will oftentimes read alone outside of class (Pilgreen, 2000).

5.5 Some theories of the reading process

Bottom up, top-down and interactive views of L2 reading

Although there are a large number of theories of L2 reading, three in particular will be briefly discussed here because of their influence on a considerable amount of the development of first and second language reading materials. These more widely-disseminated theories of L2 reading are bottom up, top down, and interactive views of reading.

A bottom-up view of reading

This view of the reading process holds that reading begins with the reader's ability to make connections between phonemes (i.e., sounds) and graphemes (i.e., letters) to decode the words in a text (Gray & Rogers, 1956). For example, if the reader sees the word "cat," he can connect those letters with the sounds / kæt/and the concept of a four-legged feline animal. If the reader is able to decode a word, she then proceeds to the next word in the sequence until the end of the sentence is reached. The meaning of the sentence is built up from word to sentence to paragraph until understanding of the text is complete. That is, meaning construction proceeds from part to whole. In this theory, the meaning of the text resides in the text itself and it is the reader's job to extract that meaning from the text (Nuttall, 2005). This means that reading is thought to be a somewhat of a passive activity. Accuracy of word recognition is considered to be a vital element of reading and phonics tends to be the instructional approach that is most often associated with bottom up views of reading (Villanueva de Debat, 2006).

Phonics instruction teaches the systematic relationship between letters and combinations of letters in written words as well as how to use this knowledge to read and write (Honig, Diamond & Gulohn, 2008). Phonics has also been described as examining the relationship between phonemes (sounds), graphemes (letters) and spelling patterns (Tompkins, Campbell, Green, & Smith, 2015). A widely used approach to phonics instruction is known as systematic phonics instruction aims to use a logical instructional sequence to introduce the key sound-letter correspondences necessary for effective reading through explicit explanation of the rules of phonics.

According to Mesmer and Griffith (2005), the term systematic relates to lesson scope (i.e., what letter–sound correspondences will be covered) and sequence (i.e., the order in which they will be taught). Explicit lessons have the teacher directly explain to learners what the lesson content is unlike an implicit approach where the teacher prompts learners to notice sound letter connections without directly explaining what they are. Instructional techniques are explicit or implicit while a syllabus can be thought of as being systematic.

A top-down perspective on reading

Bottom-up views of the reading process are typically contrasted with the top down perspective. Top-down theories of reading claim that we read for meaning and rely on our background knowledge to construct meaning from the text. Unlike bottom-up views, text understanding proceeds from whole to part. That is, before the reader begins to read the text, she makes predictions about the content of the text based on her prior background knowledge about the world, context clues (e.g., pictures), other similar texts and how language functions in general. Then she reads primarily to confirm her expectations about the content of the passage (Goodman, 2014). As she reads the text, she does so to sample it to confirm or adjust her predictions and not read every word. When she experiences difficulty, she re-reads as necessary to make sense of the text (Smith, 2004). In contrast to bottom-up views, there is more of an emphasis on fluency and readers are not expected to understand every word in a text to make sense of it.

A top-down perspective on the reading process is commonly associated with the whole language approach to reading instruction (Barnyak & Paquette, 2010). In this instructional approach, teachers are encouraged to focus on learner meaning making and enjoyment of literate activities by integrating authentic texts (i.e., children's literature) into their lessons rather than the more abstract and decontextualized texts commonly used for phonics instruction (Goodman, 2005). Whole language teachers are encouraged to focus mainly on developing learners' reading comprehension through giving them chances to engage in pleasure reading of predictable texts. Whole language also integrates multiple language skills such as listening, speaking reading and writing (Bergeron, 1990). This integration is achieved through classroom activities such as teacher interactive read aloud, and facilitating opportunities for learners to use written language and texts to communicate for authentic purposes. Learners are also encouraged to focus on the writing process over product with multiple opportunities draft and revise while seeking feedback from the teacher and peers. Whole language teachers are encouraged to create a print-rich classroom environment by using word walls and classroom libraries and other literate materials (Freeman & Freeman, 1992; Lems, 1995).

A third more recent theory of the reading process is known as the interactive model. This perspective aims to combine the most valid and useful insights from both the bottom up and top-down models. One of the main claims made by this model is that reading is both perceptual (bottom up) and cognitive (top down)(Grabe, 1988). The most recent iteration of interactive theory is the interactive-compensatory model. This theory holds that our mind contains several different processors for orthography, syntax, lexical, and semantic processors (Stanovich, 1984). In the interactive model, successful readers are both effective decoders and accurate interpreters of text because both interact as the reader uses both prior background knowledge and information from the text to construct meaning (Bernhardt, 2010; Grabe, 1991). Is this perspective, the reader uses a top down or bottom up processing depending on the text she is reading. For example, if the reader is faced with text that he is unfamiliar with he will draw more on bottom up processing to carefully process the text. However, if there are sections of that text that connect more to his linguistic and schema knowledge then he will read those parts in a more top down manner by drawing on background knowledge to make sense of those sections.

An approach to literacy pedagogy that is informed by this theory is balanced literacy instruction (Pressley, 2002). This perspective incorporates the most effective components of phonics and whole language instruction to develop literacy skills and strategies in a meaningful context. In essence, it allows teachers to integrate the best insights from both phonics and whole language (Schumm, 2006). A balanced literacy approach also encourages the integration of oral and written language so that learners are able to benefit from using their existing language knowledge as a scaffold to understanding written text genres through activities such as shared reading or shared writing (Taylor, Branscombe, Burcham, & Land, 2010). It is also important to point out that balanced literacy instruction does not mean using an eclectic "grab bag" of "fun activities" that lack any coherent rationale for why they have been combined.

With regard to classroom practice, the balanced literacy instructional approach is comprised of three main components which include reading, writing, and word study. Typical reading activities that happen in the balanced literacy classroom are teacher read aloud, shared reading, guided reading, and independent reading (Fisher, Frey, & Lapp, 2008). The writing activities are usually handwriting, shared writing, guided writing, and independent writing. To supplement the reading and writing skill development activities, opportunities for word study incorporate classroom tasks that support the development of learners' phonological awareness, phonics, and vocabulary knowledge (Kamps et al., 2007). These sorts of activities tend to take place in a wide range of grouping configurations such as whole class, small group and individual work (Pressley, 2002).

Literacy skills and strategies within a balanced perspective are also often introduced and practiced through what has been called the "gradual release of responsibility" framework (Pearson & Gallagher, 1983). This theory works by the teacher first modeling how to do a particular activity such as use a reading strategy like inferring. Next, the teacher and students engage in joint completion of the task or activity. After that, the students attempt the activity in small groups with input and feedback from the teacher as needed. Lastly, the learners perform the task themselves with assistance for the teacher as needed.

5.6 Reading lesson planning

Stages of an intensive reading lesson

When preparing L2 learners to learn to read in a second language, it is also important to point out that those who are beginning to learn to read in and L2 should have a strong literate foundation in their L1. If they do, so many of the literacy skills they have learned from learning to read in their L1 will transfer to their L2 (Cummins, 1980, 2016). If they are not literate in their first language, they will have considerable difficulty as they try to engage in the highly abstract task of using phonics to match sounds with letters. The difficulty of this task is compounded by the fact that they would not know the meaning of many words after they decoded them so it would be very difficult to make sense of a text written in a language they do not yet fully understand (Williams, 1996).

L2 reading lesson format

Lesson plans that practice reading skills are somewhat different than those that are used to teach speaking (e.g., PPP) lesson format. Instead, the ESL/EFL reading lesson is more comparable in structure to a listening lesson format. That is, a typical intensive reading lesson is arranged to have before, during, and after reading activities. Each phase of the lesson is included to enhance the reading experience and allow the learner to receive maximum benefit from it while also being able to integrate other language skills and learning strategies. The following section will present the components of an intensive reading lesson.

Pre reading

The first stage of the lesson happens before the reading starts. There are several important aims at this stage which include engaging the learners' interest in the topic, activating and filling in gaps in the knowledge or language that learners will need to understand the text, understanding the purpose for reading and making predictions about the text. Many of these pre-reading aims can be achieved simultaneously through doing a variety of activities such as teaching key vocabulary from the text, discussing related visuals, organizing pictures into a sequence and guessing the story that they tell. Many of the activities that were suggested as pre-listening activities would work here as well. Learners could also be allowed to guess the answers to during reading tasks. Vocabulary can be taught through showing realia or pictures, acting out the meaning, explanation, example sentences, synonyms or antonyms and - as a last resort - translation. As much as possible, try to elicit rather than explain vocabulary because students thinking about the relevant vocabulary they know activates their background knowledge as well.

Most of these pre-reading activities allow the learners to preview the text and reflect on what is happening in the story prior to reading. In accordance with an interactive theory of reading, these kinds of activities allow learners to practice the key reading comprehension strategies of activating relevant background knowledge and predicting.

During reading

The primary aim of activities used in the during reading phase of the reading lesson facilitating learners' development of reading skills such as phonemic awareness, decoding (phonics), fluency, and vocabulary knowledge. As well, learners should be exposed to pleasurable reading experiences so that not only will they be literate but they will also have a strong desire to read. As much as possible, when choosing activities and tasks, we should try to assign ones that reflect the kinds of literate events that learners would engage in beyond the classroom. For example, it would generally not be good practice for learners to memorize facts from a story because few readers would do this with stories they read in their everyday life.

When deciding what during reading activities to include, the aims of reading lessons will largely depend on the learners' specific literacy developmental needs. Therefore, most beginners will need to focus primarily on phonics and word identification. As their proficiency develops, lessons will gradually shift toward an emphasis on fluency and comprehension. However, all lessons should pay some attention to comprehension so that learners will ultimately understand that the point of reading is to make sense of the print.

English reading instruction should generally begin with an emphasis on phonics. Without a foundational knowledge of how the sounds and letters of English connect to each other, learners will struggle to decode and make sense of text. However, this does not mean that learners need to receive excessively detailed intensive phonics instruction. It is more beneficial for learners to have a firm grasp of the most common sound-letter correspondences than an inadequate understanding of a broader range of the phonics rules. Fortunately, with a solid understanding of the most common phonics generalizations, learners will be able to deduce many other phonics principles themselves through reading (Gunderson et al., 2013). A wide variety of activities can be used to teach phonemic awareness and phonics including activities such as sound-letter matching games that allow learners to manipulate the phonemes of English, explicit instruction of common sound-letter correspondences, and practice making sound-letter connections through independent reading and writing activities like dictation.

An example of a game that can be used to reinforce the sound-letter connections is "jumping phonics." This game allows kinesthetic learners to engage in making sound-letter associations learners with their feet. Preparation requires cut outs with the letters of the alphabet on them that the teacher scatters on the floor. After that, the class can be divided into two teams. A representative from each teach will do rock, scissors, paper and the winner will be told a word they have to spell. They must then jump from letter to letter to spell the word. If they successfully spell the word then their team gets a point and the process repeats.

Another versatile and easily prepared phonics practice activity is a board race. To prepare for this activity, the teacher would write several decodable words on the board and divide the students into two or more groups. The teacher would then call out one of the words on the board and representatives from each group would run to the board and try to be the first to touch the word the teacher said.

Once learners begin to have some facility with decoding the sounds of words in English, it is necessary to start developing learners' reading fluency. Fluency has been called the bridge between decoding and comprehension. It acts as a bridge because it is reading with sufficient speed that allows the learner to shift from focusing on decoding the text to paying attention to its meaning (Pikulski & Chard, 2005). Fluency can be developed through a wide range of activities such as timed reading, repeated reading, games like "Mad Libs", songs and chants among many others.

The third vital element that must be addressed in almost all reading lessons is comprehension. There are a substantial number of methods and techniques to teach L2 learners how to understand written text. When selecting from the plethora of methods available, it is important to bear in mind that learners need to practice using reading strategies such as predicting, self-questioning and monitoring understanding to comprehend the text.

There are several objectives that the teacher should seek to achieve when undertaking activities to promote learner comprehension of the reading text. These aims will include facilitating their use of a variety of reading strategies to comprehend the text. The teacher will also want learners to reflect on, evaluate and react to the text while they explain their developing understanding of it in class discussions. When guiding learners through a text, the teacher should also remember not to ask comprehension questions that the learners could work out the answer to without reading the passage.

Reading comprehension strategies can be developed through a variety of instructional techniques such as read aloud, shared-reading, guided reading, and independent reading. These techniques provide learners with opportunities to practice using comprehension strategies such as predicting, visualizing, monitoring comprehension, inferring, questioning, finding details, connecting and synthesizing among others. One reading instructional approach that has been growing in popularity is called modeling with a gradual release of responsibility (GRR)(Pearson & Gallagher, 1983). The purpose of this approach is to teach learners reading comprehension through the modeling and guidance of an expert L2 reader (i.e., their teacher).

This approach has the teacher demonstrate how to use reading strategies then learners try them out while receiving feedback from the teacher regarding their use of the strategy. According to this model, reading and writing instruction best proceed through several stages. The four-step process of GRR begins with the teacher modeling how to do it. The teacher first reads a text and thinks aloud to demonstrate how she uses the reading comprehension strategy. As the teacher reads through the text, she pauses to think out loud in front of the class so that they can hear what she is thinking as she reads. The choice of text is also important as the teacher models the comprehension strategy using a text that best showcases the effectiveness of the strategy (Duffy, 2009). The text used should contain the features that best highlight the strategy that the teacher wants to demonstrate. If the teacher would like to show the strategy of predicting, she should select a text that has a predictable story. For example, to model the strategy of predicting, it is best to choose a predictable text like "Brown Bear, Brown Bear, What Do You See?" by Eric Carle or "No, David" by David Shannon. These books easily show the strategy of making predictions. If she is reading a predictable text, she will stop occasionally to make predictions and check those predictions.

The next stage in the GRR process is the shared think aloud. After the teacher has sufficiently demonstrated the reading comprehension strategy, she can begin to increase student involvement in the think aloud. The teacher continues to demonstrate the strategy but this time she asks to students to contribute to the demonstration by offering their own first attempts to use the strategy. She may do this by asking them share their own predictions about the text in a class discussion. As learners offer their predictions, the teacher provides feedback and guidance as necessary. At this point, the teacher and students think aloud together but the teacher is still leading the process.

The third phase of the GRR process is similar to the second in that it is a shared think-aloud. However, the key difference is that most of the responsibility for thinking aloud has shifted to the learners who are working in small groups by doing cooperative activities like reciprocal teaching. They engage in reading the text and thinking aloud with each other while the teacher circulates among the groups and offers support and clarifications as needed.

The final step in the gradual release of responsibility procedure is for the learners to use the new reading strategy independently. For this independent practice, they have to read books that are at their appropriate level silently by themselves while attempting to use the new strategy. If they experience problems, they can call on the teacher and receive one-on-one feedback and individualized guidance on how to use the strategy more effectively.

As learners develop their strategic knowledge and competence, they will also need to develop their ability to use a wide variety of reading strategies be comfortable L2 readers. Therefore, in addition to demonstrating the use of individual strategies, the teacher must also show learners how to choose the best strategy from among several to suit their reading purpose. Learners also need to know how to use strategies flexibly in combination in order to adjust their reading approach to best suit their reading purpose. This strategy coordination process should be modelled and practiced as well.

There are a number of other helpful methods and techniques that we can use to teach reading comprehension to second language learners. There are the more commonly-used during reading comprehension tasks including comprehension questions, gap fills, re-ordering sentences or paragraphs and answering multiple choice or true/ false questions.

In addition to these more traditional tools, there are several less widely known techniques that can facilitate learners' reading comprehension development. One such method is the language experience approach (LEA). In essence, LEA works by the teacher and students first sharing an experience like a field trip or watching a short film. From there, the students dictate a text to the teacher about their shared experience. That text then becomes the basis of the class's reading lesson as the students read it together or individually to themselves.

Reading aloud is another excellent often undervalued classroom activity that can support learners' literacy development in many ways such as augmenting their vocabulary knowledge and stimulating their interest in L2 books and reading (Krashen, 2011; Trelease, 2013). Beyond reading aloud, the teacher may do shared reading or interactive read aloud where students can see and follow along with the text the teacher reads as it in from a "big book" or projected on an overhead. During the reading, the teacher can stop periodically to discuss everyone's reactions to the story.

Another type of reading comprehension instruction method for beginning L1 readers that may also be helpful for beginning L2 readers is known as guided reading. In guided reading, the teacher works with a small group of four to six learners who share some common reading challenge. Each learner takes turns reading from their own copy of the reading text while the teacher guides their reading by modeling or providing prompts, questions or feedback on the learners' problem areas with respect to print concepts, relevant background, vocabulary or conceptual knowledge, decoding, fluency, or comprehension (Nation, 2008).

Directed Reading Thinking Activity (DRTA) is a proven approach for L1 readers whose primary objective is to practice using the comprehension strategies of prediction and checking comprehension (Maarof & Suharjo, 2010). The teacher prepares for DRTA by choosing an engaging story that is somewhat predictable and deciding on where in the story she can to ask guiding questions.

During DRTA, the teacher directs and activates students' thinking before reading a passage by scanning the title, and pictures in the story (but not the last couple of pages). While the teacher and students read the text together, the teacher should use open-ended questions to direct students as they make predictions about the story (e.g., "What do you think the passage will be about?"). The teacher reads up to the first pre-selected stopping point. She then prompts the students with questions about specific information and asks them to evaluate their predictions and refine them if necessary. Before reading each section, the teacher should ask questions like "what will happen next? Why do you think so?" At the end of each section, she can ask "Were we right? How do you know?" Students should be prompted to use the text to justify their answers. This process should be continued until the book is finished. Having learners make predictions and then check their predictions against the story allows them to practice two key comprehension strategies of predicting and then confirming predictions.

A number of L2 reading comprehension instructional techniques also draw upon the principles of cooperative learning to practice reading comprehension. For example, literature circles have learners read a common text and meet to discuss their reactions to the text (Furr, 2004). Each group member assumes a different role within the group such as the summarizer, discussion director, vocabulary expert, questioner, or inference maker. The teacher can designate other possible roles if desired. These roles allow the learners to have accountability within their group and ensure that important aspects of the discussion receive appropriate attention. Literature circles can be used for non-fiction texts as well (Williams, 2010).

Reciprocal reading is another similar cooperative reading activity that can be used to promote reading comprehension strategy use. As with literature circles, learners get into groups of four where they each have their own role. The unique feature of this technique is that each role allows the learner to practice one of four commonly-used reading comprehension strategies including predicting, summarizing, questioning and clarifying (Soonthornmanee, 2002).

Two more cooperative learning strategies are jigsaw reading and radio reading. In the case of jigsaw reading, learners must divide into several expert groups. Each group is given a section of a task that they are responsible for. They must study their section of text and agree on what the most important information from it is as well as the meaning of any key words in it. After they have completed this first task, they must then move into home groups that contain members that have each read one of the various sections of the assigned text. In the home groups, they will take turns reporting on their expert group's answers for their section of the text (McCafferty et al., 2006). For radio reading, each group assigned part of the text to read and make comprehension questions about. They then read their section to the others who have to discuss and answer their questions (Tierney, Readance, & Dishner, 1990).

A final form of reading practice that is vital to developing learner comprehension abilities is independent reading. This type of reading is characterized by students silently reading texts at their ability level on their own. Independent reading also has also been referred to in several different ways by different scholars. Some other commonly used terms include sustained silent reading, free voluntary reading, and extensive reading. Extensive reading is a widely used term in L2 contexts (e.g., Day & Bamford, 1998; Renandya, 2007) whereas the term sustained silent reading tends to be more widely used in L1 contexts (Gardiner, 2005; Pilgreen, 2000). As part of independent reading, there may be a conferencing component where teachers set reading goals with learners or conduct mini-lessons where they model and practice reading strategies that learners can use to facilitate their comprehension (Atwell, 2007; Miller, 2010).

Post reading

Once the reading itself has been completed, other tasks or activities should be used to follow up on the reading. There are two main purposes for post reading activities which are to integrate the other language skills (listening, speaking and writing) and to work with the content of the reading. The four skills could be integrated in several ways. First, learners could listen to a story about the same topic that they just read about and discuss differences between the two texts. They could also practice writing by journaling a personal response to what they read or writing a letter to one of the characters. Art could also be incorporated into the lesson by having learners design a comic strip or book jacket for a text that they read. Indeed, an almost limitless variety of arts-based activities could be used as a follow up to reading.

In addition to working with the language skills, learners need to engage with the content of their reading on a deeper level. That is, they should have chances to process, reflect, and discuss the themes and content presented in the reading through cooperative learning activities such as think-pair-share, stand up, hand up, pair up or role plays. These cooperative learning activities allow learners to share their understandings of and reactions to the content of what they read. At the same time, learners are able to practice listening and speaking with each other. These small group cooperative learning activities can be followed up by with class discussions where teachers can provide feedback to learners or their own perspective on the topic.

We may also want to ensure that learners have the chance to learn the L2 from their reading. This language learning can happen through allowing them to focus on making form-meaning connections in the reading text. The use of consciousness raising activities such as highlighting grammar features in a text (i.e., input enhancement)(Han, Park, & Combs, 2008) or seeing many examples of a target structure through an input flood may help the learner acquire the target structure (Reinders & Ellis, 2009). Teachers can also spend time explicitly instructing learners about the key language features that they hope students will learn from the text. This direct instruction may also facilitate their consciousness raising and language learning (Hernández, 2011).

As well, when selecting activities to use at this stage of the lesson, it is helpful to choose activities that are based upon as authentic responses to the reading passage as possible (Duke, Purcell-Gates, Hall, & Tower, 2006). Selection of suitable follow up activities entails pausing to reflect on what learners would actually do after reading a text outside the classroom. For example, after reading a storybook at home, we can ask ourselves how likely learners would be to start filling out phonics worksheets. Recognizing that they would probably be more likely to talk to their friends about their reaction to the story, we should give them the chance to this kind of activity in class. This is not to say that learners should never do follow up activities that do not naturally follow from the reading but rather that we should strive to choose authentic follow up activities as often as we can.

5.7 Writing in a second language

A brief history of L2 writing instruction

L2 writing instruction has gone through some significant shifts in approach over time. Initially, second language writing instruction was focused upon having learners follow a model of the type of text that they wanted to write as closely as possible. This was known as a product based approach. Learners were expected to produce a text that was structurally very similar to the model that also contained grammatically well-formed sentences. Thus, there is a heavy emphasis on imitation of the model (Nordin & Mohammad, 2006). The main differences between the model text and the learner's version of it would be that the content relates directly to the learner. Another important characteristic of this model is its strong emphasis on accuracy of the final written product in terms of its grammar, spelling, mechanics and structure (Silva, 1990).

Although, text structure receives some attention, the primary emphasis in the model is on sentence level grammatical accuracy. Given this focus on accuracy, the activities used in the product-based approach are more controlled and guided in that they involve learners copying others' examples before producing their own. While Badger and White (2000) acknowledge that a product approach teaches text features and offers the scaffold of imitation, its serious limitation is that it does not emphasize the actual steps in writing enough. As well, the product-based approach fails to meaningfully incorporate the unique understandings and abilities that learners bring to the writing event.

Another approach to writing developed based on researchers' increasing attention to the process that expert writers actually follow when they write. Unlike a product-based approach's focus on grammatical accuracy, researchers studying competent writers noticed that they spent time planning and producing multiple drafts through an iterative process of ongoing refinement of their work based upon feedback from others (Kroll, 2001). As its name hints, the process approach follows a series of stages which include pre-writing (i.e., brainstorming), drafting, receiving feedback, revising, proofreading and publishing (Peregoy & Boyle, 2005).

The major strength of the process approach is that it pays attention to writing abilities and makes space for learners' background knowledge. However, it also tends to view writing as a consistent sequence of steps regardless of genre being written, and it typically does not give sufficient guidance on the actual language needed to produce various genres of writing (Badger & White, 2000). Based on these limitations, some educators in the new millennium are beginning to advocate for writing instruction to incorporate more precise direction on how to construct texts according to appropriate genre conventions (Hyland, 2004). For example, explicitly teaching learners how the structure and language of a genre like a description differs substantially from that of narrative (Knapp & Watkins, 2005).

Fortunately, writing teachers do not have to choose one approach to writing instruction and exclude the others. Indeed, some educators argue that learners benefit most when their writing teachers combine the best aspects of various approaches in an "informed eclectic" manner (Howard, 2000; Kumar, 2013). Such an approach promises to allow us to help learners experience the benefits of a process-based approach that facilitates fluent and confident writing. At the same time they learn to produce texts that are both linguistically accurate and appropriate to the sociocultural context (Badger & White, 2000).

The written product

Before we begin to consider what the final product should be for a piece of writing, we should first ask ourselves what the key elements of any piece of writing are that we need to pay attention to if we want our learners to produce accurate texts that are easily understood. Beginning with a somewhat broader perspective on the text, it is important to help students recognize the unique features of a given genre of text. Many students may not be aware that unique genre features permeate all levels of a text from its overall organization down to unique grammatical structures and word choices that are made in its construction. For example, we can quickly recognize the genre of a recipe by the way it is organized into ingredients and procedures. We can also observe the unique grammatical features of the text such as the use of number and measurements in the ingredients section as well as imperative sentences in the procedures.

Besides these key text characteristics, writers also need to know how to organize information into coherent and cohesive paragraphs so that it is logically organized and flows well. They need to consider mechanics and appropriate language choices to create the style, voice and tone they desire as well. In addition to these important considerations, those writing by hand or without the aid of word processing software must remember to take into account the need for legible handwriting, conventional spelling, and appropriate punctuation.

5.8 Instructional techniques

Product-based techniques

There are a variety of useful techniques that L2 writing teachers can draw upon to facilitate beginning L2 writers' development that originate in a product-based approach to writing instruction. Some examples of relevant activities include the use of letter and word tracing. These tasks can help learners familiarize themselves with new letters and become fluent in forming letters and words. Delayed copying and dictation can also help learners develop fluent access to phrases (Nation, 2008).

Other product-based activities that can scaffold learners' writing include fixing errors in example sentences or paragraphs. Learners can also rearrange words into sentences or sentences into paragraphs. Another commonly-used exercise is gap-fill. These types of exercises can include completing speech bubbles for cartoons made by sites like www.makebeliefscomix.com or being shown a model text and having to reproduce the model with one's own information in it. Exercises that provide a bit less scaffolding include supplying learners with content words in a sentence and they have to add in the grammar (i.e., dictogloss or grammar dictation). The key benefit of these kinds of controlled writing activities is that they help learners to "practice the art of putting words together in well-formed sentences, paragraphs and texts" (Harmer, 2006, p. 55)

Process writing techniques

As with product-based approaches, process-based writing still has plenty to offer L2 writers. As discussed above, the process-based view of L2 writing separates writing into several stages including pre-writing, drafting, revising, editing and publishing. It should be noted that although they have been presented in a linear manner, these "stages" are actually iterative meaning that while they follow and build on each other, the writer can freely move among them as necessary to ensure a more well-written piece (Peregoy & Boyle, 2005). The purpose of pre-writing is for the writer to generate possible ideas and structures for her writing to follow through a number of invention techniques such as free writing and mind mapping. The purpose of pre-writing is to generate as many creative ideas as possible so learners should be encouraged to think outside the box and not edit themselves at this stage. The drafting phase is where the writer attempts to produce a rough version of the writing without worrying too much about its accuracy or quality as long as she can get ideas down on the page. The learner should not be too worried about producing accurate writing when drafting. The aim is simply to get words on the page. Once the learner has a draft that she can work with, it is time to begin the revision process.

During revision, the writer should focus on making the meaning clear and structuring and organizing the text appropriately. At this stage, the writer should still not be overly concerned with the accuracy of the language but rather the clarity of the meaning and expression. After revising the text, the learner can move on to the editing and proofreading stage. This is where she should begin to refine and polish the accuracy of its language. The learner may engage in activities such as reading the text aloud or peer evaluation that allow her to catch any remaining linguistic errors in the text. Once the learner is satisfied that the writing is relatively error-free, she may then "publish" it in a number of ways such as putting it on the classroom or school corridor wall or even posting it online for a potentially much wider audience to read. The benefit of publishing student work in this way is that it gives them a real audience to write for.

Process-based writing lessons are also generally structured somewhat differently than product-based. Unlike a product-based approach which assumes a more teacher-centered and lockstep methodology, process-based approaches encourage more of a workshop atmosphere (Strech, 1994). This situation more realistically represents the kind of environment writers could expect in most writing events outside of the classroom. There are also numerous educational advantages of a workshop approach. For instance, it is more student-centered in the sense that learners can express themselves more creatively and seek input and feedback from the teacher and each other (Atwell, 1998). Another benefit of writing workshops is that learners can share their work with an audience beyond their teacher (Calkins, 1986). Thanks to online tools, they can publish their work through an ever-expanding variety of venues such as author's chair, student made books, sites like Storybird, and even Kindle KDP.

Process writing can also supported by cooperative learning activities (DeBolt, 1994). Some examples of cooperative-learning writing tasks that can connect to a process-based writing include jigsaw writing and group composition. For both tasks, learners are divided into groups or pairs. Each group then plans and writes one composition. Within the groups, each learner suggests sentences and corrects the sentences recommended by the other learners. Both of these tasks assume that learners can work together to creatively generate a story with input and feedback from each other.

Genre-based approach

A more recent perspective on L2 writing instruction is the genre-based approach. In essence, genre-based writing instruction is based on the insight that all written texts are designed to serve particular social purposes and the language contained within those texts is structured in such a way as to achieve that purpose (Johns, 1997). For example, a greeting card is written to express well wishes. In accordance with this purpose, it includes features such conciseness, focus on the addressee, greetings and thanks that help to achieve that aim (Mullagayanova, 2016). The primary aim of most genre-based instruction is to directly teach learners the particular features of specific written genres so that they produce those genres appropriately (Hyland, 2004). Domains of L2 writing where genre-based instruction tends to be particularly influential are EAP and ESP.

Hyland (2003) proposes a writing instructional sequence for introducing and practicing a new written genre. First, the teacher is recommended to build the context for the genre by explaining the kinds of social context that the target genre could be found in and the typical social purposes that it would serve. After that, the teacher will demonstrate how to deconstruct a particular genre through a genre analysis. This genre analysis can allow learners to observe the breakdown a genre to see what its core components are as they are identified and described by the teacher.

Next, the teacher can model how to create an example of such a genre through thinking aloud as she writes a sample text in front of the learners. The teacher can then enlist the participation of the learners to co-construct another version of a genre. After learners seem to have an adequate understanding of how to create the genre, they can be given the opportunity to try producing their own text. Once learners have written their own examples of the genre, the teacher can then discuss with them how that particular genre connects to other related genres commonly used within the same social context. For instance, if they have written an academic essay, they could be shown how it relates to other supporting genres like class lectures or presentations.

5.9 Connecting reading and writing

In addition to teaching reading and writing separately in the L2 classroom, a number of L2 literacy scholars have also begun to advocate for instruction that connects L2 reading and writing. Krashen and Lee (2004) argue that reading and writing instruction should be integrated because reading "provides writers with knowledge of the language of writing, the grammar, vocabulary, and discourse style writers use" (p. 10). Hirvela (2004) adds that reading can support writing in that through reading learners are able to expand their knowledge of the rhetorical characteristics of written texts. Likewise, realizing that reading and writing are both composing processes whereby learners use their own world knowledge to create meaning from language (Tierney & Pearson, 1983) helps us to see that on some level reading and writing development may be mutually reinforcing. Indeed, Hedgcock and Ferris (2005) argue that "research and practical experience have demonstrated overwhelmingly that one cannot become a proficient writer in any language without also developing an array of literacy skills, including the ability to comprehend written text efficiently—fluently and accurately" (p. 31).

5.10 Connecting reading and writing in the L2 classroom

Reading and writing can be connected in the L2 classroom in a wide variety of ways. Connecting these dual aspects of literacy fall into two broad categories which are reading-to-write and writing-to-read (Hirvela, 2004). In the case of reading to write, one way of connecting the two is through the use of model texts and "text mining." Essentially, this procedure has the students using a text that is of the same genre that they want to produce. Following the prompting and guidance of the teacher, the learners examine the text and note the key features and characteristics that they must include when they reproduce the genre themselves. This instructional technique differs from a product-based approach to writing. Rather than learners simply being taught to mindlessly imitate a model, they are carefully guided on how to identify the key features of a text, reflect on the purposes those characteristics serve as well as how to reproduce them in their own writing.

A second method for using reading to teach writing is through the use of summaries or paraphrase. Both of these tasks teach learners how to extract information as well as understand the content of a text on a deeper level (Hirvela, 2004). When learners summarize, they have to engage with the content of the text on a deeper level (Zamel, 1992). Paraphrase similarly pushes learners to rephrase complex or technical content into more comprehensible terms while learners hone their writing fluency (D'Angelo, 1979).

A third way that reading to write can be instantiated is through note taking. These notes could be more informal as with notes that learners might take in the margins of the texts that they read. The main advantage of these type of notes is that they enable the learner to summarize, comment, react, and make inter or intra-text connections to other information (Hirvela, 2004). Notes may also be more formal as with note-taking systems such as the Cornell system. Formal note taking methods offer the added advantage that it encourages learners to better recall and condense information from reading.

Other suggestions of incorporating reading to write include study guides and exit slips. Study guides can benefit learners through directing their attention to key information in the text (Alvermann, Phelps, & Ridgeway, 2007). Likewise, exit slips can be a simple way for learners to demonstrate their comprehension of main ideas in a text by offering "...a physical space to digest ideas, to question, to ponder, to ruminate over what has been shared and discussed in class...[that provides] powerful clarification of how students are making sense of content..." (Leigh, 2012, p. 190).

Hirvela (2004) also discusses how teachers can connect reading and writing through writing-to-read. In this instance, learners are given opportunities to write prior to, during or after reading. These brief writing sessions can help them better make sense of a text by pushing them to reading and think about it more carefully to determine how well the text matches their own ideas about it. Another approach to writing-to-read is known as writing to learn. In essence, this technique entails the learner writing in order to recall, organize, reflect and understand information or course content. This kind of writing can also be used to demonstrate their knowledge of material.

A number of classroom activities can be used to support both writing to read and writing to learn. Some examples of such activities that can facilitate writing to read include free writing where learners quickly write about anything that comes to mind prior to reading to generate and gather their thoughts on the reading topic. The aim of freewriting is for learners to freely generate ideas rather than worry about the quality or accuracy of their writing. Journaling is another classroom activity that can support writing to read because it can allow learners to clarify their thinking on the topic in a private manner. Dialogue journals can also be used as opportunities for the student and teacher to engage in some exchange about the learner's ideas.

Writing to learn can also be accomplished through a variety of activities as well. One example is the use of "entry slips" that encourage students to focus their attention on the reading topic or demonstrate their relevant subject knowledge to give the teacher an idea of where to begin. Learning logs are an additional tool that teachers can use to help learners to process their thoughts about the content of their reading. Students can use learning logs to write about their reflections on what they felt they have learned from their reading. In the process, they can reflect on and process the content they studied so writing becomes a means of processing the content on a deeper level. Writer's notebooks are yet another way that students can write to learn. They allow learners to stretch their imagination as they write or draw in their notebook for a few minutes daily. Textual or visual prompts can be used to stimulate learners' thinking and they can chances to share their ideas orally with their classmates.

5.11 Summary

This chapter offers an introduction to planning a reading and writing lesson and well as some suggestions for how to combine the skills together in the ESL/EFL classroom. It began by looking at some of the more prevalent theories of L2 reading including bottom-up, top-down and interactive views of the reading process. From there, the "big 5" concepts in reading instruction which included, phonemic awareness, phonics, fluency, vocabulary and comprehension were overviewed. As well, the main stages in a reading lesson which include pre-reading, during reading and post reading received some attention. The next section of the chapter dealt with L2 writing instruction. It covered approaches to teaching writing which included the gradual release of responsibility model and another writing instructional sequence that is based on a genre-based approach to writing pedagogy. The final section discussed making reading-writing connections. This included activities that involve reading to write as well as activities that entail writing to read.

The reader can use the information outlined in this chapter to plan, structure and integrate reading and writing lessons for the L2 classroom. It is important that we teach L2 literacy skills because an understanding of how to read and write in English can be invaluable to learners for numerous reasons. For instance, the ability to read in English provides our learners with access to information from around the world via the internet. As well, the internet has made English writing into an increasingly valuable skill as learners can communicate with people in other countries online for both personal and professional purposes.

Chapter 6

Multicompetence and Professional Development

Chapter 6

Multicompetence and Professional Development

6.1 Introduction

The previous chapters of the book have focused mainly on teaching methods for the various skills including listening, speaking, reading and writing. From this point forward, the book's emphasis will shift somewhat to discussion of topics related to second language acquisition. This chapter begins with some discussion of what it means to be bilingual. The various competing definitions of bilingualism are discussed as well as whether most L2 teachers could be considered bilingual by those definitions. After that, the chapter explains the notions of multi-competence and translanguaging what these concepts might mean for helping L2 learners and their bilingual teachers more comfortably assume the identity of a bilingual person. The chapter wraps up with some discussion of suggestions for how bilingual teachers can continue to develop their abilities in their target language as part of their commitment to ongoing professional development.

This chapter can help new teachers reflect on what a bilingual person is and to realize that it does not mean that they have to use the L2 at a native speaker level. Hopefully, this discussion will help non-native speaking bilingual teachers feel more confidence in the unique and valuable skills that they bring to the language classroom rather than unfairly comparing themselves to native speakers. The chapter also helps teachers to consider ways to continue to develop their L2 proficiency. This way they can feel as though they are continuing to grow and that they have some control over their growth. They may also want to continue striving to improve as an L2 speaker and be an inspiring model of a life-long learner for their learners.

6.2 What does it mean to be a bilingual?

Some of the more common definitions of bilingualism contrast two different types. For instance, balanced bilinguals who have equivalent mastery of their L1 and L2 are often compared with dominant bilinguals who are more proficient in one language. Similarly, early bilinguals who have learned the L2 from childhood are typically contrasted with late bilinguals who did not acquire their L2 until later in life. Another type of bilingual that sometimes is mentioned is receptive bilinguals. These individuals can understand their L2 without necessarily being able to produce it. They have often learned the L2 as a heritage language while they were growing up.

It is commonly believed that "bilingual" people are equally fluent in both languages. However, one could surely argue that if someone can communicate effectively in two languages then she is bilingual irrespective of whether or not she can use both languages to the same level of proficiency. Indeed, it is not easy to find bilinguals who actually have entirely equivalent proficiency in both languages (Harris & Nelson, 1992).

The criteria typically used to decide whether or not someone is bilingual is that they can use both of their languages in the same way as a monolingual native speaker. Brown and Larson-Hall (2012) argue that using a native speaker as the standard for bilingualism is unrealistic because we cannot be a native speaker if we have not grown up in the community of target language speakers. Of course the definition of the term "native speaker" is surrounded by considerable debate but the distinction between "native" and "non-native" speakers persists (Medgyes & Celce-Murcia, 2001).

Multi-competence (Cook, 1991) is another concept with relevance to bilingualism. In essence, this is the perspective that a bilingual language user is qualitatively different than a monolingual. The term is used to describe an L2 user's knowledge and use of two or more languages. The difference lies in the fact that the bilingual has two languages inside his head instead of one. A number of implications exist for this bilingualism such as the L2 user's ability to consciously draw on features of the L1 to fill in gaps in L2 knowledge. Equally, the L2 user can be unwittingly influenced by cross-linguistic interference from the first language as when their L2 pronunciation is strongly affected by their L1.

A multi-competence perspective does not insist that the L2 user must demonstrate native speaker level competence in the L2 to be considered bilingual. Instead, Cook(1999) argues that "[the] ultimate attainment of L2 learning should be defined in terms of knowledge of the L2. There is no reason why the L2 component of multicompetence should be identical to the monolingual's L1..." (p. 191). Therefore, a multicompetent L2 user will probably not communicate exactly like a native speaker. That is, they may speak with a foreign accent and display non-standard errors in their L2 use. However, they are able to meet their needs and productively contribute to the community of L2 speakers. Well-known examples of multi-competent L2 English users might include Angela Merkel and Jackie Chan. The point is that using the monolingual native speaker as the standard for L2 proficiency is deeply flawed from a multicompetence perspective (Cook, 2016).

Translanguaging is another relevant concept that has been developed recently that also connects to teacher bilingual competence. In essence, translanguaging is based upon the claim that the L1 and L2 are not two separate entities inside the mind of the learner. Rather, they are deeply intertwined such that languages are really just collections of linguistic features that the user mentally keeps distinct because national identity has them wrongly believe that the languages are discrete in the mind (García & Wei, 2014).

One major implication of this perspective on L1-L2 relationships is that unlike traditional monolingual approaches to language teaching that encouraged L2 only in the classroom, this view holds that the L1 can be effectively used as a scaffold to help learners better comprehend the L2 through activities such as code mixing and translating (García, 2009). Nevertheless, translanguaging does not mean that students can use the L1 however they want. In fact, specific guidelines have been suggested for effectively using the L1 in the second/foreign language learning classroom (García, Johnson, Seltzer, & Valdés, 2017). Translanguaging connects to multicompetence in that both perspectives agree that the L1 is a valuable resource that should be strategically used in the L2 classroom. The increasing recognition of the valuable role of the L1 expands the importance of the bilingual or multicompetent L2 teacher who can effectively use the L1 as a scaffold for effective L2 learning (Butzkamm & Caldwell, 2009).

6.3 The implications of these insights for bilingual language teachers

Reves and Medgyes (1994) point out that historically bilingual teachers who were "non-native" teachers of English have been rather self-deprecating. They have tended to view themselves as inferior to native speaking teachers. The cause of this negative self-perception is typically attributed to their relatively less proficient command of the target language than native speakers. Reves and Medgyes (1994) also note that this unhealthy interchange between L2 competence and professional image can turn into a vicious circle whereby "A constant realization of their limitations in the use of English may lead to a poorer self-image, which may further deteriorate language performance, and in turn may lead to a cumulatively stronger feeling of inferiority" (p. 364). This sense of inferiority has also often been exacerbated by the widespread myth that native speakers are naturally better teachers than bilinguals (Cook, 2010). However, non-native speaking teachers need to move beyond this mindset and begin to change their perspective to see the unique and valuable insights and information they can offer to their students.

A key aspect of re-framing their perspective begins with sincerely believing that they are bilinguals and not faulty native speakers. This shift in perspective can go a long way towards building their confidence as an L2 user. Likewise, internalizing concepts such as multicompetence and translanguaging can help bilingual teachers to move away from the limiting identity of being a "non-native" teacher towards the more positive self-perception of being a bilingual teacher. Naturally, accepting our bilingual identity should not give us license to lower our expectations of ourselves or our learners. As life-long learners, we should identify L2 learning strategies and activities that suit our strengths to continue to develop ourselves as an L2 user as we model this behavior for our learners. At the same time, we need to encourage our learners to continuously build their L2 proficiency through identifying and accessing materials that communication opportunities that capture their interest.

L2 teachers and learners also need to accept the fact that assuming the identity of being a bilingual user of the target language does not put an end to their challenges as an L2 learner. Inevitably, there will be people who will try to denigrate your skills for their own personal reasons. They may try to position you as being "non-native" so that they can claim expertise over you or just to be cruel. However, we must ignore these negative influences and model the kind of positive attitude that we want our learners to have as L2 users. That attitude is being a confident user who seeks to communicate to the best of her ability while acknowledging that she may make some mistakes along the way.

6.4 Your ongoing L2 development

An example of a challenging long-term goal would be to eventually get to an advanced level (e.g., C1 on the Common European Framework of Reference for Languages). Having this kind of ambitious goal is important for a number of reasons. First, language teachers are model L2 users for their learners. This is why bilingual teachers serve as role models for their learners that monolingual native speakers never can. Many of your students will look to you as an example for what they can realistically hope to achieve in the L2 (Medgyes & Celce-Murcia, 2001). Learners seeing that their teacher is not a confident user of the L2 may place unnecessarily restrictive limits on what they think they can achieve as well.

We also have to remember that we are not just role models of a bilingual person but as a lifelong learner. When we show students what we do to improve and talk with them about our language learning process, we demonstrate that it takes time to develop high proficiency and that becoming fluent is largely a self-directed task that is achieved over many years of practice. The reality is that your learners will usually believe what you do over what you say. So, if you fervently promote the value of learning the L2 without showing them that you actually do this yourself then they will likely conclude that L2 learning is something we should spend more time praising than actually doing.

6.5 Suggested activities for the teacher's personal language development

An important caveat is that for sustained L2 development, it is necessary to engage in activities that we enjoy. The suggestions presented in the following section will probably not work if you do not enjoy doing those kinds of activities. This is because you will likely give up shortly after choosing materials that are too difficult or uninteresting to you. A good rule of thumb is that if you do not like doing the activity in your mother tongue then you probably will not like doing it in your L2 either. Some people seem to think that when it comes to language learning "no pain, no gain." That is, they seem to think that if they are not studying materials that are too difficult and boring then they are not "really" learning. Remember, that the good news is that you can choose anything that you want to learn with, follow your own pace and, best of all, there are no tests that you will have to take. In the modern world of technology, worldwide media and a shrinking global village it is easy to gain access to input that can satisfy anyone's tastes.

This section contains some recommend activities that may be beneficial for your own ongoing L2 development. However, remember that you should find works best for you and do that. My first suggestion is that you approach this process as "low and slow." That is, see the process as a marathon rather than a sprint and plan accordingly. One corollary of this statement is that it is better to spare 30 minutes to an hour for language study every day rather than try to engage in long sessions one or two times per week.

After deciding on how much time you have available to spend with the L2, you should set some realistic goals for your L2 learning. When setting your goals, you will want to make sure that they are as concrete, measurable and achievable as possible. For example, "learn English" or "become fluent" are unrealistic goals because they are not concrete or measurable. A more specific and reasonable goal would be to say that you will watch a whole drama series with same-language subtitles and look up 10 words per episode. Another more specific goal could be to finish a graded reader in a week. You can always adjust your goals if you find them to be too easy or challenging. The most important thing is that your goals help you stay motivated and moving forward.

Besides having clear goals for what you want to achieve in your language learning, it is helpful to explore of the ever-proliferating assortment of tools that are available to facilitate self-directed language learning. These tools can allow you to practice the various language skills on your own time and at your own pace. An example of a tool that can assist learners with developing their L2 reading ability is the website Readlang.com. This free resource allows the learner to read any material found online with the ability to click on any unknown words to receive an instant translation.

A number of excellent resources also exist that can be used to improve your listening skills through watching videos online using tools like Captionpop.com. If you would like to do listening and speaking practice, it is possible using a website called conversationexchange.com that allows you to connect with other language learner native speakers around the world who want to learn your language. You can do a language exchange with them and practice your target language while also giving them the chance to practice theirs. Another site where an online tutor or conversation partner can be hired is italki.com.

A helpful resource for those who want to improve their writing is Lang-8.com. It works on the principle that you submit your writing to be corrected but you have to reciprocate by correcting someone else's writing. If you would like to continue to develop your vocabulary knowledge, there are a number of excellent spaced-repetition (SRS) apps like Anki and Memrise (among numerous others) that will allow you to continue to efficiently practice and build your vocabulary knowledge. To practice grammar, you might try Duolingo or the English Grammar Practice app. Of course, these tools are constantly changing so it is important to always watch for new online tools with improved features to make your learning more efficient and enjoyable.

Extensive reading or narrow reading are two other valuable means by which teachers can continue to refine their target language knowledge. The progress through the stages of extensive listening from graded readers has been described by McQuillan (2016) where he recommends beginning with graded readers and reading one hour every day. Once you feel as though graded readers are too easy, he suggests then moving on to light novels such as comic books, young adult fiction or popular adult fiction. Cho, Ahn, and Krashen (2005) also recommend engaging in narrow reading where you read several books about the same topic or a series of novels by the same author. Both of these types of reading are argued to build up a store of L2 language and schema knowledge that the reader can draw upon to make their reading easier and more pleasant.

In addition to the input achieved through reading. It is also important to access input through listening. Listening skills are most profitably developed when we engage in both intensive and extensive listening (Renandya & Farrell, 2010). The difference between the two activities is that intensive listening is practiced when the learner sits down and listens with attention while doing exercises or tasks that demonstrate his comprehension of the text. Intensive listening tends to involve listening to the same text several times while gradually listening for increasing levels of detail. Materials used for intensive listening also tend to be more challenging with more unknown vocabulary and structures. The unique benefit of this intensive listening is that learners can practice bottom up listening whereby they learn to discriminate sounds and makes sense of connected speech (Field, 2003). This intensive listening should then be combined with extensive listening where the learner listens to longer texts that contain less unknown language. Such extensive listening practice gives the learner the opportunity to engage in listening for pleasure while also improving their L2 listening comprehension (Chang & Millett, 2013).

Extensive reading and listening themselves may not be the most efficient way to continue your L2 development. You may also need to supplement this practice with some focused "study" of the language. One effective tool that can be easily used to reinforce the more complicated aspects of the language is spaced repetition software (SRS). SRS includes software such as Anki, Supermemo, and Memrise among others. It is essentially a mobile flashcard app that works by presenting the information that its user has included on her flashcards at increasing time intervals depending on the difficulty she indicated when she last reviewed the flashcard. So, for example, if she taps the button that indicates a card was difficult, it will reappear for review one day later. If she selects that same card was moderately difficult, it returns in three days. If she indicates that it was easy, it will come back in seven days. The next time she sees that same word, the intervals will be even longer. The interval for "easy" the first time was one day. The second time, the "easy" interval would be three days. In this way, the intervals for when previously seen words get spaced out grow longer over time.

Something else that you will want to eventually do with your SRS study is to gradually transition from relying on English definitions of unknown words to using target language definitions of those words. Changing to target language definitions will allow you to eventually be able to understand English through English. This ability to understand English in terms of itself will also benefit you in that you will begin to understand the target language in terms of itself rather than through the oftentimes erroneous filter of your first language. As well, using more L2 in SRS study provides extra comprehensible input that can move you away from translating towards actually thinking in the L2. This method of L2 learning has been enthusiastically promoted by a growing number of successful autodidactic learners of multiple languages around the world such as Antimoon.com, Mass Immersion Approach, and Japanese level up.

When making the "monolingual transition" to studying only in the target language using your SRS cards, try to focus on understanding the meaning rather than translating though you may continue to rely on translation a bit at the beginning to avoid feeling overwhelmed by words and definitions that you do not know. Bearing this in mind, you should also realize that there may be a period that you go through during the transition where you feel like you have a less-than-complete grasp of the meaning of the word even though you know all of the words in its definition. It will probably take some time to become accustomed to studying entirely in English but gradually you will come to feel comfortable understanding the English definitions.

This monolingual transition, of course, does not mean that you should put yourself in a position where you are spending inordinate amounts of time trying to make sense of definitions that are too difficult. Rather, ease yourself into English only study by putting in monolingual definitions that you know all of the words in. If you encounter a definition that contains only one word that you do not know then turn that definition into a new sentence card. If the definition has more than one word and you can still understand it then use it. If you cannot understand it then just use the English translation. As your stock of known words grows from input and language study, you will eventually be able to replace most of these L1 definitions with target language definitions.

With regard to the content of the card itself, the front of the card should contain an example sentence that can be pulled from native material that you are reading. Alternatively, you may take example sentences from a learner's dictionary or even online sentence databases such as tatoeba or sentencedict.com. The example sentences that you choose should be i+1 which for these purposes (although not necessarily Krashen's) means that there is only one word in the sentence that you do not know. Ideally, the example sentences should be memorable and somewhat interesting so that you will remember them as the Anki time intervals grow farther apart. On the other side of the card, include anL1 translation of the unknown word but gradually transition to these definitions being in the target language.

In addition to the SRS reviews, you will want to spend as much time as possible in contact with the target language through extensive or narrow reading or listening as well where you are using enjoyable materials at a level of at least 95% known words. This alternating between SRS study and immersive contact with the L2 is beneficial because it allows you to spend time paying attention to the features of the L2 while also enjoying interesting content in the L2. These two activities can help you maintain your motivation as you continue to build your knowledge of the L2. One related suggestion for an activity to try as you read and listen is to spend some time shadowing the listening text. Shadowing means repeating after the speaker on the audio track. Déjean Le Féal (1997) notes that "shadowing is a good way to improve a foreign language precisely in that it draws attention to every single word of an utterance, especially structure words which normally do not even register when heard" (p. 621).

In addition to gaining regular exposure to input, you should also seek out opportunities to interact with English speakers (who do not necessarily have to be native speakers). This interaction could involve taking a conversation class at a local language school. Look around for clubs or organizations in your community that promote language exchange or language meetups. For example, some cities have language exchange meetup groups or even dedicated café spaces. If you are shy about meeting face-to-face, a more comfortable may be to find potential conversation partners online through websites like www.mylanguage-exchange.com or www.language-exchanges.org that allow you to connect with native speakers from around the world to practice your English from the comfort of your own home.

Of course, as you continue to develop your professional knowledge about L2 learning, you will also gain more insights into how to study your L2 more efficiently and effectively. This ongoing professional self-development can be done in a wide variety of ways such as though professional books, professional journals, blogs, YouTube videos and any other resources you can find that expand your thinking on L2 teaching and learning. You can use these resources to find additional information about various aspects of L2 learning. However, you should take care not to spend too much time learning about how to learn languages instead of actually learning your target language.

6.6 Making classroom English comprehensible

In addition to developing our own L2 proficiency, we need to ensure that we make the target language our learners hear is as comprehensible as possible to them. Creating a classroom environment where learners feel comfortable hearing the target language can increase their motivation and confidence in communicating in the L2. This section discuss three main topics related to making your lessons as comprehensible as possible. First, we will define what comprehensible input (CI) is. From there, we will look at some techniques that we can use to make our teacher talk more comprehensible. Finally, we will discuss how you can make the other language that learners will be exposed to in the classroom comprehensible.

6.7 What is comprehensible input?

Stephen Krashen (1982) is credited with introducing the concept of comprehensible input to the language education mainstream. According to his description, comprehensible input is language that is just a little beyond the learners' current level (what he has called "i + 1"). It is language addressed to learners that they should generally understand although it might still contain some language that they do not know. This unknown language should be in the next step of their English development. Other key characteristics of comprehensible input are that it is clear and organized so that learners are able to follow it easily. It should also be meaningful in the sense that it makes sense to the learner because it connects to what they know about the world. Ideally, CI should also be highly interesting to the learner. In fact, Krashen (2011) states that the best CI in a story is so compelling that the learner might even forget that the story is in English!

6.8 Why should we make our language comprehensible?

Although this may seem to be an obvious question, it is still worth taking a moment to reflect on the reasons why we need to provide students with comprehensible input. First of all, CI is generally agreed to be a vital ingredient in English learning. Therefore, if learners are not exposed to enough comprehensible input, they miss out on a relatively easy and enjoyable way that they can learn English. They also will not be able to learn language that they do not understand.

In a similar vein, when students learn English that they can understand, it allows them to reinforce structures that they are becoming familiar with in a natural way. More importantly, it enables them to begin to make form-meaning connections between the unknown language in the input and the meaning that the context and other scaffolds provide. For example, when a complete beginner watches the teacher point to the door and say "door" they make the connection between the spoken word "door" and the thing we open when we enter a room. Creating these form-meaning connections is necessary for them to learn English.

Thirdly, giving learners chances to learn English from comprehensible input encourages them to pay attention to and reflect on how the English language works. They may begin to notice frequently occurring features of English such as the fact that past tense verbs often end with "-ed" or they may pause to ask themselves why English speakers put the verb in the middle of the sentence instead of at the end like Korean. These moments help to incrementally develop their English proficiency.

A final important reason for making our English comprehensible has to do with helping learners feel more comfortable when they study English. Many of our learners experience serious anxiety when they study because of pressure to do well at what is believed to be an important subject. They feel stressed when they are confronted with a stream of unfamiliar noise that they are supposed to make sense of and respond to. They may also be worried about their classmates' reactions to their incorrect pronunciation or awkward expressions. Easing them into English through exposing them to comprehensible language can help to build their confidence and show them that learning English does not have to be so daunting. They may grow to sincerely enjoy and look forward to English class. At the same time, exposing students to English that is just a bit beyond their current level can help them develop some tolerance for when they do not know every word that they hear. This ability to tolerate some unknown language is useful when they actually try to communicate in English outside our classroom.

6.9 Making your own language as comprehensible as possible

Having considered why CI is important, it is also necessary to review some suggestions for how we can make sure that we are comprehensible to our learners. There are essentially two main ways that you can make the English in your classroom more comprehensible. The first is by paying closer attention to the language that you use in class to ensure that it is comprehensible. The second is by carefully controlling the other input that learners are exposed to in class.

You can roughly tune the level your language to suit your learners' needs either through altering your language or through clarifying its meaning through non-linguistic means. When considering what linguistic adjustments to make, probably the first thing to pay attention to is your manner of speaking. Make sure that your pronunciation and enunciation are as clear as possible. Just to clarify the distinction, pronunciation means using the standard phonemes of your variety of English when you speak.

Enunciation means articulating the sounds clearly and not mumbling. In addition to using clear pronunciation, try to speak a bit more loudly than you might normally and do not be afraid to exaggerate your intonation a bit (though not in a cartoonish way). When you speak, try to put a bit extra stress on content words. Also, try to speak a bit more slowly than usual without sounding unnatural. Rather than speaking too slowly, it is usually best to pause after every phrase to give students more time to process what you just said before adding more information.

Besides being a bit more aware of the way that you speak, pay attention to the language that you choose. To begin with, use simple common vocabulary that you are confident they will probably know. Realize that it will take a bit of time to develop your "radar" for choosing suitable words. To facilitate your word choices, reuse stock phrases or create a common word/phrase wall for learners to reference. Also, speak in phrases and short sentences rather than is long or complex sentences but never speak using grammatically incorrect "Tarzan" language. For example, never say something like "open book please" in the hope that it will be more comprehensible. Remember that we always want to model standard grammar. Another simple but effective strategy is that when you are not sure if they have understood, slow down and repeat yourself. Do it again if you feel you need to. Rarely does it hurt to repeat yourself. A final linguistic strategy is to translate a few key words that seem to be causing comprehension problems. Try not to rely on translation too much though or students might begin to overuse it as a crutch. Remember, the need for translation means that the input may not be comprehensible enough.

Besides adjusting your language itself to be more comprehensible, you can also make non-linguistic adjustments to your classroom presentation that can enhance student understanding. Probably your most readily available and versatile language clarification resource is you. The ample use of facial expressions, body language and gestures can often effectively clarify unclear language. Likewise, other forms of visual support can make content more comprehensible and engaging at the same time. Realia, drawings, pictures, gifs, maps, timelines, videos, infographics, graphic organizers etc. are tools that every language teacher should not be without. In the same vein, teacher demonstrations of how to do activities arc oftcn more effective than explanations alone.

A third way to ensure greater comprehensibility is to seek feedback from your learners about how well they understood what you said. However, be careful not to just say "do you understand?" If you ask that question, they will say "yes" even if they do not understand because they do not want to look like they do not, their friends are all saying yes, and they are not accountable for their answer. A more effective way to check learner understanding is to ask learners more specific comprehension check questions whose answers will more definitively demonstrate their understanding. For example, you could ask a question with a yes or no answer such as "Is the book round?" Alternatively, you might ask "Is the book round or square?" For a bit more of a challenge, ask them to supply an answer in one or two words to a question like "What shape is the book?"

Several other techniques can be used to get feedback on the comprehensibility of your input can be used as well. For one, probably the most important tool you will have is to develop your "sixth sense" for when students seem to have gotten lost. Do not be afraid to backtrack as much as you need to. Remember that you are teaching students and not lessons. As well, teach learners how to ask you for clarification when they do not understand. Praise them when they do show their confusion. You might also seek feedback from your colleagues about what you could do to be more comprehensible. In particular, consider asking your co-teachers for pointers on how you can be more understandable. You could even record yourself to see what you actually sound like and be your own judge.

To further maximize your comprehensibility, you should also preview and review as much as you can. Having a sense of what is coming makes listening much easier. The same goes for reviewing what has been covered in class. Review games can be a very effective way to recycle language across lessons and fill a few leftover minutes at the end of a lesson. Second, it is worthwhile to be mindful of your demeanor as well. Be friendly and enthusiastic because it will not matter much if students can understand you if they do not want to hear what you have to say. Finally, be patient with yourself. It will take some time to develop an ear for input that is suitable for your learners. However, with practice and experimentation, at some point, you will find that you are able to do it with minimal conscious awareness.

6.10 Making our materials more comprehensible

The first key for making sure that the materials you use in your lessons are comprehensible is topic selection. Your main aim in this regard is to bring in topics that your learners are interested in and that they know something about. Also, do not be afraid to stretch the topic of the textbook a bit to make it more engaging to the learners. For example, you might use national sports stars to introduce and talk about the generic topic "sports".

Second, it is important to provide meaningful context for the lesson. For example, make sure students know the objectives of your lesson. Also, start with pre-listening and pre-reading activities like talking about relevant pictures or guessing the answers to comprehension questions. These activities give learners the chance to activate their related background knowledge and make some predictions about the content of the listening or reading passage. Likewise, teach key vocabulary before or while listening or reading. One of the best ways to help learners prepare for listening and reading is to introduce some of the important new words that they will need to comprehend the passage. Videos (or at least pictures) accompanying sound or text is also better to increase its understandability.

Use of simplified materials can make your lessons more understandable as well. For instance, you can tell short stories that have a lot of repetition of the same key words or phrases. Ideally, you would also want to have student engage in total physical response (TPR) to demonstrate their comprehension of the story and have the experience be more interactive. Similarly, repetitive picture books like "No, David!" can serve an analogous function. On the other hand, you can create your own repetitive stories yourself. You could use screen grabs from a non-copyrighted story online and made up simple stories to go with them. Students absolutely love these kinds of stories. You might also try the language experience approach where learners tell you a story from a series of pictures that you show them you write down the story and that can become the text for the class.

6.11 Other scaffolds to ensure maximum comprehensibility

If you have prepared to the best of your ability using the tips suggested and you find your students in the classroom are still struggling a bit to follow you. There are a few more tips that may help. First, you might include some Korean glosses for unknown words. As mentioned above, try not to rely on this strategy too much because you want learners to work in English as much as possible. As well, do not be afraid of repeated reading and narrow reading. We often only ask learners to read or listen to something only once but they usually get much more from it if they can read or hear it a few times. Another way to ensure greater comprehensibility in your lessons is to incorporate plenty of pair work, and small group work. Give students plenty of opportunities to talk to each other because they are often more comprehensible to each other than we are to them. Finally, do a lot of hands on activities like TPR, listen and draw, reader's theatre etc. to take some of the pressure of them having to talk too much.

6.12 Summary

This chapter discussed the concept multicompetence and its relevance to helping bilingual teachers shift their perspective from viewing themselves as being non-native speakers to being multicompetent L2 users. The chapter also covered a number of suggestions for your ongoing professional development as a L2 learner including extensive reading, listening, using SRS and shadowing. The final section reviewed some ways to produce input comprehensible for learners. It explained what comprehensible input is and offered suggestions for what you can do to make your language and lesson materials as understandable as possible.

It is hoped that bilingual readers can use the insights on multicompetence to see yourself in a new light. That is, not as a non-native teacher but as a bilingual teacher that has so much to language skill and learning knowledge to offer your students. I also hope that you have picked up a few new ideas for how to develop your L2 ability so that you continue to grow as an L2 user and as a model of life-long learning for your own students. Lastly, I hope that you could reflect on ways to make your lessons more comprehensible so that your learners will feel more at ease and come to share your passion for language learning.

SLA in Plain English

Chapter 7

Theories of Second Language Acquisition

Chapter 7
Theories of Second Language Acquisition

7.1 Introduction

This section of the book aims to provide you with a firm understanding of second language learning theories that will allow you to fully engage in many facets of the language teaching profession. In particular, an understanding of theories of second language acquisition will enables you to more effectively pursue autonomous professional development as you strive meet the ever-changing needs of the increasingly diverse learners that you teach.

This chapter deals primarily with various influential theories of second language acquisition (SLA). These theories are presented in order to familiarize you with the various theoretical perspectives that exist with respect to L2 learning. As a concise definition of SLA, "SLA refers to the process of learning another language after the native language has been learned…in a classroom situation, as well as in more 'natural' exposure situations" (Selinker & Gass, 2008, p. 7). The theories discussed below aim to account for both types of language learning. The chapter presents a variety of viewpoints on SLA to give you a sense of the plurality of perspectives that exist with respect to how one learns another language. It is organized in a roughly chronological order in that the monitor model was one of the first theories to emerge in the newly developing field of SLA research. Several of the theories reviewed subsequently incorporate responses to claims made by the monitor model. Some other theories have emerged from separate disciplines and offer quite different perspectives on how second languages are acquired. The bulk of the chapter contains an explanation of the various theories of SLA including the monitor model, interaction hypothesis, pushed output hypothesis, input processing model, information processing and sociocultural theory.

7.2 What is SLA?

Second Language Acquisition (SLA) is the study of individuals and groups who are learning a second (or third, etc.) language as well as the process of learning that language. An additional language is called an L2, even though it may actually be the third or tenth. It is sometimes also called a target language (TL). SLA includes informal L2 learning in naturalistic contexts. For example, if a learner moves to a country where the target language is commonly used and "picks up" the language through self-directed learning and attempting to communicate with local speakers of the TL. Instructed SLA, also known as ISLA, includes formal L2 learning in classrooms such as when a learner takes a foreign language class, or participates in a bilingual or immersion program. Of course, it is also possible to combine both of these approaches to L2 learning and SLA researchers study learners who do this as well.

SLA is contributed to primarily by other academic disciplines such as linguistics, psychology, sociology and education. The three main questions that SLA seeks answers to are what learners know when they "know a language," the process the learner undergoes to acquire that knowledge, and why some are more successful L2 learners than others.

7.3 Components of SLA

The formal study of SLA is subdivided into three main categories which are the study of the L2 in a natural and instructed (i.e., classroom) environment. Language acquisition in a natural environment also has some overlap with first language (L1) research in that L1 researchers are also interested in how first language learners (typically babies) acquire their mother tongue in a natural environment (i.e., in their home and community). This research is normally comprised of investigations of developmental sequences that L1 learners go through as they learn their first language. This kind of research often analyzes typical errors that learners make as they progress through learning their L1. Researchers in this area also study the developmental sequence that L1 learners follow as they acquire the grammar morphemes in their first language. Another domain of inquiry connects L1 with L2 learning through the study of cross-linguistic influence that the mother tongue may have on learning the L2.

In addition to the overlapping topics discussed above, second (or third, fourth, etc.) language learning pays a great deal of attention to classroom or instructed L2 learning. As part of instructed learning, researchers generally focus on the kinds of language input that learners have access to, the types of tasks and exercises they do with that input and the sorts of interactions that they engage in with each other and their teacher. Looking at input, researchers will be interested in the role of the comprehensibility of L2 input in second language learning. They are also curious about whether form focused (e.g., grammar explanation) or meaning focused (e.g., communicative language teaching) instruction, or some combination of both, is more effective for promoting L2 learning. Besides input, investigators consider tasks and exercises that encourage implicit, explicit knowledge, or intentional or incidental learning and their effectiveness for short and long-term language learning. Research has also been probing the impact of classroom interaction on L2 development. For instance, the teacher's role in classroom interaction is explored through investigation of the types of questions he or she asks during a lesson. Interest in classroom interaction also relates to how learners interact with each other and negotiate potential breakdowns in communication. A final aspect of classroom interaction connects to how both teachers and fellow classmates can offer feedback and error correction to a speaker and whether or not this feedback gets incorporated into the learner's L2 interlanguage system.

A final area of researcher interest in is individual differences that learners have and how those differences shape their experience of learning an L2. Two background variables that have been long thought to affect L2 learning are the learner's age and aptitude. Likewise, learners' personality and level of motivation is also believed to shape their L2 development. These and other background variables will be discussed in chapter 8.

7.4 How can SLA help EFL teachers?

Those new to second and foreign language education may understand that there is an obvious relationship between SLA research and L2 teaching but they may still wonder about exactly how knowledge of SLA can improve their teaching skills. SLA insights can actually be useful for L2 teachers in several ways. First, SLA can provide you with a more complete understanding the overall goals of language teaching (e.g., literature appreciation/ cultural awareness etc.) that you can use to inform curriculum and syllabus development. Secondly, SLA insights may help teachers to understand the student's unique contribution to learning (e.g., knowledge, attitude, strategies etc.). That is, insights from SLA research can help us to see how their background and prior experiences shape the learner and provide them with the unique strengths and needs that you must help them to build upon.

In addition to knowledge of the learner, SLA can enable teachers to more fully appreciate the theory behind specific teaching methods and techniques. For example, exploring SLA theory in a bit more depth can help the teacher to see that methods like grammar translation are based upon particular views of the L2 learning process such as it being explicit rather than implicit. The results of SLA classroom-based research can also tell us how effective specific techniques (e.g., recasts) are so we can decide whether we want to use them in our teaching. For the L2 learner, SLA can help them develop strategies they need to learn more efficiently by showing us teachers efficient methods by which we can train them in appropriate L2 learning strategy use.

7.5 Interlanguage development

Before reviewing the various theories of second language acquisition, it is necessary to first briefly discuss a central concept in SLA developed by Selinker(1972)known as interlanguage (IL). It has been defined as the developing permeable and transitional abstract system of rules containing the learner's second language knowledge. The IL contains appropriated patterns from the L1, learner postulated rules from the L2 and unique structures not found in the L1 or L2 that may originate from universal grammar influence. Linguistic investigations have revealed interlanguage to be a systematic and rule-governed linguistic system so we must not think of IL as an inferior form of "broken English." It cannot be considered to be the L1 or L2 but it contains characteristics of each. The IL is also argued to be comprised of mainly implicit knowledge. The learner's IL continually evolves as they are exposed to L2 input that allows them to adjust their understanding of how the L2 works. The IL is what lie beneath the learner's L2 comprehension and production. It is thought to be primarily shaped by a number of factors including learners' L1, literacy levels, knowledge of language as an abstract entity (i.e., metalinguistic knowledge), background characteristics, and universal features of language. Learners' exposure to L2 input and their hypotheses they form based on the patterns they see in the L2 input are commonly believed to be the main cause of their IL development.

7.6 The Monitor Model

Stephen Krashen has been an influential figure in the field of second language acquisition research. He is credited with originating the "monitor model" theory of second language acquisition. This theory is based on Noam Chomsky's innatism which essentially claims that unique language acquisition device (LAD) exists in the brain that is used exclusively for language learning. The monitor model is not without some controversy as some critics contend that several of the claims made by the theory are not falsifiable which basically means that research cannot be used to prove them wrong. Despite these criticisms, Krashen has played an instrumental role in the shift to communicative approaches to second language instruction. In particular, his introduction of the concept of comprehensible input has had a significant impact on the field. Indeed, while other scholars may debate about what comprehensible input is or the exact role that it plays in language acquisition, few would disagree that it is vital in L2 learning.

The following section will briefly introduce the monitor model and review its main features. To begin with, the monitor model is comprised of five interdependent hypotheses which are the acquisition-learning hypothesis, the monitor hypothesis, the natural order hypothesis, the input hypothesis, and the affective filter hypothesis. Let us have a look at each of these in turn.

The acquisition-learning hypothesis maintains that there is a key distinction in language learning between language learning and language acquisition. Learning, inKrashen's(1982)view, can be thought of as the kind of learning that occurs in traditional language classrooms. It involves conscious learner attention as well as study of the L2 form and rules of the target language. It is also typically associated with explicit teacher explanation and rote learning. Learning is contracted with acquisition.

Krashen(1982) argues that acquisition is an unconscious process analogous to the one we went through when we learned our first language. We are said to acquire the L2 when we are exposed to messages in the L2 we understand. It is the acquired language, and not the learned, that we use when we communicate in the L2. The acquired system is responsible for our actual spontaneous language use. In his theory, Krashen is also careful to emphasize that what is learned cannot become acquired. That is, learning about the form and structure of the L2 in a way that leads to conscious knowledge of its rules will not enable learners to be able to actually use the L2 for real communication. Therefore, Krashen contends that teachers must focus on encouraging acquisition through exposing learners to interesting and comprehensible language rather than spending too much time instructing them about the rules and structure of the L2.

Krashen (1982) claims that learned knowledge is not totally useless. According to his "monitor hypothesis," knowledge that learners have about the rules of the L2 can play a somewhat minor role in the L2 communication and use. In essence, he contends that learned knowledge can act as a kind of filter or monitor on the language produced from the acquired knowledge. That is, as learners are formulating the message that they want to produce in the L2 based on their unconscious acquired language, just before they actually produce an utterance they can activate their learned knowledge to perform a kind of final check of the structural accuracy of the language based on the rules of the L2 that they consciously know.

An illustration of how this process might work is as follows. The learner formulates the utterance "I play with my friends yesterday" in her mind. Just before she states the utterance, she mentally reviews it in light of her knowledge of past tense rules. She realizes that, according to the rule, she should add an "-ed" and phrase it as "played" rather than "play". In this way, "monitor" can allow learners to make corrections to and better ensure the accuracy of their acquired language. Krashen also points out that monitor overuse also poses a danger to learners as it may cause them to become hyperconscious or hypervigilant about their L2 use and consequently they may become more reticent to speak.

The third hypothesis in the monitor model is known as the "natural order hypothesis." This proposition holds that the grammatical morphemes of the L2 are acquired in a specific order. For example, the grammatical morpheme for "-ing" as in "I'm going" is acquired before "-'s" as in "the boy's hat." This order of grammar morpheme acquisition is quite similar despite learners' L1 background. It is also quite resistant to instruction so teaching late-acquired morphemes to beginners does not result in their acquisition. As well, language rules that are relatively easy to consciously learn are not necessarily early acquired. For instance, the rule for third person singular "-s" (e.g., "he sing<u>s</u>") is easy to consciously learn and recall. However, research demonstrates it to be relatively late acquired(Hieronymus, 1993). Interestingly, research indicates that the order of L2 acquisition is generally similar to children acquiring L1 although there also appear to be some differences (Lightbown & Spada, 2013).

The input hypothesis is arguably the centerpiece of the monitor model. Essentially, it is the claim that comprehensible input is mechanism by which a second language becomes acquired. Krashen(1982) describes comprehensible input as language that is just a step beyond the learner's current level or what he calls "i+1". This connects to the natural order hypothesis in the sense that "i+1" would theoretically be the next linguistic feature in the natural sequence that the learner has to learn. When the learner is exposed to input just a little beyond her level containing that target structure, she will acquire the structure. An important corollary of this hypothesis is that, in Krashen's view, speaking is the result of acquisition and not its cause. That is, even if learners do not have opportunities to practice using new structures in speech or writing, exposure to sufficient comprehensible input will allow them to acquire the target language and they will be able to produce the L2 in speech or writing.

The final component of Krashen's model is known as the affective filter hypothesis. This proposition states that there is an affective barrier related to learners' emotions and attitudes that can potentially short circuit their L2 acquisition. That is, when a learner experiences excessive stress or anxiety associated with his language learning, a psychological block will prevent the learner from acquiring new language from potentially comprehensible input. Therefore, language teachers must ensure that learners' affective needs are taken into consideration. The affective filter hypothesis can help to account for why some learners do not acquire the target language in circumstances where they are ostensibly being exposed to comprehensible input. However, some critics also complain that this postulation can make the model unfalsifiable and thus deflect legitimate criticism of it (Kiraly & Signer, 2017).

Numerous of classroom techniques have found their genesis from the monitor model. Early on, Krashen and Terrell (1983) developed what they referred to as the "natural approach". This method incorporated numerous classroom activities such "total physical response", storytelling and class discussion among other input-based communicative activities that focused on meaning rather than teaching grammar. Content based language teaching (CBLT) also draws upon the monitor model for its theoretical basis(Brinton, Snow, & Wesche, 1989). CBLT includes a variety of different approaches to using subject matter content as the vehicle to teach the L2. Immersion or sheltered instruction programs are examples of this approach as are less intensive versions where a teacher in a regular foreign language class organizes the syllabus according to themes that interest the learners rather than grammatical structures.

Figure 7.1 Illustration of Krashen's Monitor Model adapted from Krashen (1982)

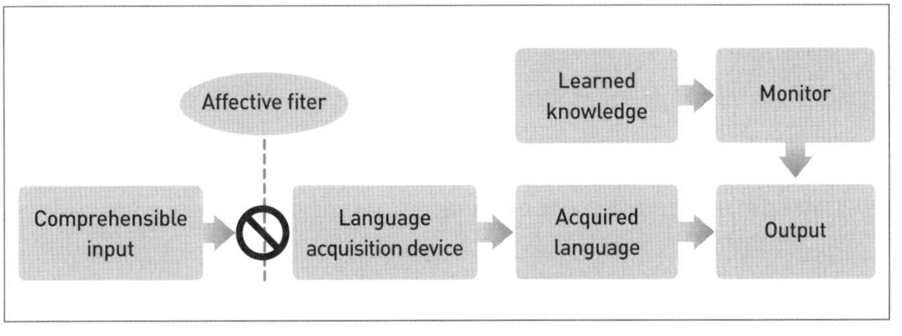

Another more recently developed language teaching approach that draw on Krashen's theories is known as Teaching Proficiency through Reading and Storytelling (TPRS)(Ray & Seely, 1998). TPRS uses highly interactive and repetitive storytelling that incorporates high frequency target language expressions along with a high volume of reading in the target language. TPRS is rapidly growing in popularity within North American foreign language education circles. Support for free voluntary reading (FVR) in the L2 classroom also grows out of the monitor model. In essence, FVR encourages learners to read large amounts of self-selected comprehensible materials in the target language to understand the general gist. The primary aims of this technique are for learners to acquire the L2 through comprehensible input while they obtain pleasure from reading and develop a habit and love of reading.

7.7 Interaction hypothesis

Other scholars have responded to Krashen's ideas with their own theories on the L2 learning process. In some cases, they partially agree with Krashen and in others they are diametrically opposed to him. Long (1990) argued that Krashen was basically right about comprehensible input being the catalyst for language acquisition but he wanted to better understand exactly how it is that input becomes comprehensible. His research eventually led him to conclude that learners create comprehensible input through interaction with each other. That is, SLA happens through negotiation of meaning conversational interactions. Long (1996, 1985) describes negotiation for meaning (NOM) as interactional modifications that interlocutors make after a communication breakdown, which serve to clarify meaning of previous utterances. Thus, it is through NOM that input becomes comprehensible.

The types of specific interactional modifications that interlocutors would make include using extra and paralinguistic cues such as body language or intonation to clarify meaning. They can also repeat and paraphrase their utterances to provide their listener with additional support. Of course, the listener needs to take an active role in providing feedback to the speaker. This feedback includes making requests for clarification when they believe they have misunderstood the speaker. Listeners should occasionally confirm their understanding as well. Interlocutors can clarify each other's statements by asking comprehension confirmation questions and paraphrasing what they heard. Checking comprehension in this way avoids confusion or misunderstanding.

7.8 The pushed (comprehensible) output hypothesis

Another response to Krashen's theory came from Swain (1985) in the form of the "pushed output hypothesis". This theory was based on the idea that comprehensible input is insufficient for language acquisition. During her research with Canadian learners of French as a second language in French immersion programs, she observed that many had been exposed to comprehensible input for many years and yet continued to display non-native characteristics in their L2 output (Swain, 2008). Swain (1985, 1993) also argued that output may compel the learner to focus less on text meaning as when seeking comprehension and pay more attention to the form of the appropriate grammatical structures necessary when formulating a spoken utterance.

In contrast to Krashen, Swain argued that producing output that was comprehensible to one's interlocutor required learners to engage in complete syntactic processing of all the language in an utterance. Additionally, she claimed that the social dynamic of communication requires the learner to push her output to more closely resemble community standards to be comprehended by her interlocutor. These efforts in turn destabilize the learner's interlanguage and thus lead to interlanguage restructuring and L2 development (Swain & Lapkin, 1998). This theory and the interaction hypothesis have some clear distinctions that must be highlighted. For instance, the interaction hypothesis holds that interaction makes input comprehensible through negotiation of meaning. In contrast, the pushed output hypothesis is not focused on comprehensible input. This view maintains that interaction demands that learners pay attention to the form and meaning of their output and strive to produce more accurate language thus propelling their L2 growth forward.

Swain (1985) posits that the process of making their output more comprehensible has a number of specific benefits for learners. First, producing comprehensible output forces learners to notice the gap between what they want to say and what they can say. This noticing then "This [realization] may trigger an analysis of incoming data, that is, a syntactic analysis of input, or it may trigger an analysis of existing internal linguistic resources, in order to fill the knowledge gap" (Swain & Lapkin, 1995, p. 375). In this way, out may push restructuring of learners' interlanguage system. Second, opportunities to use the L2 can serve a hypothesis testing function that allows learners to experiment with new language and structures that they are unsure of to get feedback about their comprehensibility and determine whether they are correct in their usage. Lastly, learner output may provide occasions for metalinguistic reflection on the features and properties of the target language. For example, learners may engage in discussion about why an expression is phrased, structured or pronounced in a particular way.

7.9 Input processing

A final theory that has emerged in recent years is VanPatten's (1996) input processing. Input processing is an approach to grammar instruction that guides learners to process what they see or hear. This approach helps learners connect language forms with their intended meanings. Input processing helps address what VanPatten saw as a limitation of Krashen's theory. Similarly to Swain, Van

Patten maintained that learners tended to focus on the meaningful content words in the input so we need a way to compel them to pay attention to the grammatical morphemes as well. Another important feature of input processing is that unlike the interaction hypothesis or pushed output hypothesis it does not require the learner to produce any output in the form of speech or writing to ensure the acquisition of new language. In that regard, it is somewhat more in line with Krashen's original view.

Van Patten argued that, contrary to Krashen's view, the process of L2 acquisition is not simply from comprehensible L1 input directly to acquisition. Otherwise all comprehensible input would be acquired. Instead, Van Patten held that there is a transitional step between input and acquisition that he identified as "intake" where some, but not all, of the input becomes acquired. VanPatten (2004) claimed that in order for input to become intake learners must engage in input processing. This is because learners have limited processing capacity and cannot pay attention to form and meaning at the same time. They naturally process content words in input before grammatical items because they focus on meaning. When the content words and context helps them make sense of an utterance, they do not notice the details of the language form. That is, they do not pay attention to the grammar morphemes. Input processing pushes learners to focus their attention on both the form and meaning of an unknown target structure from the input and attempt to connect the form and meaning in their mind. To successfully accomplish input processing, learners have to pay attention to both the form and meaning of the input they receive.

VanPatten (2004) devised input processing instruction with the aim of changing the way learners pay attention to input by having them engage in activities that induce them to make form-meaning connections from the input. One of the main classroom activities used to help learners do this is called structured input. While completing structured input activities, learners are pushed to process the meaning -structure connection for the target structure found in the input. These form-meaning connections are made because the input in the task is manipulated in such a way that it encourages learners to rely on the target structure to make sense of the input enough to complete the task. An example of a structured input activity can be seen in table 7.1 below. The task here is for students to indicate whether the event is happening now or in the past.

Table 7.1 Example structured input activity

Instructions: Read each sentence and decide whether they are doing the action now or did it in the past.
1. Geoff is going to the movies.
2. Barbara danced at a club.
3. Pat is riding a motorcycle.
4. Susan talked on her cell phone.
5. Mike is visiting his friends.

To complete the task the learner has to focus on the grammatical structure that conveys whether the action is occurring now or in the past. There is no other information in any of the sample sentences that can aid the learner in accomplishing the task of determining when the event occurred. The example sentences could have included time adverbs like 'yesterday' or 'now' but the learner would use those words to realize when the event was happening instead of noticing the inflections on the verbs. That is why these tasks are called structured input. The input in the form of these example sentences, has been altered (i.e., structured) in such a way as to make the learner pay attention to features of it (i.e., grammatical morphemes) that he might ordinarily overlook. Other examples of tasks learners could do to demonstrate their connecting the meaning with the form of the target grammatical structure include responding to true/false or multiple choice questions, matching, gap fills or short answer items that compel them to make form-meaning connections with the target grammar structure. See table 7.2 for example tasks.

Table 7.2 Example input processing tasks

Instructions: Choose the sentences that show an ongoing action is happening now.	
True or false	I am eating a hamburger (T-F)
Multiple choice	I am (eat, eating, eaten) a hamburger
Matching (choose the best answers)	I am ________ saw eating did running
Gap fill	I am eating ________
State the rule	"You add ________ to the main verb when talking about ongoing action in the present"

According to VanPatten (1996b), there are several guiding principles associated with input processing that language teachers should keep in mind. First, focus on one grammar element at a time so as not to overburden learners. Second, the focus should be on meaning before form. That is, when doing structured input tasks, learners should be spending most of their time trying to make sense of the meaning rather than analyzing the structure of the sentences. They should only be paying attention to the target structure to allow them to more clearly comprehend the example sentences. Third, learners should do some sort of task that compels them to make a form-meaning connection with the target grammatical structure. These tasks can require closed responses (e.g., true or false) and open-ended (gap fill) answers. Lastly, after completing structured input activities with example sentences, learners should have opportunities to produce the target grammar in activities that have them interact with the target structures in longer stretches of discourse.

7.10 Information processing

The information processing theory of language learning grows out of a cognitive perspective within psychology. It is based on the study of cognition or how humans acquire, process, store, and retrieve information. One major difference between this perspective and others like the monitor model is that many cognitive psychologists do not acknowledge the existence of Chomsky's language acquisition device (LAD). Consequently, in their view, L1 or L2 learning is based on the same cognitive processes of perception, memory, categorization and generalization that all other learning is. In other words, language learning is not a unique form of learning. An obvious implication of this stance is that learning circumstances and learners' prior knowledge of language shapes their perception of a new language. For example, a Korean beginning learner of English will probably initially hear English phonemes in terms of Korean phonology.

Information processing scholars contend that language is a complex cognitive skill that is composed of simple self-contained processes. These language subskills should be identified and isolated to be practiced and learned (McLaughlin & Heredia, 1996). Thus, second language learning involves practicing several various subskills and then combining those skills into a unified fluent use of the target language. In this model, it is necessary for simple skills to become automatic before more complex ones can be addressed. To illustrate this point, in order for learners to effectively comprehend a spoken utterance, they must first have in place prerequisite L2 listening subskills such as phoneme identification, aural word recognition, syntactic parsing and the ability to make suitable inferences based on world knowledge.

For L2 learners to be able to use the target language fluently their control over the component subskills must be automatic. In essence, the theory claims that language acquisition is the building up of subskill knowledge that can eventually be used automatically for understanding and producing the L2.When language skills are automaticized, learners are able to use them unconsciously and with minimal effort. Language skills become automatized through practice. For example, L2 reading is arguably comprised of a number of subskills such as decoding print, word identification etc. that can be practices and then combined into fluent reading practice. With practice and ongoing improved L2 use, a constant restructuring of the internal L2 interlanguage occurs as learners refine and elaborate their L2 system.

In contrast to other theories like the monitor model, learners must pay conscious attention (use cognitive resources to process information) in order to learn in the information processing model. The information processing model maintains that there is a limit to the amount of focused mental activity we can engage in at one time. Since there are natural limits on the amount of information that learners can pay attention to, they must learn to process information somewhat selectively (McLaughlin, Rossman, & McLeod, 1983). This selective attention might help to explain why beginners fail to notice grammatical morphemes in the input they receive because they are more focused on attempting to extract meaning from the text by making sense of the key meaning-bearing content words.

Nevertheless, information processing theorists maintain that with experience and practice, information that was new becomes easier to process and automatically accessed. In this way, increased L2 proficiency frees up processing resources that enable learners to notice previously ignored language features. As lower level skills become automatized, mental capacity is freed up for more demanding activities (McLaughlin & Nayak, 1989). To take another example from reading, once learners know how to decode text with sufficient speed and fluency, they are then able to focus more upon comprehending the meaning of the text. Lack of automatic access to meaning while reading or listening may also help explain why L2 learners struggle to understand the text. They may need more time to process it.

Mitchell and Myles (2004) point out that controlled processing involves learning new skills where only a few new elements can be retained. In contrast, automatic processing entails using more practiced skills so learners can handle more information simultaneously. Controlled processing also relies upon slow access to the novel skill being learned while automatic processing demands rapid access to a familiar skill. Another distinction between controlled and automatic processing is that controlled skills are relatively temporary, if not reinforced, and open to alteration through continued practice. However, automatic processing skills are difficult to modify or delete once they are acquired.

In an information processing perspective, repeated practice with new language eventually enables learners to automatically and subconsciously activate structures that initially needed to be produced with controlled and conscious use. Thus, with practice, learners gradually shift from controlled to automatic L2 processing. This change entails a number of qualitative transformations in their cognitive access to the L2. A key difference between controlled and automatic processing is that controlled processing is achieved through considerable conscious attention and relies on short-term memory which is quite limited in capacity. In contrast, automatic processing relies on limited peripheral attention and long-term memory which has substantially greater capacity. Minimal learner attention is required to rapidly access automatized language whenever necessary. Because cognitive space is freed up through automatic processing, the learner becomes able to focus on other aspects of the L2. For example, after a learner has automatized print decoding and word recognition skills, they can engage in the higher-level processing necessary to make sense of unfamiliar text much more effectively.

According to information processing theory, the route by which new information is internalized (i.e., learned) is first as declarative knowledge (learner is aware of the information) or through conscious, controlled practice depending on the version of information processing that one subscribes to. Anderson (1989), for instance, claims that language sub-skills are learned first as declarative knowledge. For example, learning to decode print would first begin with explicit explanation of phonics rules so that learners consciously know the rule. Next, they would practice consciously applying the rule. Through continued practice, the rule gradually becomes proceduralized, and the learner is able to automatically and unconsciously apply the rule appropriately with minimal effort. At that stage, the learner will often have forgotten having consciously learned the rule at the outset of their learning.

A contrasting view on the process of language learning within an information processing perspective is that declarative knowledge is not essential in the beginning stages of learning a new complex skill (McLaughlin, 1987). Instead, advocates of this stance claim that having learners deliberately practice with the information is enough for learning to occur. As an example of this version of information processing theory, a beginning L2 reader would practice verbally decoding (i.e., sounding out) words to apply a new rule about a previously unknown sound letter correspondence without having the rule explicitly explained to her. Instead, the teacher might read aloud some words that have the new letter in them to demonstrate the sound-letter connection. In this instance the focus is on applying the rule rather being able to explicitly state what it is.

The concept of restructuring is also integral to the information processing model. In the information processing model, the typical route by which a skill becomes automatized is through incremental improvement in its use over a sustained period of practice. However, a second way that language growth is posited to occur within this model is restructuring. That is, not all skill development follows from the gradual build up from declarative/ controlled to procedural and finally automatic. In some instances, learners display a sudden burst of progress that cannot be accounted for by the steady development of proficiency from continued practice of the skill (McLaughlin, 1990a).

Restructuring itself involves a qualitative change in the learner's knowledge so that they gain a deeper insight into acceptable patterns of L2 use than they had prior to the restructuring. As learners continue to learn the L2, they continually experience restructuring episodes as they notice patterns and gain new insights into how the L2 functions. This ongoing restructuring then allows them to refine and consolidate their L2 knowledge. In essence, restructuring is the process of the learner making a generalization about how some aspect of the L2 works. An example of restructuring is when a learner works out a grammar rule from input over time. Thus, if the learner were realize that regular past tense verbs end with "-ed" through exposure to many examples of this grammatical feature over time this would be an example of restructuring.

An unexpected way that restructuring can reveal itself is through what seems to beL2 backsliding. This apparent L2 regression occurs when a learner overgeneralizes a newly understood grammar pattern and appears to revert to an earlier stage in their L2 development despite the fact that she is actually continuing to develop. For instance, a learner might initially use the correct irregular past tense verbs like "went" or "wear" but after recognizing the "-ed" generalization she may switch to using non-standard forms like "goed" or "weared". Thus, while it may initially seem as though the learner has regressed in her development, she has actually gained knowledge of an L2 structural pattern that will facilitate more accurate L2 production overall.

Various classroom activities can be used to engage in controlled practice of a new target language skill. This new skill should be performed both with focused attention on its development and less focused attention (McLaughlin et al., 1983).Classroom activities that promote focal attention include explicit explanation of grammatical patterns and grammar pattern practice drills and fill-in-the-blank exercises. These activities concentrate learner attention on the new grammar item by guiding them to consciously pay attention and manipulate its structure as they complete the exercises. In addition to using activities that promote focus learners' attention, opportunities should also exist for learners to practice newly learned language with more peripheral attention. Examples of classroom activities that require less focused attention on the form of newly introduced language include total physical response (TPR) and information gap. These tasks require less learner attention on language structure because learners need to concentrate more on either grasping the meaning of the teacher's commands or expressing their intended meaning to their partner.

Along with the activities that allow learners to do controlled practice of new language, tasks that provide learners with opportunities to rehearse previously automaticized language are also necessary. As with the activities used for controlled practice. These controlled activities also can be divided into those that train learners with focused attention and those that rely more upon peripheral attention. Examples of classroom activities that draw on learners' concentrated awareness to practice proceduralized language include having learners engage in self or peer editing through either recording a conversation and listening to it to identify their errors or using a checklist to self or peer edit a written assignment. These kinds of tasks require focused attention because the learner has to consciously attend to the language being used in order to give feedback on it. However, they also rely on automaticized language because the learner has to produce language extemporaneously to complete the task.

Classroom activities to practice proceduralized language that allow the learner to do them with peripheral attention are also beneficial for promoting learner fluency. Examples of these types of activates include extensive reading of easy text and free talking about a topic that interests learners. These tasks practice automatized language with peripheral attention by encouraging the learner to work on communicating confidently in the target language.

7.11 Vygotsky's sociocultural theory

Vygotsky (1980) argued that language and cognitive development are deeply intertwined and closely connected to social interaction. He developed the concept of mediation to account for the process of language use. He maintained that mediation is central to language development and use. Essentially, in his view, language is a symbolic tool that we use to relate to our environment. This linguistic mediation is necessary because we cannot experience our environment directly. We have to experience it through thought. He reasoned that language is the tool that we use to express our thought both outwardly to others as well as inwardly to ourselves.

Vygotsky also claimed that thought is the internalized language of our community. That is, the language of our speech community is internalized to become our language (Vygotsky, 1980). This internalization process happens through mediations in the Zone of Proximal Development (ZPD). The mediation occurs when conversations scaffold children's development by helping them use their existing knowledge to acquire new knowledge. The mechanism by which the language (and thought) of the community is internalized is private speech. This is the kind of self-talk that we all engage in when we are faced with a somewhat challenging task. We often slow down and talk ourselves through the task. Vygotsky claims that over time our private speech gradually transforms into inner speech which is verbal thought (Lantolf & Appel, 1994).

A key construct that has grown out of Vygotskian sociocultural theory is the notion of scaffolding. Bruner (1985) explains that scaffolds enable the child to learn with guidance from an adult or more knowledgeable partner who lends the learner her consciousness until the learner can control his own actions to properly complete the task. The child can use a new skill or idea once she has conscious control over it. Thus, "...the tutor in effect performs the critical function of 'scaffolding' the learning task to make it possible for the child, in Vygotsky's words, to internalize external knowledge and convert it into a tool for conscious control" (pp. 24-25).

Scaffolds can assume a variety of forms including verbal, procedural and material. Examples of verbal scaffolds that can be used in the L2 classroom include providing a synonym for an unknown word, or using songs and chants as a mnemonic for new language. Teachers might also think aloud to verbally demonstrate complex thought processes such as making inferences while reading. In addition to verbal scaffolds, there are also procedural scaffolds that include activating learners' background knowledge through brainstorms or class discussions. Another type of procedural scaffold is the think-pair-share activity whereby learners offer each other their individual perspectives and feedback on the language content or skill that they are learning. A third category of scaffold is that found in learning materials. Examples of this type include pictures, diagrams and graphic organizers. Materials scaffolds provide the distinctive advantage of learners being able to interact with them individually and at their own pace.

7.12 Summary

This chapter has provided an overview of several of the various theories that have been developed to explain the process of L2 acquisition. Although this collection of models is certainly not exhaustive, it does contain theories that are relatively widespread. These theories included the monitor model, the interaction hypothesis, the pushed output hypothesis, input processing, information processing and sociocultural theory. Each of these theoretical perspectives offers a unique outlook on how languages are learned and often places particular emphasis upon the role of input, output and practice in the process. We can also see that many of the theories are in some sense connected in that the interaction hypothesis, the pushed output hypothesis, input processing are in many ways varied responses to the hypotheses put forth in the monitor model.

Knowledge of these SLA theories can provide language teachers with a lens to gain additional insight into some of the idiosyncrasies of their students' L2 learning process. As a result, teachers can enter their classrooms with greater confidence that their classroom practice is buttressed by a firm theoretical basis and that they have access to SLA learning models that can allow them to more effectively address some of the specific and distinctive challenges that their learners face. With the rapid proliferation of technology and growing diversity of our students, the second/foreign language classroom will only become more complex over time. This increasing complexity demands that teachers take more interest in SLA theory to provide them with a solid basis for their increasingly sophisticated instructional decision making.

You should bear in mind that this chapter is only an introduction to these various theories so if there are any that are of particular interest, you should follow up with particular theories that pique your interest. You should also continue to study these theoretical perspectives and reflect deeply on which theory or combination of theories most closely aligns with your values and philosophical orientation as a language teacher. However, be aware that some of these theories are contradictory (e.g., the monitor model and the pushed output hypothesis) so you may need to choose one to ensure that your classroom activities do not work at cross purposes. As you continue to build on this beginning knowledge base by learning more about the theories that interest you at your own pace, the slow and constant study over a long period of time will add up to a solid grounding in theoretical knowledge that will serve you well as a language teacher and lifelong learner. The key is to enjoy the process as much as possible by learning about topics that suit your interests.

SLA in Plain English

Chapter 8

Individual Differences in SLA

Chapter 8

Individual Differences in SLA

8.1 Introduction

This chapter primarily identifies the various background factors that students bring with them to the L2 classroom and explains how these factors affect their L2 learning. The chapter begins with discussion of background characteristics like aptitude, intelligence, and learning styles as well as language learning and communication strategies. Next, it discusses personality characteristics such as extroversion, willingness to communicate (WTC), risk taking, and anxiety, as well as various conceptions of motivation. Other learner background characteristics that also receive some attention include learner agency and beliefs.

With the information presented in this chapter, should be able to provide the reader with some additional insight into various puzzling issues that we face as L2 teachers. For instance, we often ask ourselves why some learners are unmotivated or believe that they cannot "really" learn English without extensive explicit grammar instruction. As a result of reading and reflecting a bit more about these factors, you should also be able to take into account your learners' individual idiosyncrasies to tailor lessons to their individual needs.

8.2 Research on learner characteristics

For a long time, researchers have shown an interest in understanding the impact that L2 learner personal characteristics may have on their performance in second language learning classrooms. Some of these learner attributes include their aptitude, intelligence, learning styles and personality factors (e.g., anxiety and motivation). This interest might be attributed to the common belief among second language educators that these characteristics can have an important influence on language learning. Therefore, gaining a clearer understanding the impact of learner personal attributes may allow teachers to more effectively take these characteristics into account in their instructional planning.

However, a number of issues make research into the impact of learner differences upon L2 learning somewhat challenging. One such difficulty is sampling learners' language in a way that provides enough examples to ensure realistic representation of how they actually use the language. A representative sample of language use is important to ensure that when the language learners' background factors are compared with their language performance, researchers can be confident that the differences that they observe in L2 performance accurately reflect genuine differences in learner background characteristics rather than flawed language samples that were collected.

One solution to this problem draws upon tools from corpus linguistics that facilitate the collection of large volumes of naturally occurring authentic L2 data. This data can be analyzed to detect patterns that reflect realistic use of the L2 in naturally occurring contexts. Such data may provide researchers with a more accurate representation of specifically how differences in learner backgrounds can impact particular aspects of their L2 performance.

Unfortunately, appropriate language sampling is not the only potential obstacle to accurately teasing out the influence that various background variables can have upon L2 use. A second potentially troublesome barrier is how to accurately define and measure the variables themselves. That is because many of the variables that researchers and teachers are most interested in are also notoriously difficult to agree on a definition that satisfies everyone. For instance, variables like motivation have continually shifting definitions that most researchers within the same discipline of psychology have serious trouble agreeing upon. It is even more difficult to find common ground with scholars from other disciplines like second language studies or sociology. Equally complicated is the accurate measurement of these variables in a way that most researchers would agree upon as being valid measurements. This widespread disagreement over variable measurement is largely due to it being impossible to directly observe and measure characteristics such as motivation, or anxiety. That is, these variables are latent and thus we cannot peer directly into the learner's head to observe them. Instead, we have to devise measurement instruments that allow us to make inferences about what this learner is thinking. The problem is that these measurement tools are always based on particular assumptions we must make that leave us open to being wrong.

Another issue with this type of research is that much of it is correlational. Correlational research is often contrasted with experimental research which is widely believed to more clearly establish causation. This means that a well-designed experimental study allows its author to make stronger claims about the specific effect that a particular experimental variable had upon another variable. For example, I could design an experiment that allows me to test the effect of varying amounts of extensive reading on vocabulary acquisition. However, in the case of learners' background variables like intelligence or aptitude, it is not possible to manipulate these variables in the same way as we can manipulate an instructional approach. Therefore, we can only say that one variable is associated with another such that as one increases so does the other or that as one increases the other decreases. That problem with such claims, is that we often cannot say with any certainty which variable is influencing which. For instance, is it motivation that causes achievement or vice versa? Equally, we cannot be certain whether there is a third as yet unidentified variable (or combination of variables) that accounts for the relationship that we have observed.

Finally, socio-cultural factors also have substantial bearing on many learner background variables and interact with these variables in varied and unpredictable ways. For instance, the learner's identity has a significant impact upon learners' L2 development (Norton, 2000). If a learner defines herself as someone who can be a successful L2 learner, then she may be more likely to persist through the inevitable challenges that come with learning an additional language. A similar outcome is also more likely if she is positioned as being an adept L2 learner by the teacher and other members of the classroom community. Another notion that is closely connected to learner identity is the concept of imagined communities. These are the communities that the learner aspires to become a member of once he has acquired the L2. If the imagined community of L2 speakers is one the learner would want to affiliate with then he will appear to be "motivated". However, if the imagined community is not one that he would want to join then he would not appear to be "motivated" (Peirce, 1995). Thus, we can see the profound affect that social context can have on the psychological construct of motivation.

An additional socio-cultural factor that strongly influences L2 learning is the power relationships between the L1 and L2 (Cummins, 2000). These power relationships relate to the socio-political context of the L1 and L2 in terms of which language has higher status in a particular context. An example of these power dynamics can be seen in the power struggle between Spanish and English in the US. They can also be witnessed in the differential treatment of learners from various L1 backgrounds in the classroom. For instance, linguistic discrimination exists in some classroom environments where learners face barriers to access to social and material resources because of others' perceptions of their cultural and linguistic affiliations (Toohey, 1996). Psychologically-oriented approaches to studying L2 learning do not often take these socio-cultural factors into full consideration. As a consequence, the impact of underlying socio-political dynamics upon what appear to be psychological issues is largely overlooked. This issue is something that language teachers need to bear in mind.

8.3 Learner characteristics in second language learning

A language learning related construct that is thought to have a relationship with L2 learning is intelligence. Intelligence has been defined "a general mental ability for reasoning, problem solving, and learning" (Colom, Karama, Jung, & Haier, 2010, p. 489). Some debate surrounds the issue of the relationship between intelligence and language learning aptitude. On the one hand, some claim but these are two separate constructs (Gardner & Lambert, 1965). However, others contend that there is considerable overlap between the two constructs (Li, 2016).

Discussions have also been had in the research literature regarding the precise role of intelligence in language learning. Some have found that intelligence is helpful with allowing learners to develop their cognitive academic language proficiency (CALP)(Genesee, 1979). This is the academic language that we find in school. However, intelligence may play less of a role in the development of basic interpersonal communication skills (BICS) which is the language that we use in everyday communication.

Traditional descriptions of intelligence have mainly been limited to verbal/ linguistic and mathematical/logical intelligence. However, newer conceptions of intelligence have also begun to make their way into debates on the role of intelligence in language learning. In addition to traditionally identified verbal/ linguistic and mathematical/ logical, Gardner (1992) argues that there are several other types of intelligence (e.g., spatial, musical etc.) that should be taken into account by the education system. He refers to this notion as multiple intelligences (MI). Christison (1996) contends that L2 teachers can benefit from discovering more about MI theory because it can allow them to integrate a variety of learning experiences into their classes that allow learners to build upon their strengths.

MI is not the only alternative conception of intelligence that has begun to enter second language education. Goleman's (1995) notion of emotional intelligence (EQ) seems to have unique relevance to language teaching and learning. EQ has been described as "the subset of social intelligence that involves the ability to monitor one's own and others' feelings and emotions, to discriminate among them and to use this information to guide one's thinking and actions" (Salovey & Mayer, 1990, p. 189). It is thought to enable people to manage their positive and negative emotions in ways that aid effective thinking (Ciarrochi & Mayer, 2007). EQ is an important aspect of language learning because language learning is an emotional experience (MacIntyre, 2002). Research exploring the connections between EQ and language learning has revealed that L2 learners continue to experience high levels of anxiety despite having spent many years learning the target language (Shao, Yu, & Ji, 2013). Existing research on EQ and second language learning has demonstrated that those with higher levels of EQ tend to be more strategic L2 learners (Aghasafari, 2006) and they experience lower levels of communication and foreign language anxiety (Dewaele, Petrides, & Furnham, 2008). Other research has begun to show that learners who have higher L2 achievement also tend to have greater levels of EQ (Mohammadi, 2012; Pishghadam, 2009) although some conflicting results have been reported on this (Zarafshan & Ardeshiri, 2012). Increased EQ has also been argued to support learners' acceptance of other cultures (Riemer, 2003).

8.4 Learning styles

Learners have been observed to differ with respect to their learning styles as well. Learning styles are categorized in several ways. Learning styles are defined as natural and preferred ways of processing and retaining new information and skills (Reid, 1995). Keefe(1979) has described learning styles as "the characteristic cognitive, affective and physiological behaviors that serve as relatively stable indicators of how learners perceive, interact with and respond to the learning environment...that reflects underlying causes of behavior" (p. 4).

Learning styles have been categorized in various ways depending on what personal characteristics of the learner they emphasize. Cognitive learning styles include the commonly acknowledged distinction between field dependent and field independent (Witkin, Moore, Goodenough, & Cox, 1977). According to this model, field-independent learners tend to be better able to analyze language well because they are "free – or independent – of the influence of the whole [visual] field when they look at the parts and therefore can notice details that their field-dependent counterparts simply cannot 'see'" (Dornyei & Ryan, 2015, p. 124). In other words, these learners can skillfully select and analyze the separate components in a field (e.g., hidden objects in a picture) becoming confused by the other parts in the same field. For example, they would have less difficulty noticing the novel grammatical features in a text. In contrast, field-dependent learners tend to be better at seeing a broader perspective. However, what they gain in having a wider perception, they lose in analytical capability.

In terms of language learning, research findings indicate that field-independent learners have an advantage with regard to their relative facility completing cognitive tasks (Johnson, Prior, & Artuso, 2000). In contrast, and to their advantage, field-dependent learners' display greater ability to pay attention to the broader context has been shown to facilitate their superior performance on inductive (Nel, 2008) and communicative tasks (Johnson et al., 2000) than their field-independent counterparts.

In addition to this cognitive view of learning styles, there is also a personality-based theory of learning styles. The personality-based model holds that L2 learning is shaped by the degree to which a learner is more or less extroverted. learners who are more introverted are inclined to be quieter, avoid over-stimulation and meeting many people (Eysenck & Chan, 1982). In contrast, an extroverts are sociable and gregarious so they typically choose to focus more on people and happenings (Wenden & Rubin, 1987). Extroverts are more gregarious and tend to talk more during instructed (Cook, 1991) and naturalistic language learning situations (Swain, 1985). Consequently, extroverts are believed to benefit more from their efforts to connect with other L2 users and access more target language input as well as practice opportunities. They may also try out a wider variety of word types and grammatical structures in their L2 interactions with others.

Several personal variables have also been investigated with regard to how they interact with introversion/extroversion and other L2 learning related variables. For instance, introversion was found to affect both communication anxiety and self-perceived communicative competence (Horwitz, Horwitz, & Cope, 1986; MacIntyre & Charos, 1996). They also display less willingness to communicate (MacIntyre, Babin, & Clément, 1999). Extroversion relates to language learning strategy use in that extroverts use more functional and social-affective strategies and pay more attention to meaning than form (Wakamoto, 2000).

With regard to academic achievement, some findings have suggested that introverts have higher academic achievement than extroverts (MacIntyre & Charos, 1996; Skehan, 1989). Ellis (1994) notes that extroversion correlates with Basic Interpersonal Communication Skill (BICS) while introversion aids learners' development of cognitive academic language ability (CALP). However, there has been at least some research that reported no academic advantage for either personality type and that both types so language teachers should focus their attention on meeting the unique needs of both introverted and extroverted learners (Gardner & Clément, 1990).

Furnham (1990) claimed that extroverts talk more and take more risks in their L2 use than introverts who tend to pay more attention to their spoken accuracy. Dewaele and Furnham (1999) investigated personality type and speaking ability and concluded that bilingual extroverts tend to be more fluent L2 speakers particularly when faced with mentally taxing interactions. Likewise, Hassan (2001) reported extroverts in his study demonstrated more accurate English pronunciation than the introverts. However, Busch (1982) did not find Japanese extraverts to be more or less skilled English speakers than the introverts. Other researchers have also expressed uncertainty regarding whether introversion/extroversion is directly related to success in language learning (Carrell, Prince, & Astika, 1996).

Yet others have pointed out that it can be difficult to establish for certain whether it is the learner's personality or the learning context and methods that most account for their observed differences in proficiency. Indeed, it may depend more on the learning environment and teaching approach with respect to whether or not it is more advantageous to be introverted or extroverted in L2 learning (MacIntyre & Charos, 1996).

A third classification scheme of learning styles is in accordance with sensory and perceptual preferences that learners are believed to have. Pritchard (2008) explains that learners can be categorized into three types that include visual, auditory and kinesthetic learners. First, there are those who prefer and benefit most from instruction and learning experiences that provide visual information such as written instructions, images and diagrams, mind maps and graphic organizers (Scarcella, 1990). The second type is the auditory learner. They are characterized by their aptitude for and enjoyment of discussion and exceptional verbal memory. They benefit most from classroom discussions and debates as well as the incorporation of music and listening into lessons (Carbo, Dunn, and Dunn, 1986). The final category of learners is the kinesthetic learner. They are most easily recognized by their difficulty sitting still for long periods and effective use of body language (Scarcella, 1990). These learners benefit most from having the chance to move while they learn. So, in the language classroom, these learners thrive when they can do activities like "mingle/mixers" based on information gaps or drama/ role plays.

Previous studies into the learning styles of ESL and EFL students have looked at their preferences for visual, auditory, kinesthetic and tactile styles. Learners across a wide variety of English L2 learning contexts indicated a preference for kinesthetic and tactile learning. Chinese university students in both Taiwan (Jones, 1997) and the PRC (Melton, 1990) favored kinesthetic and tactile styles. Similarly, Cantonese-speaking Chinese vocational school students (Wu, 2010) and university students (Peacock, 2001) in Hong Kong expressed preferences for kinesthetic learning styles.

EFL learners in other contexts also favored kinesthetic and tactile learning including Tibetan (Hong, 2007), Thai (Khmakhien, 2012), and Vietnamese learners (Tuan, 2011). Interestingly, Hyland (1993) observed that Japanese learners also expressed a preference for tactile but not kinesthetic learning styles. Research in ESL contexts also demonstrated that most ESL students strongly preferred kinesthetic and tactile learning styles (Reid, 1987; Rossi-Le, 1995).

A number of other studies also revealed that students in both ESL and EFL contexts indicated that they were auditory learners. Students is a Cantonese-speaking Chinese vocational school (Wu, 2010) and university in Hong Kong (Peacock, 2001)favored auditory learning styles. The same was also true for Thai (Khmakhien, 2012), Japanese (Hyland, 1993), and Iranian EFL learners who stated that they enjoyed listening to tapes in particular (Riazi & Riasati, 2008). Arabic, Chinese, Korean, and Indonesian learners of English in the US likewise selected auditory learning as a favorite learning style (Reid, 1987).

A preference for learning through the visual modality was less commonly expressed. In her investigation of various L1 groups studying in the US, Reid (1987) observed that Korean, Arabic and Chinese language groups were the most visual learners. Similarly, Iranian EFL learners indicated a preference for visual learning through reading, pictures and posters (Riazi & Riasati, 2008).

With respect to individual versus group learning styles, the findings of extant research appear to be somewhat mixed. On the one hand, Cantonese-speaking Chinese vocational school students in Hong Kong (Wu, 2010) and Taiwanese university students (Jones, 1997) both claimed to like working in a group. Comparable results were reported for Thai EFL learners (Khmakhien, 2012) as well as Iranian EFL learners who enjoyed interactions with others and working in groups (Riazi & Riasati, 2008). An investigation of Russian EFL and ESL students as well as Asian ESL language learners reveled their clear preferences for group over individual work (Wintergerst, DeCapua, & Verna, 2003). However, contrasting findings from a number of other studies showed that Japanese (Hyland, 1993) and Chinese (Melton, 1990) learners disliked group learning styles. In a survey of ESL learners studying in the US, most L1 groups did not like group work except for the Malaysian students (Reid, 1987).

Peacock (2001) also pointed out that that students' preferred learning styles can sometimes conflict with the teaching methods they most commonly encounter. Therefore, we need to watch for this mismatch and do our best to acknowledge the preferred learning style of our students. However, we should also be aware that everyone has his or her own learning style so no single teaching method can suit all learners all of the time. Besides, students should be encouraged to occasionally learn through less preferred modalities because they will not always be able to learn through the methods they prefer. As we consider our methods and materials selection in light of our students' learning style preferences, we also need to remember that no one style is inherently better than the others. We should also bear in mind that our main challenge is to identify instructional approaches and materials that meet the needs of learners with a variety of learning styles.

8.5 Language learning and communication strategies

Language learning strategies

Just as L2 learners differ from each other in their learning styles, they also vary in the learning and communication strategies that they use. Rubin (1987) defines learning strategies as "... any sets of operations, steps, plans, routines used by the learner to facilitate the obtaining, storage, retrieval, and use of information" (p. 19). They are thought to be valuable because they allow learners to perform beyond their current capabilities. Language learning strategies enable learners to learn independently which is critical to developing their communicative ability (Oxford, 1990). Indeed, learners need a firm knowledge of learning strategies to be autonomous learners (Griffiths, 2013) and the development of learner autonomy and strategy use are mutually reinforcing (Oxford, 2017).

Learning strategies are typically categorized in several ways depending on the views of the individual researcher. One widely used categorization scheme was put forth by O'Malley, Chamot, Stewner-Manzanares, Russo, and Kupper (1985). According to this arrangement, learning strategies are divided into metacognitive, cognitive and socio-affective. Metacognitive strategies draw upon executive function to plan and monitor one's learning and include such strategies as self-management (e.g., arranging a productive learning environment) or self-monitoring (i.e., checking that one is using a strategy appropriately), and evaluating one's learning at the conclusion of an activity. Examples of metacognitive strategies include advance organizers, directed attention, selective attention, self-management, self-monitoring, delayed production, and self-evaluation.

Cognitive strategies are typically restricted to specific learning tasks and focus more on the thinking the learner does while actually learning the L2. They also tend to relate to the handling of the actual learning materials. Examples of these kinds of strategies include repetition, translation, note taking, mental imagery, contextualization, elaboration, transfer, and making inferences.

Socio-affective strategies are primarily associated with facilitating social interactions and transactions as well as managing one's emotions while using the

L2. Particular strategies that fall into this category include asking ones intralocular clarification of an unknown utterance or cooperating with interlocutors to ensure that communication proceeds as smoothly as possible.

Communication strategies

These learning strategies can also be contrasted with communication strategies. Learning and communication strategies can sometimes overlap in the sense that it is possible to learn through the process of using a communication strategies such as testing one's supposition about how an L2 structure functions. However, we cannot generally assume that they are the same thing (Tarone, 1980). Unlike learning strategies, the focus of communication strategies is on using certain verbal tactics to facilitate oral communication. Tarone (1980) defines communication strategies as "mutual attempts of two interlocutors to agree on a meaning in situations where the requisite meaning structures do not seem to be shared" (p. 420).

Communication strategies usually fall into two broad categories. These are avoidance and compensatory strategies. Avoidance or reduction strategies are used when the L2 user is unable to produce what she wants to say. Topic avoidance, message abandonment or meaning replacement allows learners to evade unfamiliar topics and potential communication problems but can also limit the content of the interaction. Through achievement or compensatory strategies, learners devise alternative plans to address their communication problems and achieve their aims. These strategies can be divided into several groupings. One such category is compensatory strategies which includes both cooperative and non-cooperative strategies. The main cooperative strategy relies upon learners appealing to their interlocutor for help when they have difficulty expressing their message.

Non-cooperative strategies are further subdivided into interlanguage and intra-language strategies. Interlanguage strategies include those like code switching, "foreignizing" an L1 word by pronouncing it with the phonology of the L2 hoping that there might be a similar word in the target language, and translation. Intra-language strategies involve such tactics as circumlocution (explaining the meaning of the unknown target word), approximation through synonym use, and substituting a word like "thing" for an unknown word. More examples include offering examples of an unknown word, coining a new word, restructuring one's message and using non-verbal strategies like miming. Other strategies that can be used to facilitate verbal communication are using fillers and memorized prefabricated phrases. All of these communication strategies help the learner to perform slightly better in their communication than they otherwise might have been able to without them.

8.6 Research on language learning strategy training

Research has begun to establish the link between language learning strategies and the development of L2 proficiency. Indeed, Wharton (2000) reported that learners who rated their own L2 proficiency highly also claimed to use more L2 learning strategies. Other studies comparing learner strategy use at various proficiency levels have demonstrated increased use of learning strategies among more proficient learners (Bremner, 1999; Green & Oxford, 1995). Similarly, language learning strategies were significantly correlated with the TOEFL scores (Park, 1997). With respect to strategy use and L2 acquisition, Cohen and Aphek (1980) found that the paired associates vocabulary memorization strategy led to improved vocabulary acquisition. However, at least one conflicting result also exists. Nunan (1995) created a program to teach learning strategies to English learners but could not establish a correlation between their strategy training and L2 acquisition.

Listening and speaking strategies have also been associated with skilled L2 listening (Vandergrift & Goh, 2012) although this has not been the case in all investigations. Indeed, O'Malley et al. (1985) found that strategy training had no effect on listening but it did have a positive effect on speaking. Other research into speaking has revealed that strategy use correlates with speaking proficiency (Oxford & Ehrman, 1995) and strategy instruction improves EFL learners' oral ability (Dadour & Robbins, 1996).

Research into the use of reading strategies has generally revealed that more proficient readers typically rely on more top-down meaning-based strategies. Hosenfeld (1977) studied self-reported reading strategies of successful and less successful students studying various L2's. He reported that successful learners used "top-down" strategies (e.g., inferring) while less successful readers excessively relied upon bottom-up word-by-word decoding. Block (1986) reached similar conclusions after comparing learners who were more and less proficient readers among two groups of less successful postsecondary learners. The better readers drew upon their background knowledge of text structure (i.e., top-down strategies), while the less proficient readers reacted to the text rather than using strategies to analyze its structure. Likewise, Zhang, Gu, and Hu (2008) examined Singaporean ESL elementary grade learners' reading strategies in English medium schools using think-aloud procedures. Findings were that learners with high proficiency tended to use meaning-based strategies (i.e., predicting and summarizing) while less proficient learners used fewer and less varied kinds reading strategies.

However, not all findings concurred that reading strategy use clearly related to L2 reading proficiency. For instance, Oxford and Ehrman (1995) studied adult learners of several different L2's and observed that their cognitive strategy use was not related to their reading proficiency. As well, while Anderson (1991) agreed that there were no obvious differences in top-down or bottom-up strategy use by more or less successful readers, but he found that more successful readers could more effectively coordinate their strategy use (Anderson, 1991).

Strategic writing has also been the focus of a number of investigations. Studies associated with the process writing approach have identified some of the strategies that learners use during the various phases of the writing process. For example, investigations of the planning for writing have demonstrated that high proficiency L2 writers who planned in the L2 produced superior plans and compositions than low-proficiency L2 writers (Akyel, 1994). Additional studies have shown that skilled L2 writers planned more (Victori, 1999) and wrote from their plans (Skibniewski & Skibniewska, 1986). Their plans were also focused on global organization and open to ongoing alteration while writing (Sasaki, 2000).

Findings from studies of drafting show that L2 learners revise substantially more in the L2 writing than in their L1 writing (Hall, 1990). Additionally, as L2 writers develop, they increasingly move from lower to more global revisions as they proceed through consecutive draft (Butler-Nalin, 1984). They also experience considerably more difficulty in producing text in their L2 compared to their L1 regardless of their proficiency level (de Larios, Marín, & Murphy, 2001). More skilled L2 writers have a clearer sense of what they want to accomplish as well as how they can put their plan into action as they more effectively move between their overall plan and more fine-grained paragraph and sentence level text construction (Cumming, 1989).

With respect to text revision, target language ability appears to differ from text level organizational knowledge as writing task familiarity seems to contribute more to revision strategy use than L2 ability (Yasuda, 2004). As well, skilled L2 writers revise more (Raimes, 1987), and focus more on text-level organizational and structural revisions (Skibniewski & Skibniewska, 1986).

Self-regulation strategies are another area of research related to the use of second-language writing strategies. Examples of important self-regulation writing strategies are goal-setting, self-monitoring, self-evaluation, and time management (Harris, Graham, MacArthur, Reid, & Mason, 2011). Some debate exists with regard to the relationship between L2 proficiency and L2 writing strategy use. On the one hand, Cumming (1989) concludes that L2 proficiency does not influence the use of L2 composition strategies. In contrast, others have found that learners with greater L2 proficiency used writing strategies comparable to those of L1 writers (Kamimura, 1996) while lower L2 proficiency learners used fewer compensatory writing strategies (Smith, 1994). Those who are proficient writers in their L1 also tend to be stronger L2 writers (Skibniewski & Skibniewska, 1986). L2 writers share a similar range of composing strategies, but differ in the ease with which they can use particular strategies based on their L2 proficiency level (Wong, 2005).

The effectiveness of strategy instruction has also received some previous research attention. With regard to L1 research, results show that strategy instruction helps learners develop their writing skills. MacArthur, Philippakos, and Ianetta (2015) evaluated self-regulated strategy instruction in college developmental writing classes. This strategy instruction improved learners' self-efficacy and mastery motivation as well as the quality and length of their persuasive essay writing but not their written grammar. Other research in L1 contexts revealed that both strategy instruction and combining self-regulation with strategy instruction had a positive effect on L1 learners' writing (Graham, McKeown, Kiuhara,

& Harris, 2012). As well, a meta-analysis of the efficacy of various writing interventions, strategy instruction was found to be an effective writing instructional practice for adolescent first-language writers (Graham & Perin, 2007). As for L2 students, those who received strategy-based instruction in task-specific metacognitive self-regulation training in their academic writing program improved their ability to plan, monitor and evaluate a writing task (Nguyen & Gu, 2013).

8.7 Language learning aptitude

Aptitude is another background variable that has been widely acknowledged as contributing to L2 language learning. A learner with language learning aptitude has been characterized as "the ability to successfully adapt to and profit from instructed, or naturalistic exposure to the L2" (P. Robinson, 2005, p. 57). It has also been characterized as "a specific talent for learning foreign languages which exhibits considerable variation between individual learners" (Dörnyei & Skehan, 2003, p. 590). The concept of language aptitude is built on top of several assumptions outlined by Skehan (1991). These are that (1) a talent for learning languages exists that is not associated with intelligence (2) the talent is not the result of previous learning (3) it is somewhat stable and (4) it varies between individuals.

Aptitude has traditionally subdivided into several different components (Carroll, 1981). These include phonemic coding ability which is the ability to discriminate new sounds in the L2. Associative memory is the ability to create and remember associations between new words. Inductive learning ability is the capability to see patterns and make generalizations from language input. Finally, grammatical sensitivity allows learners to deduce the grammatical function of words in sentences. Language aptitude is typically measured by using tests like the MLAT (modern language aptitude test) & PLAB (Pilmsleur language aptitude test). These assessment contain subtests that assess learners' ability to (1) identify and memorize new sounds, (2) understand the function of particular words in sentences, (3) work out grammatical rules from language samples and (4) remember new words. At present, it is generally agreed that analytical ability (associated with verbal aptitude and intelligence), memory and phonetic sensitivity are key components of aptitude (DeKeyser & Koeth, 2011).

There has also been some debate surrounding the construct of aptitude itself. On the one hand, there are those who contend that aptitude is an invariable personality trait that is not amenable to development through experience or instruction (Harley & Hart, 1997; Sawyer, 1992). In contrast, other researchers argue that aptitude should be viewed as developing expertise rather than a reified entity (Dörnyei, 2010; Grigornko, Sternberg, & Ehrman, 2000) because anyone can progress from beginner to expert through continued experience and practice using a skill (McLaughlin, 1990b).

A number of variables have been associated with language learning aptitude. One variable this is widely speculated to relate to L2 aptitude is L1 learning ability. For example, Carroll (1973) previously claimed that L1 skills has a residual influence on the L2 learning aptitude. Similarly, the interdependence hypotheses put forth by Cummins (1980) posited that a common underlying proficiency exists between L1 and L2 language skills and that success in L2 development is built upon L1 ability. However, these initial speculations were not based upon any empirical results. It was later empirical work that began to present a stronger case for the existence of a relationship between L1 ability and L2 aptitude.

Sparks and Ganschow (1991) created the linguistic coding differences hypotheses (LCDH) model which in essence claims that particular linguistic deficiencies (e.g., phonological processing) would also manifest themselves in both L1 and L2 learning. Subsequent research has demonstrated that L1 skills contribute to English L2 learning. Indeed, numerous investigations highlighted the influence that various specific aspects of L1 proficiency has had upon L2 development.

One characteristic of L1 ability that has been linked to L2 learning is phonological awareness. For example, L1 phonological awareness has been shown to affect the English L2 phonological awareness of Chinese bilingual children with dyslexia (Chung & Ho, 2010). Similarly, ninth graders' phonological awareness measured in their L1 Hebrew helped to account for their English word reading and reading comprehension (Kahn-Horwitz, Sparks, & Goldstein, 2012). University students in Hong Kong whose L1 did not use an alphabet did not display as much phonological awareness as students with an alphabetic first language (China, Vietnam and Australia) (Holm & Dodd, 1996).

L1 phonological–orthographic facility was also found to contribute to L2 decoding ability. Findings from a study of high school students revealed L1 word decoding to be the best predictor of L2 word decoding skills (Sparks, Patton, Ganschow, & Humbach, 2009). L1 phonological–orthographic skill was also found to predict L2 competence in college-age adults though this relationship was mediated by L2 word decoding ability (Meschyan & Hernandez, 2002).

Other research connected other L1 skills to L2 development. Based on the results of his analysis of the relationship between aptitude, L1 acquisition, and L2 achievement, Skehan (1986) concluded that the home literacy orientation appears to contribute to L2 aptitude development. He later added that learners with superior first language facility have also been found to have greater L2 learning aptitude (Skehan, 1991). Other studies have added that L1 skills (Sparks, Humbach, & Javorsky, 2008; Sparks et al., 2009) and L1 literacy (Dufva & Voeten, 1999) are important for L2 learning.

Working memory (WM) has been defined as "...the immediate memory processes involved in the simultaneous storage and processing of information in real-time" (Harrington & Sawyer, 1992, p. 26). A number of researchers have also claimed that working memory may be the most important element of aptitude (Miyake, 1998; Sawyer & Ranta, 2001). Indeed, Wen and Skehan (2011) have gone as far as to argue that working memory is equivalent to L2 aptitude. Working memory is thought to be the entry point for L2 acquisition in the sense that "what we work on in WM is what may become part of our long term memory (LTM), that is to say, WM serves as a gateway to LTM" (Wen & Skehan, 2011, p. 22).

Wen and Skehan (2011) outline the primary reasons for why WM has been implicated as a key factor in SLA. These reasons include SLA reliance upon the general learning mechanisms and controlled processing which are widely believed to be influenced by WM. As well, WM is involved in SLA input and output processing, cognitive operations like noticing and is also a central mechanism in the linguistic chunking that shapes vocabulary and grammar learning.

Empirical work has also demonstrated the vital role the working memory plays in L2 skill learning. For instance, WM has a moderate correlation with language aptitude revealing a shared commonality between these constructs (Sáfár & Kormos, 2008). With regard to receptive skills, Gu and Wang (2007) observed that L1 and L2 WM measures predicted participants' listening comprehension performance. WM (as measured by L2 reading span) correlated strongly with the reading subsection of the TOEFL test (Harrington & Sawyer, 1992) and syntactic comprehension (Miyake, 1998). WM capacity can greatly influence L2 grammar (Ellis, 1996) and lexical (Williams & Lovatt, 2005) acquisition.

Other work exploring the relationship between WM and productive skills reveals that WM predicts L2 oral lexical, narrative, and grammatical skill (O'brien, Segalowitz, Collentine, & Freed, 2006) and L2 oral fluency development (Mizera, 2005) in instructed contexts. WM is also associated with L2 oral progress during synchronous computer mediated communication (Payne & Ross, 2005). Likewise, WM relates to L2 writing proficiency (Kellogg, Olive, & Piolat, 2007; McCutchen, 2000) although there remains a relative dearth of research in this area.

Research has also been conducted into the connections between aptitude, L2 learning and L2 achievement. For instance, aptitude has been shown to correlated with second language proficiency (Ehrman & Oxford, 1995; Miyake, 1998). A relationship has also been noted between aptitude and achievement in the second language (Bain, McCallum, Bell, Cochran, & Sawyer, 2010). Other research indicates that aptitude relates primarily to speed at which the L2 can be learned (Carroll, 1981). However, since aptitude is not a unified entity, it is possible for a learner to excel at some aspects of language learning (e.g., remembering words) while struggling with others (e.g., detecting grammar patterns) (P. Robinson, 2005). New insights into the nature of aptitude also reveal that awareness of the relative strengths and weakness of individual learners can allow more efficient learning (Erlam, 2005).

8.8 Personality

Another type of learner individual difference is learner personality factors. Researchers have identified a variety of relevant personality factors. One such factor also discussed above is whether the learner is extroverted or introverted. Some research results related to extroversion are that no correlation exists between extroversion and attainment in the L2 (Dewaele & Furnham, 1999; Gardner & Clément, 1990). However, Ellis (1994) has discussed the possible connection between introversion/extroversion may be connected with the form of the L2 the student is learning. That is, the claim that the more extroverted learners acquire better basic interpersonal communication skills (BICS) while introverts may have superior cognitive academic language proficiency (CALP). A number of studies have explored the potential connection between these variables and the results generally have been mixed. On the one hand, some have reported relationships between extroversion and speech production (Dewaele & Furnham, 2000) as well as introversion and vocabulary knowledge (Carrell et al., 1996), but others have found no connection between introversion-extroversion and language ability (Ehrman & Oxford, 1995).

Willingness to communicate (WTC) is a related construct. This is the notion that has been defined as "the intention to initiate communication, given a choice" (MacIntyre, Baker, Clément, & Conrod, 2001, p. 369). WTC in more naturalistic settings can be affected by number of factors which include size of the group interacting, self-confidence, interlocutor acquaintance, their willingness to contribute to the exchange (Cao & Philp, 2006) as well as perceived of security, excitement, and responsibility to further the conversation (Kang, 2005). With respect to instructed learning related WTC factors, Zhang, Beckmann, and Beckmann (2018) reviewed the relevant research and found that a wide variety of influences affect WTC inside the classroom including the classroom atmosphere, the classmates, the class size, and the teacher. Even the classroom task itself can affect WTC. The topic being explored, the activity type, preparation time available and whether or not the task will be assessed all have the potential to feed into learners' WTC.

The impact of learners' willingness to take risks has been thought to have some relevance to language teaching and learning. Ely (1986) describes risk-taking in L2 language learning as having several dimensions such as (1) willingness to try out unfamiliar language; (2) desire to use seemingly complex or difficult language; (3) ability to accept flawed or approximate L2 production; and (4) a predisposition to practice new language before using it. Risk-averse learners carefully plan and monitor their L2 output to avoid errors while risk-takers prefer express themselves in unrehearsed manner to learn whether their output makes sense to their interlocutor (Ellis, 1994; Krashen, 1978). They also tend to be more extroverted and strategic in their L2 learning (Beebe, 1983). Learners with a low tolerance for ambiguity associated with L2 learning typically struggle with taking more appropriate risks as well (Oxford & Ehrman, 1992).

A number of variables have been found to influence risk taking in the language learning classroom. Willingness to participate in lessons seems to come from learners' perception that classes provide them with the chance to practice and improve their L2 proficiency (Ely, 1986). This willingness can also be affected by who they are conversing with (Beebe, 1983) and teacher's efforts to allay their fears about speaking in class (Lee & Ng, 2009). Access to linguistic scaffolds such as useful grammar structures or lexis helps learners to handle risk taking more effectively, but less structured activities like free conversation are threatening to risk-averse learners (Beebe, 1983). Groups also typically have a greater propensity to take risks than students working by themselves (Lee & Ng, 2009).

Both advantages and disadvantages appear to come with being a high risk-taking language learner. With regard to advantages, risk taking in the L2 classroom predicts learners' voluntary classroom participation which in turn influenced their speaking accuracy (Ely, 1986). They also learn vocabulary more effectively (Shatz, 2015). Secondly, risk-averse learners may fossilize sooner as a result of excessively relying on familiar but inaccurate language and expressions (Beebe,

1983). In contrast, risk takers exhibit reduced fossilization of their L2 due to their readiness to experiment with new language forms and seek out situations to practice their L2 (Skehan, 1989). Risk-taking L2 learners also gain access to more input which has the potential to become L2 intake that contributes to their L2 development (Beebe, 1983).

Disadvantages for risk-taking include learners' willingness to take risks causing them to focus more on simply expressing themselves than being accurate. As a consequence, they may be more fluent than accurate in their L2 output (Dewaele & Furnham, 1999; Krashen, 1978). As well, higher L2 proficiency levels has not been associated with risk taking (Dehbozorgi, 2012; Ghoorchaei & Kassaian, 2009), but high risk-takers tended to assess their speaking ability higher (Tavakoli & Ghoorchaei, 2009) and they also have a more positive attitude towards language learning (Dehbozorgi, 2012).

Anxiety has been identified has playing a role in L2 learning. Language learning anxiety has been described as "the feeling of tension and apprehension specifically associated with second language contexts, including speaking, listening, and learning" (MacIntyre & Gardner, 1994, p. 284). Anxiety has been further subdivided into trait and state anxiety. Trait anxiety is a more permanent predisposition and a core aspect of learner's personality and a learner with high trait anxiety can be thought of as a generally anxious person (Worde, 1998). State anxiety is more temporary, context specific and tends to be caused more by external circumstances (Scovel, 1978).

Kleinmann (1977) also pointed out that anxiety can been thought of in terms of whether or not it is debilitative or facilitative. Anxiety is debilitate if when it reaches a high enough level that it causes the learner to no longer be able to effectively perform the task at hand. In contrast, facilitative anxiety is that level of nervousness that the learner feels pushes her to try harder and perform better than if she were too relaxed. However, others have more recently argued that in order for the constructs of debilitative and facilitative anxiety to be helpful for L2 teachers, they need to realize that are two totally different entities that do not necessarily correlate with each other. Consequently, it can be possible for a learner to actually be experiencing both at the same time (MacIntyre, 2017).

Research has revealed that foreign language anxiety can negatively affect L2 achievement in that anxious learners have lower L2 achievement levels (Cheng, Horwitz, & Schallert, 1999; Horwitz et al., 1986) and poor performance (Gardner & MacIntyre, 1993) during the input, processing, and output phases of language learning (MacIntyre & Gardner, 1994). Other research has also shown that students may communicate less in stressful classes that lack an encouraging environment (Steinberg & Horwitz, 1986).

Horwitz et al. (1986) argued that the teacher has considerable influence on learner anxiety. Therefore, teachers need to strive to organize classroom activities and practices in such a way as to minimize learners' apprehension as much as possible. However, this need to lower students' anxiety can be doubly challenging for language teachers because many teachers also have anxiety about their own L2 proficiency that can cause them to use ineffective methods such as avoiding communication opportunities that could actually help lessen student anxiety (Horwitz, 1996). Nevertheless, research has identified several strategies that teachers can use to reduce learners' anxiety.

One suggestion has been to teach learners coping strategies to help them more effectively handle their anxiety. Although Kondo and Ying-Ling (2004) reported that use of coping strategies did not associate with levels of language anxiety, several other researchers found that they did (Kao & Craigie, 2013). Indeed, a number of specific strategies have been suggested to help reduce learner anxiety. Some effective coping strategies include maintaining positive teacher classroom presence through creating a welcoming atmosphere (Tsiplakides & Keramida, 2009) showing enthusiasm (Alrabai, 2015), patience and humor (He, 2017). Other anxiety-alleviating strategies included providing opportunities for training (Kralova, Skorvagova, Tirpakova, & Markechova, 2017), practice and rehearsal (Alrabai, 2015; Nutt, 2017) as well as using small group work (Tsiplakides & Keramida, 2009).

A final personality related factor discussed throughout the second language learning literature is motivation. Motivation is characterized by a learner who "displays some goal-directed activity, and second, that the person expends some effort" (Gardner, 1985, p. 50). Motivation "provides the primary impetus to initiate learning the second language and later the driving force to sustain the long and often tedious learning process" (Dörnyei, 1998, p. 117). In general, the greater perceived value of the activity, the more highly motivated they will be to do it.

The components of motivation have been isolated and organized somewhat differently over the years. Gardner and Lambert (1972) distinguished integrative and instrumental as two separate orientations toward motivation. Integrative motivation involves the learners studying the second language so that he or she can more closely integrate into the second language culture. That is, they desire to participate in or join the target culture. Instrumental motivation entails studying the L2 to attain certain aims from knowing the language. Examples of such goals include pursuing a career, passing an important professional test or gaining a promotion. Research demonstrates that teachers should encourage the development of both integrative and instrumental motivation to promote L2 learning success (Riemer, 2003).

Another commonly referenced view of motivation categorizes the construct quite differently. Within Ryan and Deci's (2000) Self-Determination Theory, the labels of intrinsic versus extrinsic motivation are widely used constructs to explain motivation. Intrinsic motivation is that which the learner brings with them to the classroom. It is the kind being drawn upon when the learner performs a task for its own sake. It is based on the learners own inherent interest in the subject matter and his or her desire to master it (Deci & Ryan, 1985). Intrinsically motivated learners engage in the task is pleasurable so the reward is doing the task itself. These learners are inherently interested in and curious about the task. Frequently, the learner wants to master the task so they are eager to continually challenge themselves in order to improve. As part of their drive for mastery, learners develop their own criteria for what they believe constitutes success. The prototypical example of intrinsic motivation is learning to play a video game. No parent has to remind their child to spend more time playing video games if they want to improve.

In contrast, extrinsic motivation originates from sources that are outside of the learner including rewards and punishments such as praise, candies, grades and so forth (Vansteenkiste, Lens, & Deci, 2006). Because the learner's real desire is to receive the reward (and not complete the task), the learner prefers not to challenge herself with difficult tasks. Common extrinsic rewards given are attention and praise which come with the danger of learner's excessive dependence on the teacher's approval (Kohn, 1999). The criteria for success are also decided external to the learner which does not encourage deep understanding of what constitutes quality work. An example of a task that often requires external motivation to complete is homework.

Recent theories highlight commonalities between intrinsic and extrinsic motivation in that, rather than being polar opposites, extrinsic motivation can develop into more intrinsic motivation through building social relationships and support networks (Ryan & Deci, 2000). As well, many activities often entails both types of motivation (Amabile, 1993). For instance, when we both want to do an enjoyable activity like play the piano but we also feel some pressure to practice a piece before our next piano lesson.

8.9 A socially-oriented theoretical perspective on motivation

In more recent years, the focus in second language motivation research has expanded somewhat. As it has been traditionally conceptualized, motivation has been a psychological construct that has assumed a unitary, coherent and ahistorical learner (Norton, 2000). With the recent "social turn" in second language acquisition research (Block, 2003), a more sociologically-oriented view has begun to emerge. This social conception has been termed "investment." In contrast to the construct of motivation, it presupposes that identity is complex, malleable and continually changing across time and space. They also claim that identity is reproduced in particular social interactions with the influence of other people (Peirce, 1995). A central concept that relates to learner identity is the notion of investment. According to this theory, learners invest in language learning when they believe that making the effort to learn the language will give them access "a wider range of symbolic and material resources, which will in turn increase the value of their cultural capital" (Peirce, 1995, p. 17). Thus, their willingness to try to learn the language is deeply connected to its perceived value in their life.

Advocates of the social identity and investment view of L2 learning also point out that power relationships have a substantial influence on language learning.

An example of the impact that power can have in the ESL classroom comes from the work of Morita (2004). She observed international students studying in content classes at a Canadian English-speaking university. Participants felt empowered in some classes and marginalized in others depending on whether space was made for them to participate by their peers and instructor. They were sometimes viewed as unknowledgeable or deficient L2 speakers which led to their exclusion from full classroom participation. As a result, in those classes they had limited access to the target language and opportunities to communicate with their Canadian peers.

Another more socially-oriented theoretical perspective on motivation known as Dörnyei's (2009) L2 Motivational Self System model emphasizes an "ideal L2 self" that learners want to become as an L2 user. According to this model, three factors affect learner motivation. The first is the notion of the "ideal L2 self" which is the imagined L2 speaker that the learner wants to become. The second related concept is the "ought-to L2 self" which describes what the learner believes he or she should do (e.g., duties, responsibilities etc.) to avoid negative L2 learning experiences. The third element connects the social experiences that the learner has in relation to L2 learning. For example, the learners social and educational environment. This component accounts for the effect of the learning context including previous learning experiences, classes, teachers, curricula, peers et cetera.

In essence, the more the environment supports our motivation and our ideal-self incorporates the role of being a target language speaker, the more motivated we will be. Our actions, desired identities and the social groups that we aspire to join are all deeply intertwined so social context significantly influences L2 learners' identity and motivation. Thus, a learner's observed level of motivation is heavily dependent on the social context (Ushioda, 2013). For example, an ESL learner and an EFL learner might differ in their motivation and attitude due to their access to the target language, experiences with the target culture, and socio-political climate of the country among many other factors. Of course, a myriad of factors can impact any individual learner so that specific learner's affective state cannot be predicted solely on the basis of him or her being in an ESL or EFL context.

8.10 Identity and agency in L2 learning

Identity is a key influence in the L2 learning process as well (Teng, 2018). Identity has been defined as "how a person understands his or her relationship to the world, how that relationship is constructed across time and space, and how the person understands possibilities for the future" (Norton, 2000, p. 5). Social identities include gender, ethnicity, race, nationality, religion, marital status, and language (Block, 2012; Riley, 2007) which influence how a student's view of themselves as well as how others regard them. Identity is multiple and often contradictory (Toohey & Norton, 2003) and develops in social interactions (Hawkins, 2005). Learners' identity and associated social position can limit their access to (Hawkins, 2005; Norton & Toohey, 2001), willingness, and ability to exploit language learning opportunities in or out of school (Kanno, 2003; Matear, 2008).

If a learner does not believe that people in her social category will be successful learners of the target language, then her teacher may only see an "unmotivated" student. However, as discussed above, the learner's beliefs are also shaped by the social context in that it is both those inside and outside her community send her the message that she does or does not belong in the community of target language speakers. In this way, investment is closely interconnected with the notion of an imagined community (Norton, 2001). An imagined community refers to the "...groups of people, not immediately tangible and accessible, with whom we connect through the power of the imagination" (Kanno & Norton, 2003, p. 241). The reality is that if the learner does not view themselves as being a potential target language speaker, it will be an arduous task to convince them to do the hard work required to learn the target language.

Kanno (2008) argues that some of these constructs and dynamics may help to partially explain what occurs in "subtractive" versus "additive" Japanese bilingual education contexts. That is, minority group members (e.g., immigrants and refugees) learning the language of majority groups displaying different attitudes and motivation from those of majority group members learning a minority language. Minority group members often have considerably more restricted access to the people, resources and information that would allow them to learn the target language more effectively and also have limited educational, social or economic capital that they could draw on in their attempts to learn the L2.

Kanno compares these "submersion" experiences with "immersion" programs and the contrast is readily apparent. In the case of immersion programs, it is often well-resourced, majority-group members who are confident in their identity who join the programs. They are not learning the L2 as a means to survive in a foreign and oftentimes hostile environment. They are typically coming to the program from a position of social and economic strength and learning the L2 as an optional benefit to provide themselves with even more of an economic advantage. It is likely that these dynamics are replicated in other contexts as well.

Learner agency is another construct that connects to identity and motivation. Agency has been described as a learner's ability to act as it is restricted by his or her social and material circumstances (Kalaja, Alanen, Palviainen, & Dufva,

2011). Teng (2018) observes that learners' agency shapes their identity and language learning. Agency is influenced by prior experiences and it plays a key role in learners' goal setting. It is a prerequisite for language learning but the exercise of agency is not always guaranteed because some contexts can thwart the learner's efforts to do so (e.g., a "submersion" L2 learning environment).

As language teachers, one crucial action that we can take is to find ways to help learners see that they have some agency. We can also show them how to leverage the agency that they have into more effective language learning. For example, in our classes, we might teach learners techniques like extensive reading and listening that they can use effectively engage in self-directed learning. Fostering learners' sense of agency is critical because in many cases this valuable insight is the only means that a disadvantaged learner may have to remind herself that her mindset can play a large part in determining whether or not she will successfully acquire the target language.

8.11 Learner beliefs and L2 learning

One final background factor to take into consideration is learners' beliefs. All learners, and particularly older learners, have strong beliefs about how languages should be taught. These beliefs are based on their preferences, experiences and assumptions that a particular type of instruction is better than others. Teachers need to pay attention to these beliefs because they can be a strong mediating factor in the quality of our learners' classroom experiences. That is, it may not necessarily be their actual classroom experience that affects their language learning but rather how that experience is filtered through their perception of what they think should be happening in a "proper" or "real" language class.

As a result of their cultural beliefs, previous instructional experiences and learning styles, learners often have developed particular preferences for different types of instruction (Horwitz, 1988). Accordingly, they may come to view alternative instructional approaches as unnatural or ineffective. Learners' preference for learning based on their language learning beliefs may also influence the strategies they use to learn new material. For example, a learner who is accustomed to learning primarily through translation will tend to rely on translation more than an individual who has studied through more communicative methods.

There are several areas where these beliefs can intersect with learners' classroom experiences to make them unsatisfied with the instruction that they receive. For example, if a learner has previously learned English through form-based lessons, they may experience difficulty adjusting to communicative approaches. Indeed, they may complain that they are wasting time just sitting around idly chatting and when they should be "learning the language" through explanations of its grammar. Similarly, learners may also complain if they are more accustomed to a teacher-centered class and they find them themselves in student-centered lessons. From their perspective, it may feel as though they are only learning each other's "broken English" when they need more exposure to learn the teacher's "perfect English."

Based on their preconceptions, some learners may also have complaints about the corrective feedback they receive. In many communicative classes, explicit feedback or error correction is often eschewed in the belief that it is ineffective or unnecessary (Krashen, 1982; Truscott, 1996). However, many learners who have been educated in more traditional systems expect explicit and direct feedback and may view teachers who do not provide it with suspicion (Ferris, Chaney, Komura, Roberts, & McKee, 2000). It is also important to note that these preferences are not limited to any particular method. That is, if a learner is used to communicative classes and they find themselves in a more traditional teacher-centered, grammar-focused class with a lot of direct and explicit feedback they will be equally dissatisfied as in the reverse case.

We want to be mindful of learners' preferences and expectations for language learning. We should do our best to take into consideration their expectations and not always push them to engage in learning activities that they do not believe are productive. Ignoring our learners' beliefs and expectations could create unnecessary anxiety and resistance from them which is certain to impede their L2 development. On the other hand, we should not be overly compliant in trying to cater to learners' beliefs and expectations. A key aspect of our role in creating effective and autonomous language learners is to push them to continue expanding their existing repertoire of L2 learning strategies by trying out alternative methods that they may unexpectedly enjoy and find useful. It is this exposure to new methods that will most likely contribute to their greater flexibility in their second language learning. It may also foster their ongoing interest in pursuing L2 development as a lifelong endeavor that they come to accept personal responsibility for. This aim can hardly be achieved by allowed them to remain securely within their comfort zone. We must continually strive to find the balance between what they are comfortable with and novelty in methods and techniques.

8.12 Summary

This chapter has reviewed a variety of learner background factors that can influence their L2 learning. For instance, intelligence is argued to be related to L2 learning ability although it may be related more to the development of academic language proficiency rather than conversational communication ability. Learning styles and strategies have been proposed to account for how learners are able to learn and communicate more efficiently in the L2.

Aptitude is widely acknowledged to be a separate entity than intelligence and has been put forward to explain why it is that some learners appear to progress more rapidly than others. Like intelligence, the role of aptitude does not exclude some learners from studying an additional language. In fact, aptitude research appears to indicate that while all learners may not reach the same levels of ultimate attainment, the vast majority can learn to communicate in the L2.

Likewise, learner personality factors that include extroversion, willingness-to-communicate, risk-taking, anxiety, motivation, identity, and learner beliefs have all been studied to ascertain how much they shape L2 language learning. Aspects of one's personality such as anxiety and extroversion have also been identified as potential inhibitors for some learner's L2 communication efforts. Learner motivation has received attention over the years and has been conceptualized in several different ways depending on its posited source. Learners' beliefs about themselves as learners and how languages should be learned can affect classroom experiences especially if those beliefs conflict with those of the teacher.

Socio-cultural factors have been previously overlooked, but they promise to have a wide-ranging effect on many of the other background variables. Factors such as classroom power dynamics and learner identity are just beginning to be investigated so more will be known about their influence in the years to come. However, what we know so far is that these factors have an undeniable impact upon a learner's experience of learning an additional language.

Teachers can use their knowledge about the background variables that may affect students' L2 learning to adjust their classroom practice to take into account these background factors as much as possible. For example, with respect to learning styles and strategies, teachers could find out what their students' learning styles are and use classroom activities that connect well with these preferred learning styles. Learning strategies can be addressed by teaching learners various types of strategies that students can use to learn new language more efficiently. They could also provide learners with opportunities to practice communication strategies independently with communicative tasks in the classroom. These tasks can then be supported with discussion of and feedback on their performance.

Classroom implications for learners' personality variables are that teachers want to minimize learner anxiety as much as possible although some facilitative anxiety might be productive. We should also promote willingness-to-communicate and sensible risk-taking through giving learners plenty of chances to talk in class. With regard to motivation, we teachers should realize that learners all have different goals for learning another language and in order to spark their interest we need to find effective ways to help them meet their goals. We also have to find activities that they will enjoy and topics that will capture their interest. We should also do what we can to help learners to cultivate an identity that allows them to see themselves as a successful target language user.

We should also be aware of the particular beliefs about who they are as language learners and what is supposed to be happening in L2 classrooms. These beliefs are primarily formed through their own previous classroom experiences. Teachers need to take these expectations into consideration in our planning while also being prepared to stretch our learners with new teaching methods that they may be less familiar with. We also should be able to provide convincing justifications for how our methods will facilitate their L2 development to assuage any doubts that they might have.

Teachers should be aware that socio-cultural factors also have significant bearing upon many learner background variables and interact with these variables in varied and unpredictable ways. For instance, if a learner either views herself as someone who can be a successful and wishes to join her imagined community of L2 speakers, then she will be more likely to persist through the inevitable challenges that come with learning an additional language. A similar outcome is also more likely if she is positioned as being an adept L2 learner by the teacher and other members of the classroom community. Thus, we must do what we can to help our learners see themselves as strong and confident L2 users who want to participate in a community of target language speakers.

Lastly, we should realize that each of these factors is only one piece of an exceedingly complex puzzle so they do not always account for the particular behaviors and dynamics that we observe in our classroom. Furthermore, these factors and others that as yet have not been identified interact with each other in ways that we do not yet fully understand. Therefore, we need to realize that pat or straightforward solutions to our teaching quandaries are rare.

Chapter 9

Age and L2 Learning

Chapter 9
Age and L2 Learning

9.1 Introduction

The main aim of this short chapter is to provide the reader with a clearer sense of what the research says about the relationship that age and second language learning. The substantial amount of research attention that age and second language learning has received warrants its own brief chapter. Deciding what constitutes a "young" or "older" learner in second language acquisition research has not been without substantial debate. Ellis (2015) points out that "adult" and "child" learners are not easily categorized. While learners have been classified into pre-puberty, adolescents, and post-puberty adult learners he calls attention to the fact that "there is a big difference… between a four-year-old and a ten-year-old child and perhaps an even bigger one between a 17-year-old and a 50-year-old adult learner" (p. 37). Thus, it seems that any way we attempt to categorize learners by age, we risk masking important differences within the category.

Age in L2 learning has widely been acknowledged as an important learner background variable because it has been shown to relate to both the rate and ultimate attainment in L2 acquisition. The age variable examined in L2 studies is usually the age of first exposure to the target L2. When age is investigated, researchers frequently focus on learners' rate of acquisition (i.e., how quickly they acquire the L2) in which case adults typically have an advantage at the outset (Snow & Hoefnagel-Höhle, 1978). Alternately, researchers study learners' ultimate attainment. Findings in this area typically show that those who begin at a younger age usually turn out to be more proficient in the L2 than those who begin studying when they are older (Patkowski, 1990).

The chapter begins with a description of the critical period as well as some of the debate surrounding its existence. From there, it discusses some of the unique advantages that both young learners and adults bring to their second language learning. Lastly, it reviews research conclusions with respect to age and the development of L2 pronunciation and syntax. An understanding of the role of age in L2 learning and knowledge of some of the key issues will enable you to be more aware of the age-related troubles that yours may experience at particular stages of their L2 development. You will hopefully also develop a bit more patience and have more realistic expectations for your learners with regard to how quickly they can progress in their learning.

9.2 A hypothesized critical period for L2 learning

The findings of several research studies demonstrate that child L2 learners are typically more successful at learning the L2 than adult L2 learners (Muñoz, 2010). The question is whether the cause of this result is biological, cognitive, or contextual. The explanations for these observed outcomes usually differ depending on the researcher's theoretical orientation. On the one hand, there are those who agree with Chomsky that humans are born with a unique and innate ability to learn language (White, 2003). However, describes the debate that exists among these scholars as some claim that this ability diminishes as learners age while other contend that we continue to have this ability throughout our lives. That is, older learners may depend on more general learning skills that we use to learn any complex skill (e.g., driving or playing a sport) rather than their unique language learning ability which they gradually lose access to (Gass, 1997). Both of these positions contrast with yet another that we are not born with any special language learning module in our brain at all. These researchers argue that all language learning (regardless of age) is the same kind of learning that we see with any complex skill and accordingly learners should learn language in the same way as any complex skill (Anderson, 1989; McLaughlin, 1987).

Based upon the results of studies showing that younger learners often display greater long-term attainment, a number or researchers have speculated that there is a "critical period" after which learners are unable to access the inborn language learning device either partially or completely and accordingly the are unable to learn the L2 to the same proficiency level as those who began learning the L2 at a younger age (Lenneberg, 1967). However, it is difficult to compare older and younger learners because age is not the only dimension on which they differ.

There have been a number of studies conducted whose results have indicated that there may indeed be a critical period for acquiring various aspects of the L2. For instance, in terms of L2 grammatical knowledge development, some research findings suggest that younger immigrant ESL learners are more native-like than older learners (Johnson & Newport, 1989). Other research reviews (Long, 1990a) and meta-analysis (Qureshi, 2016) have demonstrated that the younger a learner is when beginning to learn an L2, the greater the likelihood of that learner becoming a fluent L2 speaker.

9.3 Unique advantages of young learners and adults

Nevertheless, the aim of many second language learners is not to become a native speaker of the target language. In this regard, older learners may have some particular advantages that younger learners often cannot match. For example, older learners are typically considerably more efficient in their study than younger learners and can allow them to initially progress more rapidly than younger learners in the beginning (Ellis, 2015). This advantage is probably attributable to adults' greater linguistic and world knowledge that helps them to more effectively make sense of the target language input that they are exposed to. It also helps that adults have more well-developed experience learning in formal classroom environments and thus they may benefit more from traditional classroom instruction. Indeed, as a consequence of these advantages older learners are often able to acquire L2 competence at a faster rate than younger learners (Snow & Hoefnagel-Höhle, 1978) even though they typically do not match younger learners' long-term attainment (Singleton, 1989).

Based on the best evidence currently available, it appears that those who eventually want to be indistinguishable from native speakers may have to start their L2 study at a young age (Ellis, 2015). However, a growing number of others argue that it is a mistake to use monolingual native speakers as a standard for comparison when deciding whether an L2 user has successfully learned the target language (Cook, 1999; García & Wei, 2014). Murahata, Murahata and Cook (2016) contend that instead we need to recognize that we must take care when comparing L2 learners with monolingual native speakers because their learning the L2 has positioned two interacting language systems inside the mind of the learner. Therefore, language teachers should not strive to turn their learners into native speakers but rather into multi-competent L2 users. The construct of multicompetence acknowledges that learners have "knowledge of more than one language in the same mind or the same community" (Cook, 2012, p. 1). Fostering learner multicompetence enables learners to experience the many cognitive and social benefits that accompany bilingualism and multilingualism such as improved meta-linguistic awareness (Jessner, 2008), greater cultural sensitivity (Cook, 2002) and empathy (Dewaele & Wei, 2012).

While adult learners have some advantages over younger learners, the converse is also true. For instance, a number of researchers contend that if a learner intends to sound like a native speaker of the L2, it is probably best for her to begin learning at a younger age as long as she has access to plenty of opportunities to use the L2 (Muñoz & Singleton, 2011). However, a qualification for this statement is that in EFL settings an early start may not be as effective if the learners only receive a couple of hours of instruction per week. This is because their lack of gaining a sense of progress may cause them to abandon their language learning (Lightbown & Spada, 2013). Additional advantages that younger learners have include being emotionally and intellectually prepared for L2 learning (Doyle & Hurrell, 1997) and being less anxious and inhibited while also being more enthusiastic, curious and open-minded (Read, 2003). Early learners also have the advantage of being able to draw upon implicit learning rather than needing to learn through explicit instruction (DeKeyser, 2003). Some social benefits that younger L2 learners can experience from learning and using an L2 include developing their positive regard for the target culture (Nikolov & Djigunović, 2006). Communication through the L2 can likewise foster younger learners' cognitive development, language awareness, problem-solving, creativity, mental flexibility and communication skills in both the L1 and L2 (Caccavale, 2007; Liddicoat, Papademetre, Scarino, & Kohler, 2003).

Besides, the existence of a critical period cannot be thc only or factor to consider when an adult decides to study an additional language. A wide variety of other factors also need to be taken into consideration such as the learner's own unique aptitude and motivations among other socio-cultural influences such as access to and usefulness of the L2 that would probably have a much more powerful influence upon the adult L2 learners' L2 development.

The problem is that age is often conflated with other important language learning factors such as attitudes toward the TL as well as amount of exposure to the TL (Piske & Young-Scholten, 2009). When younger learners are compared with older L2 learners in ways that take into account these factors, older learners actually have some advantages over younger learners. Indeed, Brown and Larson-Hall (2012) review research findings have indicated that older children can attain faster short-term progress in an L2. As well, expectations regarding the sophistication of children's language production may cause interlocutors to unconsciously set a lower standard for them. They may then unfairly compare children's production to adult L2 learners while tacitly assuming that the older learners will produce more sophisticated language in the same amount of time learning the L2 as the younger learners (Collier, 1989).

Some scholars have claimed that for many learners in EFL contexts, it may actually be more efficient for them to begin L2 learning when they are a bit older (Ellis, 2015). Indeed, Lightbown and Spada (2013) contend that it can be counterproductive for EFL learners to begin their L2 learning too young using the traditional "drip-feed" curriculum whereby they receive L2 instruction for 2-3 hours per week. Younger learners seem to more efficiently acquire the L2 through implicit, inductive and incidental learning. However, they lack the necessary considerable exposure to the target language to learn implicitly in most EFL contexts. Consequently, Lightbown and Spada (2013) express the concern that these learners' failure to see any meaningful progress in their L2 proficiency over many years of study may cause them to become disillusioned and demotivated as a result.

We do not often consider the fact that the sociocultural context often creates very different language learning experiences and opportunities for learners as well. When comparing the L2 proficiency of younger and older learners, it is important to take into account any factors that may also have an inordinate impact on any observed differences. For instance, one important factor is the actual amount of exposure that L2 learners get to the TL. Living in the country where the language is spoken does not guarantee opportunities to use it. Amit (2007) discusses the notion of the "expat bubble" where expatriates in a foreign country will seal themselves off in their own community of monolingual speakers. Likewise, many immigrants also struggle to learn the local language of their newly-adopted home (Mazumdar, 2004). Contrast this with children who often have to interact in the L2 if they attend a school that uses the language spoken by the wider community. For example, most immigrant children usually have to attend local schools and learn through the local language. As a consequence, they typically learn the target language to conversational proficiency within three years and acquire academic language within seven to ten years (Cummins, 2008).

However, in situations where adults have had comparable access to input and output opportunities as children, they typically learn languages well. Brown and Larson-Hall (2012) review two cases where adults commonly receive access to substantial amounts of L2 exposure thereby allowing for a more fair comparison between younger and older L2 learners. One example of intensive language learners they discuss is Mormon missionaries. Over the approximately two-year period of their mission, most missionaries were able to learn the target language to at least an upper-intermediate level of proficiency and, in some cases, they achieved advanced proficiency. However, the amount of progress that they experienced in the TL partially depended upon the relationship of the TL and their L1

English. Thus, learners of languages like French saw greater growth in their L2 ability over the same period than those learning languages like Japanese.

The second example they provide is of civil servants who often have to learn a foreign language as a prerequisite for advancing in their career. The Foreign Service Institute (FSI) has been in operation since 1947 to provide training to these government employees. Over that period of time, FSI researchers have been able to determine with considerable accuracy the number of hours required to learn a particular target language if one is a native speaker of English. For instance, they have established that it takes approximately 2200 hours for a native speaker of English to learn Korean. These program results also demonstrate that the majority of adults who go through the program are able to learn the target language to a high level of proficiency. Based on the outcomes from both of these programs, it is valid to claim that adult L2 learners can reach a high standard of attainment in the target language if they are given enough time and opportunities to use the target language.

9.4 Age and particular aspects of L2 development

Those who begin learning the L2 from a young age often reach L2 proficiency level comparable to that of native speakers. However, this outcome is considerably less common for L2 learners who begin acquiring the TL in adulthood. Investigations of age and L2 acquisition have typically centered upon the connection between learners' age of arrival in the country where the L2 is spoken or their length of residence in that country and the development of their L2 phonology (i.e., pronunciation) and morphosyntax (i.e., grammar knowledge). There has been considerable research interest in the relationship between learners' age and the development of their L2 phonology. Most of the existing research indicates that a foreign accent is present for those who learn the TL after a certain age (Patkowski, 1990; Scovel, 1988) although considerable debate exists regarding exactly what that age is. Some claim that it is as young as 6 years old (Long, 1990a) while others state that it can be as late as 15 years old (Patkowski, 1990).

Speculation on why late L2 learners fail to achieve native-like pronunciation largely centers on two causes. The first hypothesis is that after the critical period has been passed, changes occur in the learner's brain physiology that prevent them from processing the L2 sounds in the same way as they would have previously. As a result, they become unable to hear the fine phonemic distinctions that they would have heard before and thus they become unable to produce those same distinctions (Scovel, 1988). Results from empirical studies have caused some researchers to modify this stance to being a sensitive rather than critical period. The sensitive period concept acknowledges the gradual rather than abrupt decline in learners' ability to sound like an L2 native speaker (Long, 1990a).

The second hypothesis is that the problem is psycho-perceptual. In this case, as learners continue to develop and strengthen their L1 proficiency with age, they also increasingly perceive the L2 through the lens of the L1 (Bialystok, 1997; Flege, 1999). Accordingly, later L2 learners then pronounce the L2 as they perceive it. Evidence of the veracity of this hypothesis could be the presence of phonemes in the learner's L2 pronunciation that are only originally found in their L1 and not their L2. Further evidence may come from the fact the learners from different L1 backgrounds exhibit pronunciation patterns that are more in accord with their respective L1 backgrounds (Major, 2008). If the second hypothesis is true, language teachers and learners can hope to continue to develop their L2 pronunciation since this there is no immutable biological hard wiring to blame for non-target-like L2 pronunciation. Thus, if learners can somehow be trained to perceive the TL phonemes on its own terms rather than through their L1, improved pronunciation might be trainable and learners can develop more target-like pronunciation.

To date, most research gave limited consideration to several other important qualitative factors in the development of L2 phonology (Moyer, 2009). However, researchers must take these potential influences into account in order to fully examine the myriad of reasons that many adults lack full command of the L2 phonological system. One important qualitative explanation for adults' limited control of L2 phonology is the contextual and geographical restrictions they face that can severely limit their access to L2 speakers. Other possible reasons are perceived threats to their identity and having fewer incentives to reach a native-like level if they are able to communicate well enough to meet their daily communicative needs (Moyer, 2009). Of course, each of these qualitative factors and others require further exploration.

The variability in learner grammar development is less apparent than in learner pronunciation. That is, late L2 learners are typically more able to achieve native-like morphosyntax than pronunciation. Research results have shown that L2 learners generally make more accurate grammaticality judgments if they began their L2 learning prior to adolescence (Johnson & Newport, 1989; Patkowski, 1990). However, results of this research has come into question in recent years. One issue is that considerable variability exists in ultimate L2 attainment as learners age because even well beyond the onset of puberty, there are still cases of learners who were able to successfully learn an L2 to a standard where they could pass for a native speaker (Bongaerts, Mennen, & Slik, 2000; Ioup, Boustagui, El Tigi, & Moselle, 1994). As well, several potential confounding variables have been identified in the research such as the amount of L2 use that learners actually engaged in and their education level which also explain learner development but are often not well accounted for in existing research (Flege, Yeni-Komshian, & Liu, 1999). The amount of use is important because, as touched upon above, it will not matter how long a learner has spent in a target language environment (i.e., age of arrival) if they have received limited exposure to the L2. Other influences on nativelike morphosyntax development include the linguistic similarity of the L1 and L2 (Cranshaw, 1998) and L2 dominance or the language that bilinguals tend to be more proficient in (Flege, MacKay, & Piske, 2002). Thus, it appears that both L2 phonology and morphosyntax are able to develop over time. However, morphosyntax seems to be the most open to change with additional exposure to the L2.

9.5 Summary

A final background factor that has been widely discussed in relevant research literature is learners' age. In the research into age and L2 learning, the language learning ability of children is typically compared with that of adults. Probably the most contentious issue with regard to learner age is whether or not there is a critical period beyond which learners can no longer learn an L2. Another question that has been rather thoroughly investigated is whether particular aspects of L2 development such as phonology and morphosyntax are differently influenced by learner age. Research does suggest that phonology is indeed more susceptible to age-related influence than morphosyntax.

As with the other background variables discussed in the previous chapter, knowledge of how age interacts with L2 learning can enlighten language teachers about some of the potential causes of issues that they observe in class. This knowledge can also aid us in considering how to handle these issues. For example, with regard to age, knowledge about the relationship between age and L2 learning can help us develop realistic expectations about the amount of time that is necessary to learn an additional language to an intermediate level and the futility of trying to explain L2 grammar to younger learners. We also need to realize that while children do better over the long term if they have sufficient contact with the L2, adults can also often progress more quickly than children over the short term. All of these age-related insights can beneficially inform our course and lesson planning.

SLA in Plain English

Chapter 10

Conclusion

Chapter 10
Conclusion

The central aim of this text has been to introduce beginning English language teachers to the key concepts in English teaching as well as the key concepts, principles and theories of SLA. Chapter 1 dealt with lesson planning as the foundation of teaching English. Its importance lies in the fact that insufficient lesson planning wastes time while effective planning ensures purposeful lessons that inspire students' confidence in the teacher. This chapter reviewed some of the reasons for planning, considerations in course planning such as syllabus design as well as materials and methods to be used. This discussion also covered writing lesson objectives, sequencing lesson activities and handling lesson enrichment, remediation and classroom assessment.

In chapter 2, we reviewed some ideas for teaching about word knowledge, and how to teach and reinforce new lexis. We also compared several L2 grammar instructional approaches including implicit, explicit, inductive, deductive, processing instruction, corpus-based, systemic functional linguistics and informed eclecticism. Knowledge of how to teach grammar and vocabulary helps us achieve our lesson aims to present the new lexis and grammar structures thereby meeting our learners' assumptions that we will effectively teach them L2 vocabulary and grammar.

Chapter 3 on teaching listening and speaking outlined how to plan a listening and speaking lesson. It covered how teachers can activate learners' background knowledge and capture their interest with pre-listening activities, guide them through the listening process with during-listening tasks and connect listening to other skills with post-listening tasks. The PPP paradigm and cooperative learning were suggested as a useful lesson structures for speaking instruction and practice. The contents of this chapter can help the reader to prepare learners for listening as well as connect listening to other skills.

Chapter 4 dealt with planning, structuring and integrating reading and writing lessons for the ESL/EFL classroom. It began by looking at some theories of the L2 reading process and the "big 5" concepts in reading instruction. The pre-reading, during reading and post reading of an L2 reading lesson were explained as were the gradual release of responsibility model and genre-based writing lesson structures. The chapter also discussed some ways that we can make reading-writing connections in our literacy lessons.

Chapter 5 dealt with multicompetence and how bilingual teachers should view themselves as being multicompetent L2 users rather than non-native speakers. It also covered suggestions for continued professional development to grow as an L2 user and as a model of lifelong learning. It concluded with an exploration of ways for the teacher to make classroom input comprehensible for learners so they will feel more comfortable in class and grow to love L2 learning.

Chapter 6 reviewed several theories of L2 learning including the monitor model, the interaction hypothesis, the pushed output hypothesis, input processing, information processing and sociocultural theory. Knowledge of these SLA theories can give language teachers greater insight into their students' L2 learning process. Accordingly, they can be more confident that their classroom practice is informed by credible SLA theory that helps them meet their learners' unique needs.

Chapter 7 explored several learner background factors that can influence their L2 learning. Research suggests that intelligence may be related more to the development of academic language rather than conversational ability. Aptitude is distinct from intelligence and might explain why some learners progress more rapidly than others. Personality characteristics such as motivation, anxiety and introversion are also potential inhibitors for L2 communication. Teacher and learner mismatched language learning beliefs, dysfunctional classroom power dynamics and learner identity may also influence their L2 learning. Equally, learning styles and strategies can facilitate learning and communication.

Teachers can use their knowledge of students' individual differences to adjust their classroom practice to account for these factors as much as possible. For example, they might teach learning and communication strategies to minimize learner anxiety while promoting willingness-to-communicate. They might also strive to find ways to consider learner expectations and goals to help them see themselves as a successful target language user who can effectively participate in the target language community.

Chapter 8 investigated the relationship between the background variable of age and L2 learning. Debate continues regarding the existence of a critical period after which learners cannot learn an L2. As well, research findings on the effect of age on various components of L2 learning suggest that phonology is more prone to age-related influence than morphosyntax. Knowledge of age and L2 learning interactions can also aid teachers in acknowledging the amount of time necessary to learn an L2, that deductive grammar instruction to younger learners is probably pointless and that adult learners actually do have some advantages over children.

I hope that you will find the information presented in this book helpful. If you are a beginning teacher, I hope this book has provided you with some fundamental and widely-used lesson structures that you can follow to teach the four skills. This gives you something of a guidebook that you can begin with as you continue to hone your craft and develop professionally. Secondly, I hope that the book acquaints new teachers with the core insights from SLA research that they would benefit most from knowing about as a language teacher. You should be able to use these insights to understand your learners better and to more effectively tailor your lessons to meet their individual needs.

I also wish that this discussion of language teaching methods and SLA topics in the same source will help you to begin to make some connections between theories of language learning and various language teaching methods and techniques. These kinds of connections can allow you to more effectively support your classroom practice with sufficient justification and be able to use your understanding of how L2's are acquired to suitably adapt and differentiate your methods.

To conclude, you can also ask yourself where you can go from here. If you are a new teacher, this is just the beginning of your professional journey and there are a number of beneficial actions that you can take to continue your development. First, you should find more resources and keep learning about the theoretical and practical foundations of language teaching. This self-development does not necessarily have to involve intensive study. Regular ongoing self-directed learning can help you to continue to expand upon your understanding of the key concepts, theories, and principles of language teaching and learning. Likewise, this type of continuing autonomous professional development allows you to further hone your pedagogical skills and instincts. Secondly, you should continue to learn about theories of language learning and develop your personal philosophy of language teaching and learning. This will allow you to find and develop variations on activities that can more efficiently help your students learn the target language. Your ongoing professional development will also aid you in thinking critically about how well your methods align with your beliefs. That is, you can carefully examine your beliefs about language learning to verify their consistency with what current theories and research tell us about how languages are best learned.

Language learning theory and practice are intimately connected so we should continue to reflect upon the connections between our beliefs about teaching and learning and their relationship to our daily practice as language teachers. We also need to learn more about our learners' strengths and areas of need. We can do this by observing them carefully and engaging in ongoing informal assessment as part of our teaching. Another way to better be able to take the perspective of our students is to begin to study an additional language yourself. If you are fluent in a second language, try learning a new one so that you are reminded of the struggles that accompany learning another language. Lastly, we need to recognize also that teaching is rarely a flawlessly performed activity. We must prepare to the best of our ability for our classes, however, we should also accept that there will be times when despite our best efforts the lesson will not proceed in the way we hoped it would. In those cases, we should reflect to learn what we can from the experience and resolve to do better next time.

References

References

Adams, M. J. (1990). *Beginning to read: Learning and thinking about print*. Cambridge, MA: MIT Press.

Aghasafari, M. (2006). *On the relationship between emotional intelligence and language learning strategies* (Unpublished master's thesis). Allameh Tabataba'i University, Iran.

Aghlara, L., & Tamjid, N. H. (2011). The effect of digital games on Iranian children's vocabulary retention in foreign language acquisition. *Procedia-Social and Behavioral Sciences, 29*, 552–560.

Akyel, A. (1994). First language use in EFL writing: Planning in Turkish vs. planning in English. *International Journal of Applied Linguistics, 4*(2), 169–184.

Alrabai, F. (2015). The influence of teachers' anxiety-reducing strategies on learners' foreign language anxiety. *Innovation in Language Learning and Teaching, 9*(2), 163–190.

Alvermann, D. E., Phelps, S. F., & Ridgeway, V. G. (2007). *Content area reading and literacy: Succeeding in today's diverse classrooms*. Boston: Pearson.

Amabile, T. M. (1993). Motivational synergy: Toward new conceptualizations of intrinsic and extrinsic motivation in the workplace. *Human Resource Management Review, 3*(3), 185–201.

Amit, V. (Ed.). (2011). *Going first class? New approaches to privileged travel and movement*. Oxford: Berghahn Books.

Anderson, J. (2016). Why practice makes perfect sense: The past, present and potential future of the PPP paradigm in language teacher education. *ELTED, 19*, 16–22.

Anderson, J. R. (1989). Practice, working memory, and the ACT* theory of skill acquisition: A comment on Carlson, Sullivan, and Schneider (1989). *Journal of Experimental Psychology: Learning, Memory, and Cognition, 15*, 527–530.

Anderson, N. J. (1991). Individual differences in strategy use in second language reading and testing. *The Modern Language Journal, 75*(4), 460–472.

Anthony, J. L., & Francis, D. J. (2005). Development of phonological awareness. *Current Directions in Psychological Science, 14*(5), 255–259.

Arter, J. A. (1995). *Portfolios for Assessment and Instruction. ERIC Digest*. (No. ED388890; pp. 1–7). Retrieved from ERIC Clearinghouse on Counseling and Student Services website: https://files.eric.ed.gov/fulltext/ED388890.pdf

Aslan, A. (2016). Language teaching models in teacher training programs. *Turkish Online Journal of English Language Teaching (TOJELT), 1*(3), 135–143.

Atwell, Nancie. (1998). *In the middle: New understandings about writing, reading, and learning*. ERIC.

Atwell, Nancy. (2007). The reading zone. *New York: Scholastic*.

Azar, B. (2007). Grammar-based teaching: A practitioner's perspective. *TESL-EJ, 11*(2), 1–12.

Bachman, L. F., & Palmer, A. S. (1996). *Language testing in practice: Designing and developing useful language tests*. Oxford: Oxford University Press.

Badger, R., & White, G. (2000). A process genre approach to teaching writing. *ELT Journal, 54*(2), 153–160.

Bain, S. K., McCallum, R. S., Bell, S. M., Cochran, J. L., & Sawyer, S. C. (2010). Foreign language learning aptitudes, attitudes, attributions, and achievement of postsecondary students identified as gifted. *Journal of Advanced Academics, 22*(1), 130–156.

Barnyak, N. C., & Paquette, K. R. (2010). An investigation of elementary pre-service teachers' reading instructional beliefs. *Reading Improvement, 47*(1), 7–18.

Barr, B. (2016). *Checking the effectiveness of Quizlet® as a tool for vocabulary learning* (Doctoral Dissertation). Tamagawa University, Tokyo.

Beebe, L. (1983). Risk-taking and the language learner. In H. W. Seliger & M. H. Long (Eds.), *Classroom oriented research in second language acquisition*. (pp. 39–66). Rowley, MA: Newbury House.

Bergeron, B. S. (1990). What does the term whole language mean? Constructing a definition from the literature. *Journal of Reading Behavior, 22*(4), 301–329.

Bernhardt, E. B. (2010). *Understanding advanced second-language reading*. New York: Routledge.

Bialystok, E. (1997). The structure of age: In search of barriers to second language acquisition. *Second Language Research, 13*(2), 116–137.

Birch, B. M. (2014). *English L2 reading: Getting to the bottom*. New York: Routledge.

Bixler, B. (2006). Writing educational goals and objectives. Retrieved April 8, 2019, from Retrieved February website: http://www. personal.psu.edu/staff/b/x/bxb11/Objectives/

Black, P. J. (1993). Formative and summative assessment by teachers. *Studies in Science Education, 21*, 49–97.

Block, D. (2000). Revisiting the gap between SLA researchers and language teachers. *Links & Letters, 7*, 129–143.

Block, D. (2003). *The social turn in second language acquisition*. Edinburgh, Scotland: University of Edinburgh Press.

Block, D. (2012). Economising globalisation and identity in applied linguistics in neoliberal times. In D. Block, J. Gray, & M. Holborow (Eds.), *Neoliberalism and applied linguistics* (pp. 56–85). London: Routledge.

Block, E. (1986). The comprehension strategies of second language readers. *Tesol Quarterly, 20*(3), 463–494.

Bongaerts, T., Mennen, S., & Slik, F. van der. (2000). Authenticity of pronunciation in naturalistic second language acquisition: The case of very advanced late learners of Dutch as a second language. *Studia Linguistica, 54*(2), 298–308.

Bransford, J. D., Brown, A. L., & Cocking, R. R. (Eds.). (1999). *How people learn: Brain, mind, experience, and school*. Washington, DC: National Academy Press.

Bremner, S. (1999). Language learning strategies and language proficiency: Investigating the relationship in Hong Kong. *Canadian Modern Language Review, 55*(4), 490–514.

Brinton, D. M., Snow, M., & Wesche, M. (1989). *Content-based second language instruction*. New York: Newbury House.

Brown, H. D. (1994). *Teaching by principles*. Englewood Cliffs, NJ: Prentice Hall.

Brown, H. D. (2000). *Teaching by principles: An interactive approach to language pedagogy* (2nd ed.). Englewood Cliffs, NJ: Prentice Hall Regents.

Brown, J. D. (2005). *Testing in language programs: A comprehensive guide to English language assessment* (2nd ed.). New York: McGraw-Hill.

Brown, R., Waring, R., & Donkaewbua, S. (2008). Incidental vocabulary acquisition from reading, reading-while-listening, and listening to stories. *Reading in a Foreign Language, 20*(2), 136–163.

Brown, S., & Larson-Hall, J. (2012). *Second language acquisition myths: Applying second language research*. Ann Arbor, MI: University of Michigan Press.

Bruner, J. (1985). Vygotsky: A historical and contemporary perspective. In J. Wertsch (Ed.), *Culture, communication, and cognition: Vygotskian perspectives* (pp. 21–34). Cambridge: Cambridge University Press.

Busch, D. (1982). Introversion-extraversion and the EFL proficiency of Japanese students. *Language Learning, 32*(1), 109–132.

Butler-Nalin, K. (1984). Revising patterns in students' writing. In A. N. Applebee (Ed.), *Contexts for learning to write: Studies of secondary school instruction* (pp. 121–133). Norwood, NJ: Ablex.

Butzkamm, W., & Caldwell, J. A. (2009). *The bilingual reform: A paradigm shift in foreign language teaching*. Tubingen: Gunter Narr Verlag.

Bygate, M. (1987). *Speaking*. Oxford: Oxford University Press.

Caccavale, T. (2007). The correlation between early second language learning and native language skill development. *Learning Languages, 13*(1), 30–32.

Calkins, L. M. (1986). *The art of teaching writing*. Portsmouth, NH: Heinemann.

Canale, M., & Swain, M. (1980). Theoretical bases of communicative approaches to second language teaching and testing. *Applied Linguistics, 1*(1), 1–47.

Cao, Y., & Philp, J. (2006). Interactional context and willingness to communicate: A comparison of behavior in whole class, group and dyadic interaction. *System, 34*(4), 480–493.

Carless, D. R. (2009). Revisiting the TBLT versus PPP debate: Voices from Hong Kong. *Asian Journal of English Language Teaching, 19*, 49–66.

Carrell, P. L., Prince, M. S., & Astika, G. G. (1996). Personality types and language learning in an EFL context. *Language Learning, 46*(1), 75–99.

Carroll, J. B. (1973). Implications of aptitude test research and psycholinguistic theory for foreign language teaching. *International Journal of Psycholinguistics, 2*, 5–14.

Carroll, J. B. (1981). Twenty-five years of research on foreign language aptitude. In K. C. Diller (Ed.), *Individual differences and universals in language learning aptitude* (pp. 83–118). Rowley, MA: Newbury House.

Cartwright, K. B. (2011). *Word Callers*. Portsmouth, NH: Heinemann.

Cavanagh, M. (2011). Students' experiences of active engagement through cooperative learning activities in lectures. *Active Learning in Higher Education, 12*(1), 23–33.

Chang, A. C., & Millett, S. (2013). The effect of extensive listening on developing L2 listening fluency: Some hard evidence. *ELT Journal, 68*(1), 31–40.

Chappuis, S., & Stiggins, R. J. (2002). Classroom assessment for learning. *Educational Leadership, 60*(1), 40–44.

Chard, D. J., & Dickson, S. V. (1999). Phonological awareness: Instructional and assessment guidelines. *Intervention in School and Clinic, 34*(5), 261–270.

Cheng, Y., Horwitz, E. K., & Schallert, D. L. (1999). Language anxiety: Differentiating writing and speaking components. *Language Learning, 49*(3), 417–446.

Chinnery, G. M. (2014). Call Me... Maybe: A Framework for Integrating the Internet into ELT. *English Teaching Forum, 52*, 2–13.

Cho, K.-S., Ahn, K.-O., & Krashen, S. (2005). The effects of narrow reading of authentic texts on interest and reading ability in English as a foreign language. *Reading Improvement, 42*(1), 58–65.

Christison, M. A. (1996). Multiple intelligences & second language learners. *The Journal of the Imagination in Language Learning, 3*, 8–12.

Chung, K. K. H., & Ho, C. S.-H. (2010). Second language learning difficulties in Chinese children with dyslexia: What are the reading-related cognitive skills that contribute to English and Chinese word reading? *Journal of Learning Disabilities, 43*(3), 195–211.

Ciarrochi, J., & Mayer, J. D. (2007). The key ingredients of emotional intelligence interventions: Similarities and differences. In J. Ciarrochi & J. D. Mayer (Eds.), *Applying emotional intelligence: A practitioner's guide* (pp. 144–156). New York: Taylor & Francis.

Clark, D. (2010). *Bloom's taxonomy of learning domains: The three types of learning*. Washington, DC: Edmonds.

Cobine, G. R. (1995). *Effective use of student journal writing* (No. EDO-CS-95-02). Bloomington, IN: ERIC Clearinghouse on Reading, English, and Communication.

Cohen, A. D., & Aphek, E. (1980). Retention of second-language vocabulary overtime: Investigating thc role of mnemonic associations. *System, 8*(3), 221–235.

Collier, V. P. (1989). How long? A synthesis of research on academic achievement in a second language. *TESOL Quarterly, 23*(3), 509–531.

Colom, R., Karama, S., Jung, R. E., & Haier, R. J. (2010). Human intelligence and brain networks. *Dialogues in Clinical Neuroscience, 12*(4), 489–501.

Cook, G. (2002). Breaking taboos. *English Teaching Professional, 23*, 5–7.

Cook, G. (2010). *Translation in language teaching*. Oxford: Oxford University Press.

Cook, V. (1991). *Second language learning and language teaching*. London: Arnold.

Cook, V. (1999). Going beyond the native speaker in language teaching. *TESOL Quarterly, 33*(2), 185–209.

Cook, V. (Ed.). (2002). Background to the L2 user. In *Portraits of the L2 user* (pp. 1–28). Clevedon, UK: Multilingual Matters.

Cook, V. (2013). Multicompetence. In P. Robinson (Ed.), *The Routledge Encyclopedia of Second Language Acquisition* (pp. 447–451). New York: Routledge.

Cook, V. (2016). Working definition of multi-competence. Retrieved from Vivian Cook Web Sites on Second Language Acquisition website: http://www.viviancook.uk/Writings/Papers/MCentry.htm

Cook, V. J. (1991). The poverty-of-the-stimulus argument and multicompetence. *Interlanguage Studies Bulletin (Utrecht), 7*(2), 103–117.

Corder, S. (1983). Strategies of communication. In C. Faerch & G. Kasper (Eds.), *Strategies in interlanguage communication* (pp. 15–19). London: Longman.

Coxhead, A. (2000). A new academic word list. *TESOL Quarterly, 34*(2), 213–238.

Cranshaw, A. S. (1998). *A study of Anglophone native and near native linguistic and metalinguistic performance*. (Unpublished Doctoral Dissertation). Universite de Montreal, Montreal, Canada.

Criado, R. (2013). A critical review of the presentation-practice-production model (PPP) in foreign language teaching. In R. Monroy (Ed.), *Homenaje a francisco Gutiérrez Díez* (pp. 97–115). Murcia, Spain: Editum.

Cross, J. (2002). "Noticing" in SLA: Is it a valid concept? *TESL-EJ, 6*(3), A2.

Cumming, A. (1989). Writing expertise and second-language proficiency. *Language Learning, 39*(1), 81–135.

Cummins, J. (1980). The cross-lingual dimensions of language proficiency: Implications for bilingual education and the optimal age issue. *TESOL Quarterly*, 175–187.

Cummins, J. (2000). *Language, power, and pedagogy: Bilingual children in the crossfire*. Clevedon, UK: Multilingual Matters.

Cummins, J. (2008). BICS and CALP: Empirical and theoretical status of the distinction. In B. V. Street & N. Hornberger (Eds.), *Encyclopedia of language and education: Vol. 2 Literacy* (2nd ed., pp. 71–83). New York: Springer.

Cummins, J. (2016). Reflections on Cummins (1980), the cross-lingual dimensions of language proficiency: Implications for bilingual education and the optimal age issue. *TESOL Quarterly, 50*(4), 940–944.

Cunningham, E. (1990). Explicit versus implicit instruction in phonemic awareness. *Journal of Experimental Child Psychology, 50*(3), 429–444.

Dadour, E. S., & Robbins, J. (1996). University-level studies using strategy instruction to improve speaking ability in Egypt and Japan. In R. L. Oxford (Ed.), *Language learning strategies around the world: Cross-cultural perspectives* (pp. 157–166). Manoa: University of Hawaii Press.

D'Angelo, F. J. (1979). The art of paraphrase. *College Composition and Communication, 30*(3), 255–259.

Darn, S. (n.d.). Eliciting [British Council]. Retrieved April 17, 2019, from Teaching English website: https://www.teachingenglish.org.uk/article/eliciting

Darn, S., & White, I. (n.d.). Checking understanding [British Council]. Retrieved April 19, 2019, from Teaching English website: https://www.teachingenglish.org.uk/article/checking-understanding

Day, R., & Bamford, J. (1998). *Extensive reading in the second language classroom*. Cambridge: Cambridge University Press.

de Larios, J. R., Marín, J., & Murphy, L. (2001). A temporal analysis of formulation processes in L1 and L2 writing. *Language Learning, 51*(3), 497–538.

DeBolt, V. (1994). *Write! Cooperative learning & the writing process*. San Juan Capistrano, CA: Kagan Cooperative Learning.

Deci, E. L., & Ryan, R. M. (1985). *Intrinsic motivation and self-determination in human behavior*. New York: Plenum.

Dehbozorgi, E. (2012). Effects of attitude towards language learning and risk-taking on EFL student's proficiency. *International Journal of English Linguistics, 2*(2), 41.

Déjean Le Féal, K. (1997). Simultaneous interpretation with" training wheels". *Meta: Translators' Journal, 42*(4), 616–621.

DeKeyser, R. (2003). Implicit and explicit learning. In C. Doughty & M. H. Long (Eds.), *Handbook of second language acquisition* (pp. 312–348). Oxford: Blackwell.

DeKeyser, R. M., & Koeth, J. (2011). Cognitive aptitudes for second language learning. In E. Hinkel (Ed.), *Handbook of research in second language teaching and learning* (Vol. 2, pp. 395–406). New York: Routledge.

Dewaele, J.-M., & Furnham, A. (1999). Extraversion: The unloved variable in applied linguistic research. *Language Learning, 49*(3), 509–544.

Dewaele, J.-M., & Furnham, A. (2000). Personality and speech production: A pilot study of second language learners. *Personality and Individual Differences, 28*(2), 355–365.

Dewaele, J.-M., Petrides, K. V., & Furnham, A. (2008). Effects of trait emotional intelligence and sociobiographical variables on communicative anxiety and foreign language anxiety among adult multilinguals: A review and empirical investigation. *Language Learning, 58*(4), 911–960.

Dewaele, J.-M., & Wei, L. (2012). Multilingualism, empathy and multicompetence. *International Journal of Multilingualism, 9*(4), 352–366.

Donley, K. K., & Reppen, R. (2001). Using corpus tools to highlight academic vocabulary in SCLT. *TESOL Journal, 10*(2–3), 7–12.

Dörnyei, Z. (1995). On the teachability of communication strategies. *TESOL Quarterly, 29*(1), 55–85.

Dörnyei, Z. (2009). The L2 motivational self system. In Z. Dörnyei & E. Ushioda (Eds.), *Motivation, language identity and the L2 self* (Vol. 36, pp. 9–11). Clevedon, UK: Multilingual Matters.

Dörnyei, Z. (2010). The relationship between language aptitude and language learning motivation: Individual differences from a dynamic systems perspective. In E. Macaro (Ed.), *Continuum companion to second language acquisition* (pp. 247–267). London: Continuum.

Dornyei, Z., & Ryan, S. (2015). *The psychology of the language learner revisited.* New York: Routledge.

Dörnyei, Z., & Scott, M. L. (1997). Communication strategies in a second language: Definitions and taxonomies. *Language Learning, 47*(1), 173–210.

Dörnyei, Z., & Skehan, P. (2003). Individual differences in second language learning. In C. Doughty & M. H. Long (Eds.), *The handbook of second language acquisition* (pp. 589–630). Oxford: Blackwell.

Doyle, P., & Hurrell, A. (Eds.). (1997). *Foreign language education in primary schools.* Strasbourg Cedex, France: Council of Europe Press.

Duffy, G. G. (2009). *Explaining reading: A resource for teaching concepts, skills, and strategies* (2nd ed.). New York: Guilford Press.

Dufva, M., & Voeten, M. J. (1999). Native language literacy and phonological memory as prerequisites for learning English as a foreign language. *Applied Psycholinguistics, 20*(3), 329–348.

Duke, N. K., Purcell–Gates, V., Hall, L. A., & Tower, C. (2006). Authentic literacy activities for developing comprehension and writing. *The Reading Teacher, 60*(4), 344–355.

Dupuy, B. C. (1999). Narrow listening: An alternative way to develop and enhance listening comprehension in students of French as a foreign language. *System, 27*(3), 351–361.

Ehrman, M. E., & Oxford, R. L. (1995). Cognition plus: Correlates of language learning success. *The Modern Language Journal, 79*(1), 67–89.

Ellis, N. C. (1995). The psychology of foreign language vocabulary acquisition: Implications for CALL. *Computer Assisted Language Learning, 8*, 103–128.

Ellis, N. C. (1996). Working memory in the acquisition of vocabulary and syntax: Putting language in good order. *The Quarterly Journal of Experimental Psychology, 49*(1), 234–250.

Ellis, R. (1994). *The study of second language acquisition*. Oxford: Oxford University Press.

Ellis, R. (1997). *SLA research and language teaching*. New York: Oxford University Press.

Ellis, R. (2001). Second language acquisition: Research and language pedagogy. In C. Candlin & N. Mercer (Eds.), *English language teaching in its social context* (pp. 44–74). London: Routledge.

Ellis, R. (2002). Grammar teaching-practice or consciousness-raising? In J. C. Richards & W. A. Renandya (Eds.), *Methodology in language teaching: An anthology of current practice* (pp. 167–174). Cambridge: Cambridge University Press.

Ellis, R. (2015). *Understanding second language acquisition* (2nd ed.). Oxford: Oxford University Press.

Ellis, R., & Barkhuizen, G. P. (2005). *Analysing learner language*. Oxford: Oxford University Press.

Elorza, I., & García-Riaza, B. (2010). FL students' input in higher education courses: Corpus methodology for implementing language representativeness. In M. C. Campoy-Cubillo, B. Bellés-Fortuño, & M. L. Gea-Valor (Eds.), *Corpus-based approaches to English language teaching* (pp. 216–232). London: Continuum.

Ely, C. M. (1986). An analysis of discomfort, risktaking, sociability, and motivation in the L2 classroom. *Language Learning, 36*(1), 1–25.

Erlam, R. (2005). Language aptitude and its relationship to instructional effectiveness in second language acquisition. *Language Teaching Research, 9*(2), 147–171.

Eysenck, S. B., & Chan, J. (1982). A comparative study of personality in adults and children: Hong Kong vs England. *Personality and Individual Differences, 3*(2), 153–160.

Faerch, C., & Kasper, G. (1980). Processes in foreign language learning and communication. *Interlanguage Studies Bulletin, 5*, 47–118.

Farrell, T. S. (2002). Lesson planning. In J. C. Richards & W. A. Renandya (Eds.), *Methodology in language teaching: An anthology of current practice* (pp. 30–39). Cambridge: Cambridge University Press.

Ferris, D. R., Chaney, S. J., Komura, K., Roberts, B. J., & McKee, S. (2000). Perspectives, problems, and practices in treating written error. *Colloquium*. Presented at the International TESOL Convention, Vancouver, BC.

Field, J. (2002). The changing face of listening. In J. C. Richards & W. A. Renandya (Eds.), *Methodology in language teaching: An anthology of current practice* (pp. 242–247). Cambridge: Cambridge University Press.

Field, J. (2003). Promoting perception: Lexical segmentation in L2 listening. *ELT Journal, 57*(4), 325–334.

Fisher, D., Frey, N., & Lapp, D. (2008). Shared readings: Modeling comprehension, vocabulary, text structures, and text features for older readers. *The Reading Teacher, 61*(7), 548–556.

Fisher, D., Frey, N., & Lapp, D. (2012). Building and activating students' background knowledge: It's what they already know that counts: Teachers must assess and build on the background knowledge students possess. *Middle School Journal, 43*(3), 22–31.

Flege, James E. (1999). Age of learning and second language speech. In D. Birdsong (Ed.), *Second language acquisition and the Critical Period Hypothesis* (pp. 101–131). Mahwah, NJ: Erlbaum.

Flege, James Emil, MacKay, I. R., & Piske, T. (2002). Assessing bilingual dominance. *Applied Psycholinguistics, 23*(4), 567–598.

Flege, James Emil, Yeni-Komshian, G. H., & Liu, S. (1999). Age constraints on second-language acquisition. *Journal of Memory and Language, 41*(1), 78–104.

Fraser, C. A. (1999). Lexical processing strategy use and vocabulary learning through reading. *Studies in Second Language Acquisition, 21*(2), 225–241.

Freeman, Y. S., & Freeman, D. (1992). *Whole language for second language learners*. Portsmouth, NH: Heinemann.

Freire, P., & Macedo, D. (2005). *Literacy: Reading the word and the world*. New York: Routledge.

Fulcher, G. (2010). *Practical language testing*. London: Hodder.

Furnham, A. (1990). Language and personality. In W. P. Robinson & H. Giles (Eds.), *Handbook of language and social psychology* (pp. 73–95). Sussix, UK: Wiley.

Furr, M. (2004). Literature circles for the EFL classroom. *Proceedings of the 2003 TESOL Arabia Conference*. Presented at the Dubai, United Arab Emirates. Dubai, United Arab Emirates: TESOL Arabia.

García, O. (2009). Education, multilingualism and translanguaging in the 21st century. In A. Mohanty, M. Panday, R. Phillipson, & T. Skutnabb-Kangas (Eds.), *Multilingual Education for Social Justice: Globalising the Local*. (pp. 140–158). New Delhi: Orient BlackSwan.

García, O., Johnson, S. I., Seltzer, K., & Valdés, G. (2017). *The translanguaging classroom: Leveraging student bilingualism for learning*. Philadelphia, PA: Caslon.

García, O., & Wei, L. (2014). *Translanguaging: Language, bilingualism and education*. New York, NY: Palgrave Macmillan.

Gardiner, S. (2005). *Building student literacy through sustained silent reading*. Alexandria, VA: Association for Curriculum and Supervision.

Gardner, H. (1993). *Multiple intelligences: The theory in practice*. New York: Basic Books.

Gardner, R. C. (1985). *Social psychology and second language learning: The role of attitudes and motivation*. London: Arnold.

Gardner, R. C., & Clément, R. (1990). Social psychological perspectives on second language acquisition. In H. Giles & W. P. Robinson (Eds.), *Handbook of Language and Social Psychology*. (pp. 495–517). London: John Wiley & Sons.

Gardner, R. C., & Lambert, W. E. (1965). Language aptitude, intelligence, and second-language achievement. *Journal of Educational Psychology*, 56(4), 191.

Gardner, R. C., & Lambert, W. E. (1972). *Attitudes and motivation in second-language learning*. Rowley, MA: Newbury House.

Gardner, R. C., & MacIntyre, P. D. (1993). On the measurement of affective variables in second language learning. *Language Learning, 43*(2), 157–194.

Gass, S. M. (1997). *Input, interaction, and the second language learner*. New York: Routledge.

Genesee, F. (1979). Acquisition of reading skills in immersion programs. *Foreign Language Annals, 12*(1), 71–77.

Ghoorchaei, B., & Kassaian, Z. (2009). The relationship between risk-taking, fluency and accuracy in English speech of Iranian EFL students. *Iranian EFL Journal*, 3, 111–136.

Goleman, D. (1995). Emotional intelligence: Why it can matter more than IQ. *New York: Bantam*.

Gollin, J. (1998). Deductive vs. Inductive language learning. *English Language Teaching Journal*, 52, 88–89.

Goodman, K. (2005). *Whats whole in whole language?* Berkeley. CA: RDR Books.

Goodman, K. S. (2014). Reading: A psycholinguistic guessing game. In Goodman, Kenneth & Y. Goodman (Eds.), *Making sense of learners making sense of written language* (pp. 115–124). New York: Routledge.

Grabe, W. (1988). Reassessing the term "interactive." In P. L. Carrell, J. Devine, & E. Eskey (Eds.), *Interactive approaches to second language reading* (pp. 56–70). Cambridge: Cambridge University Press.

Grabe, W. (1991). Current developments in second language reading research. *TESOL Quarterly, 25*(3), 375–406.

Grabe, W. (2009). *Reading in a second language: Moving from theory to practice*. New York: Cambridge University Press.

Grabe, W. P., & Stoller, F. L. (2013). *Teaching and researching: Reading*. New York: Routledge.

Graham, S., McKeown, D., Kiuhara, S., & Harris, K. R. (2012). A meta-analysis of writing instruction for students in the elementary grades. *Journal of Educational Psychology, 104*(4), 879–896.

Graham, S., & Perin, D. (2007). A meta-analysis of writing instruction for adolescent students. *Journal of Educational Psychology, 99*(3), 445–476.

Gray, W. S., & Rogers, B. (1956). *Maturity in reading: Its nature and appraisal*. University of Chicago Press.

Green, J. M., & Oxford, R. (1995). A closer look at learning strategies, L2 proficiency, and gender. *TESOL Quarterly*, 29(2), 261–297.

Griffiths, C. (2013). *The strategy factor in successful language learning*. Bristol, UK: Multilingual Matters.

Grigornko, E. L., Sternberg, R. J., & Ehrman, M. E. (2000). A theory-based approach to the measurement of foreign language learning ability: The Canal-F theory and test. *The Modern Language Journal, 84*(3), 390–405.

Gu, S., & Wang, T. (2007). Study on the relationship between working memory and EFL listening comprehension. *CELEA Journal, 30*(6), 46–56.

Gunderson, L., D'Silva, R., & Murphy Odo, D. (2013). ESL (ELL) *literacy instruction: A guidebook to theory and practice*. New York: Routledge.

Haight, C. E., Herron, C., & Cole, S. P. (2007). The effects of deductive and guided inductive instructional approaches on the learning of grammar in the elementary foreign language college classroom. *Foreign Language Annals, 40*(2), 288–310.

Hall, C. (1990). Managing the complexity of revising across languages. *Tesol Quarterly, 24*(1), 43–60.

Halliday, M. A. (1970). Functional diversity in language as seen from a consideration of modality and mood in English. *Foundations of Language, 6*, 322–361.

Halliday, M. A. K., & Matthiessen, C. (2004). *An introduction to functional grammar* (2nd ed.). London: Arnold.

Hammerly, H. (1982). *Synthesis in second language teaching*. Blaine, WA: Second Language Publications.

Han, Z., Park, E. S., & Combs, C. (2008). Textual enhancement of input: Issues and possibilities. *Applied Linguistics, 29*(4), 597–618.

Harley, B., & Hart, D. (1997). Language aptitude and second language proficiency in classroom learners of different starting ages. *Studies in Second Language Acquisition, 19*(3), 379–400.

Harmer, J. (2006). *How to teach writing*. Harlow, UK: Pearson Education.

Harrington, M., & Sawyer, M. (1992). L2 working memory capacity and L2 reading skill. *Studies in Second Language Acquisition, 14*(1), 25–38.

Harris, K. R., Graham, S., MacArthur, C., Reid, R., & Mason, L. H. (2011). Self-regulated learning processes and children's writing. In B. Zimmerman & D. H. Schunk (Eds.), *Handbook of self-regulation of learning and performance* (pp. 187–202). New York: Routledge.

Harris, R. J., & Nelson, E. M. M. (1992). Bilingualism: Not the exception any more. In R. J. Harris (Ed.), *Cognitive processing in bilinguals* (Vol. 83, pp. 3–14). Amsterdam: North-Holland.

Hassan, B. A. (2001). *Extraversion/ introversion and gender in relation to the English pronunciation accuracy of Arabic speaking college students*. Cairo: Mansoura University.

Hatch, E. M. (1978). *Second language acquisition: A book of readings*. Rowley, MA: Newbury House.

Hawkins, M. R. (2005). Becoming a student: Identity work and academic literacies in early schooling. *Tesol Quarterly, 39*(1), 59–82.

He, D. (2017). How to cope with foreign language speaking anxiety effectively? The case of university students in China. *Electronic Journal of Foreign Language Teaching, 14*(2), 159–174.

Hedgcock, J., & Ferris, D. R. (2005). Teaching L2 composition: *Purpose, process, and practice*. Mahwah, NJ: Lawrence Erlbaum Associates.

Hernández, T. A. (2011). Re-examining the role of explicit instruction and input flood on the acquisition of Spanish discourse markers. *Language Teaching Research, 15*(2), 159–182.

Hieronymus, J. L. (1993). *ASCII phonetic symbols for the world's languages: Worldbet*. Retrieved from http://www.cs.utoronto.ca/~frank/csc401/readings/worldbet.pdf

Hill, J. (2000). Revising priorities: From grammatical failure to collocational success. In M. Lewis (Ed.), *Teaching collocation: Further developments in the lexical approach* (pp. 47–69). Hove, UK: Language Teaching Publications.

Hill, J., Lewis, M., & Lewis, M. (2000). Classroom strategies, activities and exercises. In M. Lewis (Ed.), *Teaching collocation: Further developments in the lexical approach* (pp. 88–117). Hove, UK: Language Teaching Publications.

Hippner-Page, T. (2002). *Semantic clustering versus thematic clustering of English vocabulary word for second language instruction: Which method is more effective?* (No. ED445550). ERIC Document Reproduction Service.

Hirvela, A. (2004). *Connecting reading & writing in second language writing instruction*. Ann Arbor, MI: University of Michigan Press.

Holm, A., & Dodd, B. (1996). The effect of first written language on the acquisition of English literacy. *Cognition, 59*(2), 119–147.

Holt, B. J., & Hannon, J. C. (2006). Teaching-learning in the affective domain. *Strategies, 20*(1), 11–13.

Hong, Y.-R. (2007). A survey on the learning style preference of Tibetan EFL learners in China. *US-China Foreign Language, 5*(4), 39–42.

Horwitz, E. K. (1988). The beliefs about language learning of beginning university foreign language students. *The Modern Language Journal, 72*(3), 283–294.

Horwitz, E. K. (1996). Even teachers get the blues: Recognizing and alleviating language teachers' feelings of foreign language anxiety. *Foreign Language Annals, 29*(3), 365–372.

Horwitz, E. K., Horwitz, M. B., & Cope, J. (1986). Foreign language classroom anxiety. *The Modern Language Journal, 70*(2), 125–132.

Hosenfeld, C. (1977). A preliminary investigation of the reading strategies of successful and nonsuccessful second language learners. *System, 5*(2), 110–123.

Howard, R. M. (2000). Collaborative pedagogy. In G. Tate, A. Ruppier, & K. Schick (Eds.), *Collaborative pedagogies: A bibliographic guide* (pp. 54–70). Oxford: Oxford University Press.

Hu, M., & Nation, I. S. P. (2000). Vocabulary density and reading comprehension. *Reading in a Foreign Language, 13*, 403–430.

Hughes, A. (2007). *Testing for language teachers*. Cambridge: Cambridge University Press.

Hyland, K. (1993). Culture and learning: A study of the learning style preferences of Japanese students. *RELC Journal, 24*(2), 69–87.

Hyland, K. (2003). *Second language writing*. Cambridge: Cambridge University Press.

Hyland, K. (2004). *Genre and second language writing*. Ann Arbor, MI: University of Michigan Press.

Ioup, G., Boustagui, E., El Tigi, M., & Moselle, M. (1994). Reexamining the critical period hypothesis: A case study of successful adult SLA in a naturalistic environment. *Studies in Second Language Acquisition, 16*(1), 73–98.

Jacobs, G. M. (2004). Cooperative learning: Theory, principles, and techniques. *Proceedings of the First International Conference on Second and Foreign Language Teaching and Research*, 411–420. Retrieved from https://files.eric.ed.gov/fulltext/ED573881.pdf

Jacobs, G. M., & Liu, K. K. (1996). Integrating language functions and collaborative skills in the second language classroom. *TESL Reporter, 29*, 21–33.

Jacobs, G. M., Power, M. A., & Inn, L. W. (2002). *The teacher's sourcebook for cooperative learning: Practical techniques, basic principles, and frequently asked questions*. Thousand Oaks, CA: Corwin Press.

Jessner, U. (2008). Multicompetence approaches to language proficiency development in multilingual education. In J. Cummins (Ed.), *Encyclopedia of language and education: Vol. 5: Bilingual Education* (pp. 91–103). Amsterdam: Springer.

Jiang, N. (2004). Semantic transfer and its implications for vocabulary teaching in a second language. *The Modern Language Journal, 88*(3), 416–432.

Johns, A. M. (1997). *Text, role and context: Developing academic literacies*. Cambridge: Cambridge University Press.

Johnson, D. W., Johnson, R., & Holubec, E. (1998). *Cooperation in the classroom* (7th ed.). Edina, MN: Interaction Book Co.

Johnson, David W., & Johnson, R. T. (1990). Social skills for successful group work. *Educational Leadership, 47*(4), 29–33.

Johnson, David W., & Johnson, R. T. (2005). New developments in social interdependence theory. *Genetic, Social, and General Psychology Monographs, 131*(4), 285–358.

Johnson, David W., & Johnson, R. T. (2011). Cooperative learning. In D. J. Christie (Ed.), *The encyclopedia of peace psychology*. Retrieved from https://onlinelibrary.wiley.com/doi/abs/10.1002/9780470672532.wbepp066

Johnson, J., Prior, S., & Artuso, M. (2000). Field dependence as a factor in second language communicative production. *Language Learning, 50*(3), 529–567.

Johnson, J. S., & Newport, E. L. (1989). Critical period effects in second language learning: The influence of maturational state on the acquisition of English as a second language. *Cognitive Psychology, 21*(1), 60–99.

Jones, N. B. (1997, April). *Applying learning styles research to improve writing instruction*. Presented at the RELC Seminar on Learners and Language Learning, Singapore.

Jones, R., & Lock, G. (2011). *Functional grammar in the ESL classroom: Noticing, exploring and practicing*. New York: Palgrave Macmillan.

Kahn-Horwitz, J., Sparks, R. L., & Goldstein, Z. (2012). Relevance of the linguistic coding difference hypothesis to English as an additional language of literacy in Israel. In M. Leikin, M. Schwartz, & Y. Tobin (Eds.), *Literacy studies: Perspectives from cognitive neurosciences, linguistics, psychology and education*. (pp. 21–42). London: Springer.

Kalaja, P., Alanen, R., Palviainen, A., & Dufva, H. (2011). From milk cartons to English roommates: Context and agency in L2 learning beyond the classroom. In P. Benson & H. Reinders (Eds.), *Beyond the language classroom* (pp. 47–58). London: Palgrave.

Kamimura, T. (1996). Composing in Japanese as a first language and English as a foreign language: A study of narrative writing. *RELC Journal, 27*(1), 47–69.

Kamps, D., Abbott, M., Greenwood, C., Arreaga-Mayer, C., Wills, H., Longstaff, J., ... Walton, C. (2007). Use of evidence-based, small-group reading instruction for English language learners in elementary grades: Secondary-tier intervention. *Learning Disability Quarterly, 30*(3), 153–168.

Kang, S.-J. (2005). Dynamic emergence of situational willingness to communicate in a second language. *System, 33*(2), 277–292.

Kanno, Y. (2003). *Negotiating bilingual and bicultural identities: Japanese returnees betwixt two worlds*. Mahwah, NJ: Lawrence Erlbaum Associates.

Kanno, Y. (2008). *Language and Education in Japan: Unequal Access to Bilingualism*. New York: Palgrave Macmillan.

Kanno, Y., & Norton, B. (2003). Imagined communities and educational possibilities: Introduction. *Journal of Language, Identity, and Education, 2*(4), 241–249.

Kao, P.-C., & Craigie, P. (2013). Evaluating student interpreters' stress and coping strategies. *Social Behavior and Personality: An International Journal, 41*(6), 1035–1043.

Kayi, H. (2006). Teaching speaking: Activities to promote speaking in a second language. *The Internet TESL Journal, 12*(11), 1–6.

Keefe, J. W. (1979). *Student learning styles: Diagnosing and prescribing programs*. Reston, VA: National Association of Secondary School Principals.

Kellerman, E. (1991). Compensatory strategies in second language research: A critique, a revision, and some (non-) implications for the classroom. In R. Phillipson, E. Kellerman, L. Selinker, M. Sharwood Smith, & M. Swain (Eds.), *Foreign/Second language pedagogy research: A commemorative volume for Clous Farch*. (pp. 142–161). Clevedon, UK: Multilingual Matters.

Kellerman, E., Ammerlaan, T., Bongaerts, T., & Poulisse, N. (1990). System and hierarchy in L2 compensatory strategies. In R. Scarcella, E. S. Anderson, & S. D. Krashen (Eds.), *Developing communicative competence in a second language* (pp. 163–178). Boston: Heinle & Heinle.

Kellogg, R. T., Olive, T., & Piolat, A. (2007). Verbal, visual, and spatial working memory in written language production. *Acta Psychologica, 124*(3), 382–397.

Khmakhien, A. (2012). Demystifying Thai EFL learners' perceptual learning style preferences. *Southeast Asian Journal of English Language Studies, 18*(1), 61–74.

Kiany, G. R., & Shiramiry, E. (2002). The Effect of Frequent Dictation on the Listening Comprehension Ability of Elementary EFL Learners. *TESL Canada Journal, 20*(1), 57–63.

Kiraly, D., & Signer, S. (2017). *Scaffolded language emergence in the classroom: From theory to practice*. Berlin: Frank & Timme.

Klauda, S. L., & Guthrie, J. T. (2008). Relationships of three components of reading fluency to reading comprehension. *Journal of Educational Psychology, 100*(2), 310–321.

Kleinmann, H. H. (1977). Avoidance behavior in adult second language acquisition. *Language Learning, 27*(1), 93–107.

Knapp, P., & Watkins, M. (2005). *Genre, text, grammar: Technologies for teaching and assessing writing*. Sydney, AU: UNSW Press.

Koda, K., & Zehler, A. M. (2008). *Learning to read across languages*. New York, NY: Routledge.

Kohn, A. (1999). *Punished by rewards: The trouble with gold stars, incentive plans, A's, praise, and other bribes*. Boston: Houghton Mifflin Harcourt.

Kondo, D. S., & Ying-Ling, Y. (2004). Strategies for coping with language anxiety: The case of students of English in Japan. *ELT Journal, 58*(3), 258–265.

Kralova, Z., Skorvagova, E., Tirpakova, A., & Markechova, D. (2017). Reducing student teachers' foreign language pronunciation anxiety through psycho-social training. *System, 65*, 49–60.

Krashen, S. (2004). *The Power of Reading*. Westport, Conn: Libraries Unlimited.

Krashen, S. D. (1978). Individual variation in the use of the monitor. In W. C. Ritchie (Ed.), *Second language acquisition research: Issues and implications* (pp. 175–183). New York: Academic Press.

Krashen, S. D. (1982). *Principles and practice in second language acquisition*. Oxford: Pergamon Press.

Krashen, S. D. (1996). The case for narrow listening. *System, 24*(1), 97–100.

Krashen, S. D. (2011a). *Free voluntary reading*. Westport, Conn: Libraries Unlimited.

Krashen, S. D. (2011b). The compelling (not just interesting) input hypothesis. *The English Connection, 15*(3), 17.

Krashen, S. D., & Lee, S.-Y. (2004). Competence in foreign language writing: Progress and lacunae. *Literacy across Cultures, 12*(2), 10–14.

Krashen, S. D., Renandya, W. A., Mason, B., & Bose, P. (2018). Paths to competence in listening comprehension. *Beyond Words, 6*(1), 1–3.

Krashen, S. D., & Terrell, T. D. (1983). *The natural approach: Language acquisition in the classroom*. New York: Prentice Hall.

Kroll, B. (2001). Considerations for teaching an ESL/EFL writing course. In M. Celce-Murcia (Ed.), *Teaching English as a second or foreign language* (3rd ed., pp. 219–232). Boston: Heinle & Heinle.

Kumar, C. P. (2013). The eclectic method-theory and its application to the learning of English. *International Journal of Scientific and Research Publications, 3*(6), 1–4.

Langer, J. A. (2015). *Envisioning knowledge: Building literacy in the academic disciplines*. New York: Teachers College Press.

Lantolf, J. P., & Appel, G. (Eds.). (1994). *Vygotskian approaches to second language research*. Norwood, NJ: Ablex.

Larsen-Freeman, D. (2015). Research into practice: Grammar learning and teaching. *Language Teaching, 48*(2), 263–280.

Larsen-Freeman, D., & Anderson, M. (2013). *Techniques and principles in language teaching* (3rd ed.). Oxford: Oxford university press.

Larsen-Freeman, D., & Celce-Murcia, M. (2015). *The grammar book*. Boston: Heinle and Heinle.

Laufer, B., & Girsai, N. (2008). Form-focused instruction in second language vocabulary learning: A case for contrastive analysis and translation. *Applied Linguistics, 29*(4), 694–716.

Laufer, Batia. (1986). Possible changes in attitude towards vocabulary acquisition research. *International Review of Applied Linguistics, 24*, 69–75.

Lee, J. F., & VanPatten, B. (2003). *Making communicative language teaching happen*. (2nd ed.). New York: McGraw-Hill.

Lee, S. K. (1995). Creative games for the language class. *Forum, 33*(1), 35.

Lee, W., & Ng, S. (2009). Reducing student reticence through teacher interaction strategy. *ELT Journal, 64*(3), 302–313.

Leech, G., Rayson, P., & Wilson, A. (2001). *Word frequencies in written and spoken English*. London: Longman.

Leigh, S. R. (2012). The Classroom Is Alive with the Sound of Thinking: The Power of the Exit Slip. *International Journal of Teaching and Learning in Higher Education, 24*(2), 189–196.

Lems, K. (1995). *Whole language and the ESL/EFL classroom*. (No. ED384210). ERIC Document Reproduction Service.

Lenneberg, E. H. (1967). *The biological foundations of language*. New York: Wiley.

Levine, A., & Reves, T. (1990). Does the method of vocabulary presentation make a difference? *TESL Canada Journal, 8*(1), 37–51.

Lewis, M. (1993). *The lexical approach*. Hove, UK: Language Teaching Publications.

Lewis, M. (1996). Implications of a lexical view of language. In D. Willis & J. Willis (Eds.), *Challenge and change in language teaching* (pp. 10–16). Oxford: Heinemann.

Li, S. (2010). The effectiveness of corrective feedback in SLA: A meta-analysis. *Language Learning, 60*(2), 309–365.

Li, S. (2016). The construct validity of language aptitude: A meta-analysis. *Studies in Second Language Acquisition, 38*(4), 801–842.

Liamkina, O., & Ryshina-Pankova, M. (2012). Grammar dilemma: Teaching grammar as a resource for making meaning. *The Modern Language Journal, 96*(2), 270–289.

Liang, X., Mohan, B. A., & Early, M. (1998). Issues of cooperative learning in ESL classes: A literature review. *TESL Canada Journal, 15*(2), 13–23.

Liddicoat, A., Papademetre, L., Scarino, A., & Kohler, M. (2003). *Report on Intercultural Language Learning*. Canberra: Australian Government Department of Education, Science and Training.

Lie, A. (2002). *Cooperative learning*. Jakarta: Grasindo.

Lightbown, P. M., & Spada, N. (2013). *How languages are learned* (4th ed.). Oxford: Oxford university press.

Littlejohn, A., & Hicks, D. (1998). An A to Z of methodology. Retrieved August 5, 2019, from Cambridge English for Schools website: https://www.cambridge.org/elt/ces/methodology/openendedtasks.htm

Loewen, S. (2014). *Introduction to instructed second language acquisition*. New York: Routledge.

Long, M. (1996). The role of the linguistic environment in second language acquisition. In W. Ritchie & T. Bhatia (Eds.), *Handbook of second language acquisition* (pp. 413–468). San Diego, CA: Academic Press.

Long, M. H. (1985). Input and second language acquisition theory. In S. M. Gass & C. G. Madden (Eds.), *Input in second language acquisition* (pp. 377–393). Rowley, MA: Newbury House.

Long, M. H. (1990a). Maturational constraints on language development. *Studies in Second Language Acquisition, 12*(3), 251–285.

Long, M. H. (1990b). Task, group, and task-group interactions. *University of Hawaii Working Papers in ESL, 8*, 1–26.

Long, M. H., & Porter, P. A. (1985). Group work, interlanguage talk, and second language acquisition. *TESOL Quarterly, 19*(2), 207–228.

Lydon, A. (2017, October 26). The importance of whitespace in education. Retrieved April 6, 2019, from ResourcEd website: https://resourced.prometheanworld.com/whitespace-education/

Lyle, S. (2014). The limits of phonics teaching. *School Leadership Today, 5*(5), 68–74.

Maarof, N., & Suharjo, M. K. (2010). Using DRTA strategy to overcome EFL students' problems in reading literature in English. *International Journal of Learning, 17*(8), 93–103.

MacArthur, C. A., Philippakos, Z. A., & Ianetta, M. (2015). Self-regulated strategy instruction in college developmental writing. *Journal of Educational Psychology, 107*(3), 855–867.

MacIntyre, P. D. (2002). Motivation, anxiety and emotion in second language acquisition. *Individual Differences and Instructed Language Learning, 2*, 45–68.

MacIntyre, P. D. (2017). An overview of language anxiety research and trends in its development. In C. Gkonou, M. Daubney, & J.-M. Dewaele (Eds.), *New insights into language anxiety: Theory, research and educational implications* (pp. 11–30). Bristol, UK: Multilingual Matters.

MacIntyre, P. D., Babin, P. A., & Clément, R. (1999). Willingness to communicate: Antecedents & consequences. *Communication Quarterly, 47*(2), 215–229.

MacIntyre, P. D., Baker, S. C., Clément, R., & Conrod, S. (2001). Willingness to communicate, social support, and language-learning orientations of immersion students. *Studies in Second Language Acquisition, 23*(3), 369–388.

MacIntyre, P. D., & Charos, C. (1996). Personality, attitudes, and affect as predictors of second language communication. *Journal of Language and Social Psychology, 15*(1), 3–26.

MacIntyre, P. D., & Gardner, R. C. (1994). The subtle effects of language anxiety on cognitive processing in the second language. *Language Learning, 44*(2), 283–305.

Major, R. C. (2008). Transfer in second language phonology. *Phonology and Second Language Acquisition, 36*, 63–94.

Martin, J. R. (1992). *English text: System and structure*. Philadelphia/Amsterdam: John Benjamins Publishing.

Marzban, A., & Hashemi, M. (2013). The impact of opinion-gap tasks on the speaking of Iranian intermediate EFL learners. *Procedia - Social and Behavioral Sciences, 70*, 943–948.

Mason, B., Vanata, M., Jander, K., Borsch, R., & Krashen, S. (2008). The effects and efficiency of hearing stories on vocabulary acquisition by students of German as a second foreign language in Japan. *Indonesian JELT, 5*(1), 1–14.

Matear, A. (2008). English language learning and education policy in Chile: Can English really open doors for all? *Asia Pacific Journal of Education, 28*(2), 131–147.

Mazumdar, R. (2004, May 17). Coming here was a mistake: Skilled immigrants who can't get work in their trained professions end up frustrated and dispirited. *Calgary Herald*, p. A13.

McCafferty, S. G., Jacobs, G. M., & Iddings, A. C. D. (2006). *Cooperative learning and second language teaching*. Cambridge: Cambridge University Press.

McCutchen, D. (2000). Knowledge, processing, and working memory: Implications for a theory of writing. *Educational Psychologist, 35*(1), 13–23.

McDonough, J., & Shaw, C. (2012). *Materials and Methods in ELT*. New York: John Wiley & Sons.

McGrath, I. (2002). *Materials Evaluation and Design for Language Teaching Edinburgh Textbooks in Applied Linguistics*. Edinburgh, UK: Edinburgh University Press.

McGroarty, M. (1989). The benefits of cooperative learning arrangements in second language instruction. *NABE Journal, 13*(2), 127–143.

McGuire, H. (2005). Realia in academia. *Making Connections Language, Literacy, Learning*, pp. 2–3.

McLaughlin, B. (1987). *Theories of second-language learning*. London: Edward Arnold.

McLaughlin, B. (1990a). Restructuring. *Applied Linguistics, 11*(2), 113–128.

McLaughlin, B. (1990b). The relationship between first and second languages: Language proficiency and language aptitude. In B. Harley, P. Allen, J. Cummins, & M. Swain (Eds.), *The development of second language proficiency* (pp. 158–178). Cambridge: Cambridge University Press.

McLaughlin, B., & Heredia, R. (1996). Information-processing approaches to research on second language acquisition and use. In W. Ritchie & T. Bhatia (Eds.), *Handbook of second language acquisition* (pp. 213–228). San Diego, CA: Academic Press.

McLaughlin, B., & Nayak, N. (1989). Processing a new language: Does knowing other languages make a difference. *Interlingual Processes, 1*(5), 179–187.

McLaughlin, B., Rossman, T., & McLeod, B. (1983). Second language learning: An information-processing perspective. *Language Learning, 33*(2), 135–158.

McQuillan, J. (2016). What can readers read after graded readers?. *Reading in a Foreign Language, 28*(1), 63–78.

Meara, P. (1980). Vocabulary acquisition: A neglected aspect of language learning. *Language Teaching, 13*(3–4), 221–246.

Medgyes, P., & Celce-Murcia, M. (2001). When the teacher is a non-native speaker. In *Teaching English as a second or foreign language* (3rd ed., pp. 415–427). Boston: Heinle & Heinle.

Melton, C. D. (1990). Bridging the cultural gap: A study of Chinese students' learning style preferences. *RELC Journal, 21*(1), 29–54.

Meschyan, G., & Hernandez, A. (2002). Is native-language decoding skill related to second-language learning? *Journal of Educational Psychology, 94*(1), 14–22.

Mesmer, H. A. E., & Griffith, P. L. (2005). Everybody's selling it—But just what is explicit, systematic phonics instruction? *The Reading Teacher, 59*(4), 366–376.

Miller, D. (2010). *The book whisperer: Awakening the inner reader in every child*. San Francisco, CA: John Wiley & Sons.

Mitchell, R., & Myles, F. (2004). *Second language learning theories* (2nd ed.). London: Hodder.

Miyake, A. (1998). Individual differences in second language proficiency: The role of working memory. In A. F. Healy & L. E. Bourne Jr. (Eds.), *Foreign language learning: Psycholinguistic studies on training and retention* (pp. 339–364). Mahwah, NJ: Erlbaum.

Mizera, G. J. (2005). *Working memory and L2 oral fluency* (Unpublished Ph.D. dissertation). University of Pittsburgh, Pittsburgh.

Mohammadi, M. (2012). The role of emotional intelligence on English learning as a second language. *International Research Journal of Applied and Basic Sciences, 3*(9), 1953–1956.

Mohseni Far, M. (2008). An overview of syllabuses in English language teaching. Retrieved from http:/www. syllabusdesign.com

Morita, N. (2004). Negotiating participation and identity in second language academic communities. *Tesol Quarterly, 38*(4), 573–603.

Moyer, A. (2009). Input as a critical means to an end: Quantity and quality of experience in L2 phonological attainment. In T. Piske & M. Young-Scholten (Eds.), *Input matters in SLA* (pp. 159–174). Bristol, UK: Multilingual Matters.

Mullagayanova, G. S. (2016). Linguistic features typical of the greeting cards language. *Modern Scientific Researches and Innovations*, (9), 320–324.

Muñoz, C. (2010). On how age affects foreign language learning. In A. Psaltou-Joycey & M. Mattheoudakis (Eds.), *Advances in research on language acquisition and teaching* (pp. 39–49). Retrieved from http://www.enl.auth.gr/gala/14th/Papers/I nvited%20 Speakers/Munoz.pdf

Muñoz, C., & Singleton, D. (2011). A critical review of age-related research on L2 ultimate attainment. *Language Teaching, 44*(1), 1–35.

Murahata, G., Murahata, Y., & Cook, V. J. (2016). Research questions and methodology of multi-competence. In L. Wei & V. J. Cook (Eds.), *The Cambridge handbook of linguistic multi-competence* (pp. 26–49). Cambridge: Cambridge University Press.

Murphey, T. (2013). *Music and song*. Oxford: Oxford University Press.

Nakanishi, T. (2015). A meta-analysis of extensive reading research. *Tesol Quarterly, 49*(1), 6–37.

Nakata, T. (2008). English vocabulary learning with word lists, word cards and computers: Implications from cognitive psychology research for optimal spaced learning. *ReCALL, 20*(1), 3–20.

Nation, I. S. (2008). *Teaching ESL/EFL reading and writing*. New York: Routledge.

Nation, I. S., & Webb, S. A. (2011). *Researching and analyzing vocabulary*. Boston: Heinle/ Cengage.

Nation, P. (2001). *Learning vocabulary in another language*. Cambridge: Cambridge University Press.

Nation, P. (2004). A study of the most frequent word families in the British National Corpus. *Vocabulary in a Second Language: Selection, Acquisition, and Testing, 10*, 3–13.

Nation, P. (2006). How large a vocabulary is needed for reading and listening? *Canadian Modern Language Review, 63*(1), 59–82.

Nation, P. (2015). Principles guiding vocabulary learning through extensive reading. *Reading in a Foreign Language, 27*(1), 136–145.

National Reading Panel. (2000). *Teaching children to read: An evidence-based assessment of the scientific research literature on reading and its implications for reading instruction*. Washington, DC: National Institute of Child Health and Human Development.

Nattinger, J. (1986). Lexical phrases, functions and vocabulary acquisition. *The ORTESOL Journal*, 7, 1–14.

Nel, C. (2008). Learning style and good language learners. In C. Griffiths (Ed.), *Lessons from good language learners* (pp. 49–60). Cambridge: Cambridge University Press.

Nemtchinova, E. (2013). *Teaching listening*. Alexandria, VA: TESOL International Association.

Nguyen, L. T. C., & Gu, Y. (2013). Strategy-based instruction: A learner-focused approach to developing learner autonomy. *Language Teaching Research, 17*(1), 9–30.

Nikolov, M., & Djigunović, J. M. (2006). Recent research on age, second language acquisition, and early foreign language learning. *Annual Review of Applied Linguistics, 26*, 234–260.

Nolasco, R., & Arthur, L. (1987). *Conversation*. Oxford: Oxford University Press.

Nordin, S. M., & Mohammad, N. (2006). The best of two approaches: Process/genre-based approach to teaching writing. *The English Teacher, 35*, 75–85.

Norris, J. M., & Ortega, L. (2000). Effectiveness of L2 instruction: A research synthesis and quantitative meta-analysis. *Language Learning, 50*(3), 417–528.

Norton, B. (2000). *Identity and language learning: Social processes and educational practice*. London: Longman.

Norton, B. (2001). Non-participation, imagined communities and the language classroom. In M. P. Breen (Ed.), *Learner contributions to language learning: New directions in research* (pp. 159–171). Harlow, UK: Pearson Education.

Norton, B., & Toohey, K. (2001). Changing perspectives on good language learners. *TESOL Quarterly, 35*(2), 307–322.

Nunan, D. (1988). *The learner-centred curriculum: A study in second language teaching*. Cambridge: Cambridge University Press.

Nunan, D. (1995). Learner strategy training in the classroom: A case study. *Unpublished Paper*.

Nunan, D. (2002). Listening in language learning. In J. C. Richards & W. A. Renandya (Eds.), *Methodology in language teaching: An anthology of current practice* (pp. 238–241). Cambridge: Cambridge University Press.

Nutt, J. (2017). Interview testing: Focusing on repetition and increased contact with a variety of teachers to improve language retention and reduce anxiety. *The Language Teacher, 41*(2), 21–24.

Nuttall, C. (2005). *Teaching reading skills in a foreign language*. Oxford: Macmillan Education.

O'brien, I., Segalowitz, N., Collentine, J., & Freed, B. (2006). Phonological memory and lexical, narrative, and grammatical skills in second language oral production by adult learners. *Applied Psycholinguistics, 27*(3), 377–402.

O'malley, J. M., & Chamot, A. U. (1990). *Learning strategies in second language acquisition*. Cambridge: Cambridge University Press.

O'Malley, J. M., Chamot, A. U., & Küpper, L. (1989). Listening comprehension strategies in second language acquisition. *Applied Linguistics, 10*(4), 418–437.

O'Malley, J. M., Chamot, A. U., Stewner-Manzanares, G., Russo, R., & Kupper, L. (1985). Learning strategy applications with students of English as a second language. *TESOL Quarterly, 19*(3), 557–584.

Orlick, T. (2006). *Cooperative games and sports: Joyful activities for everyone* (2nd ed.). Champaign, IL: Human Kinetics.

Oxford, R. L. (1990). *Language learning strategies: What every teacher should know*. Rowley, MA: Newbury House.

Oxford, R. L. (2017). *Teaching and researching language learning strategies: Self-regulation in context*. New York: Routledge.

Oxford, R. L., & Ehrman, M. (1992). Second language research on individual differences. *Annual Review of Applied Linguistics, 13*, 188–205.

Oxford, R. L., & Ehrman, M. E. (1995). Adults' language learning strategies in an intensive foreign language program in the United States. *System, 23*(3), 359–386.

Panadero, E., & Jonsson, A. (2013). The use of scoring rubrics for formative assessment purposes revisited: A review. *Educational Research Review, 9*, 129–144.

Paramasivam, S. (2009). Language transfer as a communication strategy and a language learning strategy in a Malaysian ESL classroom. *The Asian EFL Journal Quarterly, 11*(1), 192–299.

Park, G.-P. (1997). Language learning strategies and English proficiency in Korean university students. *Foreign Language Annals, 30*(2), 211–221.

Patkowski, M. S. (1990). Age and accent in a second language: A reply to James Emil Flege. *Applied Linguistics, 11*(1), 73–89.

Payne, S., & Ross, B. (2005). Synchronous CMC, working memory, and L2 oral proficiency development. *Language Learning & Technology, 9*(3), 35–54.

Peacock, M. (2001). Match or mismatch? Learning styles and teaching styles in EFL. *International Journal of Applied Linguistics, 11*(1), 1–20.

Pearson, P. D., & Gallagher, G. (1983). The gradual release of responsibility model of instruction. *Contemporary Educational Psychology, 8*(3), 112–123.

Peirce, B. N. (1995). Social identity, investment, and language learning. *TESOL Quarterly, 29*(1), 9–31.

Peregoy, S. F., & Boyle, O. (2005). *Reading, writing, and learning in ESL: A resource book for teaching K-12 English learners* (4th ed.). New York: Longman.

Perfetti, C. A., & Hogaboam, T. (1975). Relationship between single word decoding and reading comprehension skill. *Journal of Educational Psychology, 67*(4), 461–469.

Pigada, M., & Schmitt, N. (2006). Vocabulary acquisition from extensive reading: A case study. *Reading in a Foreign Language, 18*(1), 1–28.

Pikulski, J. J., & Chard, D. J. (2005). Fluency: Bridge between decoding and reading comprehension. *The Reading Teacher, 58*(6), 510–519.

Pilgreen, J. L. (2000). T*he SSR handbook: How to organize and manage a sustained silent reading program*. Portsmouth, NH: Boynton/Cook.

Pishghadam, R. (2009). A quantitative analysis of the relationship between emotional intelligence and foreign language learning. *Electronic Journal of Foreign Language Teaching, 6*(1), 31–41.

Piske, T., & Young-Scholten, M. (2009). *Input matters in SLA*. Clevedon, UK: Multilingual Matters.

Pressley, M. (2002). *Reading instruction that works: The case for balanced teaching*. New York: Guilford Press.

Pritchard, A. (2008). *Ways of learning: Learning theories and learning styles in the classroom*. New York: Routledge.

Purcell, J. M. (1992). Using songs to enrich the secondary class. *Hispania, 75*(1), 192–196.

Purgason, K. (1991). Lesson plans and units. In M. Celce-Murcia & L. McIntosh (Eds.), *Teaching English as a second or foreign language* (pp. 419–431). Boston, MA: Heinle & Heinle.

Qureshi, M. A. (2016). A meta-analysis: Age and second language grammar acquisition. *System, 60*, 147–160.

Raimes, A. (1987). Language proficiency, writing ability, and composing strategies: A study of ESL college student writers. *Language Learning, 37*(3), 439–468.

Rasinski, T. (2004). Creating fluent readers. *Educational Leadership, 61*(6), 46–51.

Rasinski, T. V. (2012). Why reading fluency should be hot! *The Reading Teacher, 65*(8), 516–522.

Ray, B., & Seely, C. (1998). *Fluency through TPR storytelling: Achieving real language acquisition in school*. Berkeley, CA: Command Performance Language Institute.

Read, C. (2003). Is younger better? *English Teaching Professional, 28*, 5–7.

Reid, J. M. (1987). The learning style preferences of ESL students. *TESOL Quarterly, 21*(1), 87–111.

Reid, J. M. (1995). *Learning styles in the ESL/EFL classroom*. Boston: Heinle & Heinle.

Reinders, H., & Ellis, R. (2009). The effects of two types of input on intake and the acquisition of implicit and explicit knowledge. In R. Ellis, S. Loewen, C. Elder, H. Reinders, R. Erlam, & J. Philip (Eds.), *Implicit and explicit knowledge in second language learning, testing and teaching* (pp. 281–302). Bristol, UK: Multilingual Matters.

Renandya, W. A. (2007). The power of extensive reading. *RELC Journal, 38*(2), 133–149.

Renandya, W. A., & Farrell, T. S. C. (2010). 'Teacher, the tape is too fast!' Extensive listening in *ELT*. *ELT Journal, 65*(1), 52–59.

Reppen, R. (2010). *Using corpora in the language classroom*. Cambridge: Cambridge University Press.

Reves, T., & Medgyes, P. (1994). The non-native English speaking EFL/ESL teacher's self-image: An international survey. *System, 22*(3), 353–367.

Riazi, A., & Riasati, M. J. (2008). Language learning style preferences: A student's case study of Shiraz EFL institutes. *Iranian EFL Journal, 1*, 156–182.

Richard-Amato, P. A. (1988). *Making it happen: Interaction in the second language classroom, from theory to practice*. White Plains, NY: Longman.

Richards, J. (2008). *Teaching listening and speaking from theory to practice*. Oxford: Oxford University Press.

Richards, J. C. (1985). Conversational competence through role play activities. *RELC Journal, 16*(1), 82–91.

Richards, J. C. (1998). *Beyond training: Perspectives on language teacher education*. Cambridge: Cambridge University Press.

Richards, J. C., & Renandya, W. A. (2002). *Methodology in language teaching: An anthology of current practice*. Cambridge: Cambridge university press.

Riemer, M. J. (2003). Integrating emotional intelligence into engineering education. *World Transactions on Engineering and Technology Education, 2*(2), 189–194.

Riley, P. (2007). *Language, culture and identity: An ethnolinguistic perspective*. London: Continuum.

Robin, R. (2011). Listening comprehension in the age of Web 2.0. In N. Arnold & L. Ducate (Eds.), *Present and future promises of CALL: From theory and research to new directions in language teaching* (pp. 93–130). San Marcos, TX: CALICO.

Robinson, P. (2005). Aptitude and second language acquisition. *Annual Review of Applied Linguistics, 25*, 45–73.

Rossi-Le, L. (1995). Learning styles and strategies in adult immigrant ESL students. In J. M. Reid (Ed.), *Learning styles in the ESL/EFL classroom*. (pp. 118–125). Boston: Heinle & Heinle.

Rost, M. (2013). *Teaching and researching: Listening*. New York: Routledge.

Rubin, J. (Ed.). (1987). *Learner strategies in language learning*. Englewood Cliffs, NJ: Prentice-Hall.

Rubin, J. (2001). Language learner self-management. *Journal of Asian Pacific Communication, 11*(1), 25–37.

Rupley, W. H., Logan, J. W., & Nichols, W. D. (1998). Vocabulary instruction in a balanced reading program. *The Reading Teacher, 52*(4), 336–346.

Ryan, R. M., & Deci, E. L. (2000). Self-determination theory and the facilitation of intrinsic motivation, social development, and well-being. *American Psychologist, 55*(1), 68–78.

Sáfár, A., & Kormos, J. (2008). Revisiting problems with foreign language aptitude. *IRAL-International Review of Applied Linguistics in Language Teaching, 46*(2), 113–136.

Salovey, P., & Mayer, J. D. (1990). Emotional intelligence. *Imagination, Cognition and Personality, 9*(3), 185–211.

Sasaki, M. (2000). Toward an empirical model of EFL writing processes: An exploratory study. *Journal of Second Language Writing, 9*(3), 259–291.

Sawyer, M. (1992). Language aptitude and language experience: Are they related? *International University of Japan: Working Papers, 3*, 27–45.

Sawyer, M., & Ranta, L. (2001). Aptitude, individual differences, and instructional design. In W. P. Robinson (Ed.), *Cognition and second language instruction* (pp. 319–353). Cambridge: Cambridge University Press.

Schmidt, R. W. (1990). The role of consciousness in second language learning. *Applied Linguistics, 11*(2), 129–158.

Schmitt, N. (2008). Instructed second language vocabulary learning. *Language Teaching Research, 12*(3), 329–363.

Schmitt, N., & Schmitt, D. (1995). Vocabulary notebooks: Theoretical underpinnings and practical suggestions. *ELT Journal, 49*(2), 133–143.

Schumm, J. S. (2006). *Reading assessment and instruction for all learners*. New York: Guilford Press.

Scovel, T. (1978). The effect of affect on foreign language learning: A review of the anxiety research. *Language Learning, 28*(1), 129–142.

Scovel, T. (1988). *A time to speak: A psycholinguistic inquiry into the critical period for human speech*. New York: Newbury House.

Scrivener, J. (2011). *Learning teaching: The essential guide to English language teaching*. Oxford: Macmillan Education.

Selinker, L. (1972). Interlanguage. *IRAL-International Review of Applied Linguistics in Language Teaching, 10*, 209–232.

Selinker, L., & Gass, S. M. (2008). *Second language acquisition*. Mahwah, NJ: Erlbaum.

Shankar, P. (2004). *Teaching Of English*. New Delhi: APH Publishing.

Shankweiler, D., Crain, S., Katz, L., Fowler, A., Liberman, A., Brady, S., … Fletcher, J. (1995). Cognitive profiles of reading-disabled children: Comparison of language skills in phonology, morphology, and syntax. *Psychological Science, 6*(3), 149–156.

Shao, K., Yu, W., & Ji, Z. (2013). An exploration of Chinese EFL students' emotional intelligence and foreign language anxiety. *The Modern Language Journal, 97*(4), 917–929.

Shatz, I. (2015). Using gamification and gaming in order to promote risk taking in the language learning process. *Proceedings of the 13th Annual MEITAL National Conference*, 227–232. Haifa, Israel.

Shepard, L. A. (2003). Reconsidering large-scale assessment to heighten its relevance to learning. In J. M. Atkin & J. E. Coffey (Eds.), *Everyday assessment in the science classroom* (pp. 121–146). Washington, DC: National Science Teachers Association Press.

Shintani, N., Li, S., & Ellis, R. (2013). Comprehension-based versus production-based grammar instruction: A meta-analysis of comparative studies. *Language Learning, 63*(2), 296–329.

Silva, T. (1990). Second language composition instruction: Developments, issues, and directions in ESL. In B. Kroll (Ed.), *Second language writing: Research insights for the classroom* (pp. 11–23). New York: Cambridge University Press.

Singleton, D. (1989). *Language acquisition: The age factor*. Clevedon, UK: Multilingual Matters.

Skehan, P. (1986). Where does language aptitude come from? In P. Meara (Ed.), *Spoken language* (pp. 95–113). London: Centre for Information on Language Teaching.

Skehan, P. (1989). *Individual differences in second language acquisition*. London: Arnold.

Skehan, P. (1991). Individual differences in second language learning. *Studies in Second Language Acquisition, 13*(2), 275–298.

Skibniewski, L., & Skibniewska, M. (1986). Experimental study: The writing processes of intermediate/advanced foreign language learners in their foreign and native languages. *Studia Anglica Posnaniensia, 19*(3), 142–163.

Slavin, R. E. (1991). Synthesis of research of cooperative learning. *Educational Leadership, 48*(5), 71–82.

Slavin, R. E., Madden, N. A., & Leavey, M. (1984). Effects of cooperative learning and individualized instruction on mainstreamed students. *Exceptional Children, 50*(5), 434–443.

Smart, J. (2012). *Innovative approaches to ESL grammar instruction* (Doctoral Dissertation). Northern Arizona University, Flagstaff, AZ.

Smith, F. (2004). *Understanding reading: A psycholinguistic analysis of reading and learning to read*. New York: Routledge.

Smith, K. A. (1996). Cooperative learning: Making "groupwork" work. In C. Bonwell & T. Sutherland (Eds.), *Active learning: Lessons from practice and emerging issues*. (pp. 71–82). San Francisco, CA: Jossey-Bass.

Smith, V. (1994). *Thinking in a foreign language: An investigation into essay writing and translation by L2 learners*. Tübingen, Germany: Gunter Narr Verlag.

Snow, C. E., & Hoefnagel-Höhle, M. (1978). The critical period for language acquisition: Evidence from second language learning. *Child Development*, (49), 1114–1128.

Sokmen, A. A. (1988). Taking advantage of conference-centered writing. *TESOL Newsletter*, 22(1), 1–5.

Soonthornmanee, R. (2002). The effect of the reciprocal teaching approach on the reading comprehension of EFL students. *RELC Journal, 33*(2), 125–141.

Sparks, R. L., & Ganschow, L. (1991). Foreign language learning differences: Affective or native language aptitude differences? *The Modern Language Journal, 75*(1), 3–16.

Sparks, R. L., Humbach, N., & Javorsky, J. (2008). Individual and longitudinal differences among high and low-achieving, LD, and ADHD L2 learners. *Learning and Individual Differences, 18*(1), 29–43.

Sparks, R. L., Patton, J. O. N., Ganschow, L., & Humbach, N. (2009). Long-term relationships among early first language skills, second language aptitude, second language affect, and later second language proficiency. *Applied Psycholinguistics, 30*(4), 725–755.

Spolsky, B. (1989). *Conditions for second language learning: Introduction to a general theory*. Oxford: Oxford University Press.

Spratt, M. (1999). How good are we at knowing what learners like? *System, 27*(2), 141–155.

Stanovich, K. E. (1984). The interactive-compensatory model of reading: A confluence of developmental, experimental, and educational psychology. *Remedial and Special Education, 5*(3), 11–19.

Steffensen, M. S., Joag-Dev, C., & Anderson, R. C. (1979). A cross-cultural perspective on reading comprehension. *Reading Research Quarterly, 10*, 10–29.

Steinberg, F. S., & Horwitz, E. K. (1986). The effect of induced anxiety on the denotative and interpretive content of second language speech. *Tesol Quarterly, 20*(1), 131–136.

Stiggins, R. J. (2002). Assessment crisis: The absence of assessment for learning. *Phi Delta Kappan, 83*(10), 758–765.

Strech, L. (1994). *The implementation of writer's workshop: A review of the literature*. Long Beach, CA: California State University.

Street, B. V. (Ed.). (1993). *Cross-cultural approaches to literacy*. Cambridge: Cambridge University Press.

Swain, M. (1985). Communicative competence: Some roles of comprehensible input and comprehensible output in its development. In S. M. Gass & C. Madden (Eds.), *Input in second language acquisition* (pp. 235–253). Rowley, MA: Newbury House.

Swain, M. (1993). The output hypothesis: Just speaking and writing aren't enough. *Canadian Modern Language Review, 50*(1), 158–164.

Swain, M. (2008). The output hypothesis: Its history and its future. *Foreign Language Teaching and Research, 40*(1), 45–50.

Swain, M., & Lapkin, S. (1995). Problems in output and the cognitive processes they generate: A step towards second language learning. *Applied Linguistics, 16*(3), 371–391.

Swain, M., & Lapkin, S. (1998). Interaction and second language learning: Two adolescent French immersion students working together. *The Modern Language Journal, 82*(3), 320–337.

Takase, A. (2007). Japanese high school students' motivation for extensive L2 reading. *Reading in a Foreign Language, 19*(1), 1–18.

Tarone, E. (1980). Communication strategies, foreigner talk, and repair in interlanguage. *Language Learning, 30*(2), 417–428.

Tarone, E. (1981). Some thoughts on the notion of communication strategy. *TESOL Quarterly, 15*(3), 285–295.

Tarone, E., Cohen, A. D., & Dumas, G. (1976). *A closer look at some interlanguage terminology: A framework for communication strategies* (No. 9; pp. 76–90). Toronto: Ontario Institute for Studies in Education.

Tarone, E., & Yule, G. (1989). *Focus on the language learner: Approaches to identifying and meeting the needs of second language learners*. Oxford: Oxford University Press.

Tavakoli, M., & Ghoorchaei, B. (2009). On the relationship between risk-taking and self-assessment of speaking ability: A case of freshman EFL learners. *The Journal of AsiaTEFL, 6*(1), 1–27.

Taylor, J. B., Branscombe, N. A., Burcham, J. G., & Land, L. (2010). *Beyond early literacy: A balanced approach to developing the whole child*. New York: Routledge.

Teng, M. (2018). *Autonomy, agency, and identity in teaching and learning English as a foreign language*. Singapore: Springer.

The British Council. (1995). *English in the world: The English 2000 global consultation*. Manchester: The British Council.

Thomas, J., & Short, M. (Eds.). (1996). *Using corpora for language research: Studies in honour of Geoffrey Leech*. London: Longman.

Thornbury, S. (1999). *How to teach grammar*. London: Longman.

Tierney, R. J., & Pearson, P. D. (1983). Toward a composing model of reading. *Language Arts, 60*(5), 568–580.

Tierney, R. J., Readance, J. E., & Dishner, E. K. (1990). *Reading strategies and practices. A compendium* (3rd ed.). Boston: Allyn & Bacon.

Toma, I., Alexandru, C.-E., Dascalu, M., Dessus, P., & Trausan-Matu, S. (2016). Semantic taboo–a serious game for vocabulary acquisition. *Romanian Journal of Human-Computer Interaction, 10*(2), 241–256.

Tomlinson, B. (2008). *English language learning materials: A critical review*. London: Continuum.

Tompkins, G., Campbell, R., Green, D., & Smith, C. (2015). *Literacy for the 21st century* (2nd ed.). Melbourne, AU: Pearson Australia.

Toohey, K. (1996). Learning English as a Second Language in Kindergarten: A Community of Practice Perspective. *Canadian Modern Language Review, 52*(4), 549–76.

Toohey, K., & Norton, B. (2003). Learner autonomy as agency in sociocultural settings. In D. M. Palfreyman & R. Smith (Eds.), *Learner autonomy across cultures: Language education perspectives* (pp. 58–72). Basingstoke: Palgrave Macmillan.

Trelease, J. (2013). *The read-aloud handbook*. New York: Penguin.

Truscott, J. (1996). The case against grammar correction in L2 writing classes. *Language Learning, 46*(2), 327–369.

Tsiplakides, I., & Keramida, A. (2009). Helping Students Overcome Foreign Language Speaking Anxiety in the English Classroom: Theoretical Issues and Practical Recommendations. *International Education Studies, 2*(4), 39–44.

Tsui, A. B. (1996). Reticence and anxiety in second language learning. In K. Bailey & D. Nunan (Eds.), *Voices from the language classroom* (pp. 145–167). Cambridge: Cambridge University Press.

Tuan, L. T. (2011). EFL learners' learning styles and their attributes. *Mediterranean Journal of Social Sciences, 2*(2), 299–320.

Uberman, A. (1998). The use of games for vocabulary presentation and revision. *English Teaching Forum, 36*, 20–27.

Underwood, M. (1989). *Teaching listening*. London: Longman.

Ur, P. (2018). PPP: Presentation–practice–production. In J. I. Liontas & M. DelliCarpini (Eds.), *The TESOL encyclopedia of English language teaching* (pp. 1–6). London: John Wiley & Sons.

Ushioda, E. (2013). Motivation and ELT: Global issues and local concerns. In E. Ushioda (Ed.), *International perspectives on motivation: Language learning and professional challenges* (pp. 1–17). Basingstoke: Palgrave Macmillan.

Valdéz Pierce, L., & O'Malley, J. M. (1992). *Performance and portfolio assessment for language minority students*. Washington, DC: National Clearinghouse for Bilingual Education.

Vandergrift, L. (1999). Facilitating second language listening comprehension: Acquiring successful strategies. *ELT Journal, 53*(3), 168–176.

Vandergrift, L. (2005). Relationships among motivation orientations, metacognitive awareness and proficiency in L2 listening. *Applied Linguistics, 26*(1), 70–89.

Vandergrift, L., & Goh, C. C. (2012). *Teaching and learning second language listening: Metacognition in action*. New York: Routledge.

VanPatten, B. (1996a). *Input processing and grammar instruction in second language acquisition*. Norwood, NJ: Ablex.

VanPatten, B. (1996b). *Input processing and grammar instruction: Theory and research*. Norwood, NJ: Ablex.

VanPatten, B. (2004). *Processing instruction: Theory, research, and commentary*. New York: Routledge.

Vansteenkiste, M., Lens, M., & Deci, E. L. (2006). Intrinsic versus extrinsic goal contents in selfdetermination theory: Another look at the quality of academic motivation. *Educational Psychologist, 41*(1), 19–31.

Victori, M. (1999). An analysis of writing knowledge in EFL composing: A case study of two effective and two less effective writers. *System, 27*(4), 537–555.

Villanueva de Debat, E. (2006). Applying current approaches to the teaching of reading. *English Teaching Forum, 44*, 8–15.

Vygotsky, L. S. (1980). *Mind in society: The development of higher psychological processes*. Cambridge, MA: Harvard University Press.

Wakamoto, N. (2000). Language learning strategy and personality variables: Focusing on extroversion and introversion. *International Review of Applied Linguistics in Language Teaching, 38*(1), 71–81.

Walter, E. (2008). *Cambridge advanced learner's dictionary*. Cambridge: Cambridge University Press.

Wen, Z., & Skehan, P. (2011). A new perspective on foreign language aptitude research: Building and supporting a case for working memory as language aptitude. Ilha Do *Desterro A Journal of English Language, Literatures in English and Cultural Studies*, (60), 15–44.

Wenden, A., & Rubin, J. (1987). *Learning strategies in language learning*. Englewood Cliffs, NJ: Prentice-Hall.

Wesche, M., & Paribakht, T. S. (1996). Assessing second language vocabulary knowledge: Depth versus breadth. *Canadian Modern Language Review, 53*(1), 13–40.

Wharton, G. (2000). Language learning strategy use of bilingual foreign language learners in Singapore. *Language Learning, 50*(2), 203–243.

White, L. (2003). *Second language acquisition and universal grammar*. Cambridge: Cambridge University Press.

Widodo, H. P. (2006). Approaches and procedures for teaching grammar. *English Teaching: Practice & Critique, 5*(1), 122–141.

Wilkins, D. (1972). *Linguistics in language teaching*. London, UK: Arnold.

Willems, G. M. (1987). Communication strategies and their significance in foreign language teaching. *System, 15*(3), 351–364.

Williams, D. (2010). Student reactions to literature circles in content-based instruction. *KOTESOL Proceedings 2010*, 219–231. Seoul, Korea: Korea TESOL.

Williams, E. (1996). Reading in two languages at year five in African primary schools. *Applied Linguistics, 17*(2), 182–209.

Williams, J. N., & Lovatt, P. (2005). Phonological memory and rule learning. *Language Learning, 55*(1), 177–233.

Wilson, J. J. (2008). *How to teach listening*. Harlow, UK: Longman.

Wilson, R. J. (1996). *Assessing students in classrooms and schools*. Scarborough, ON: Allyn & Bacon Canada.

Winocur, S. L. (1985). Developing lesson plans with cognitive objectives. In A. L. Costa (Ed.), *Developing minds: A resource book for teaching thinking* (pp. 87–93). Alexandria, VA: Association for Supervision And Curriculum Development.

Wintergerst, A. C., DeCapua, A., & Verna, M. A. (2003). Conceptualizing learning style modalities for ESL/EFL students. *System, 31*(1), 85–106.

Witkin, H. A., Moore, C. A., Goodenough, D. R., & Cox, P. W. (1977). Field-dependent and field-independent cognitive styles and their educational implications. *Review of Educational Research, 47*(1), 1–64.

Wong, A. T. (2005). Writers' mental representations of the intended audience and of the rhetorical purpose for writing and the strategies that they employed when they composed. *System, 33*(1), 29–47.

Worde, R. V. (1998). *An investigation of students' foreign language anxiety*. Retrieved from http://www.eric.ed.gov/ERICWebPortal

Wright, A., Betteridge, D., & Buckby, M. (1984). *Games for language learning*. West Nyack, NY: Cambridge University Press.

Wright, J. (1998). *Dictionaries*. Oxford: Oxford University Press.

Wu, M. M. (2010). An exploratory study of the language-learning style preferences and language-learning motivation of ESL learners at a vocational education institute in Hong Kong. *Electronic Journal of Foreign Language Teaching, 7*(2), 222–238.

Xia, Y. U. (2016). Domestication of audiolingualism in ELT in China: From the perspective of cultural accommodation. *Studies in Literature and Language, 13*(3), 22–27.

Yamashita, J. (2004). Reading attitudes in L1 and L2, and their influence on L2 extensive reading. *Reading in a Foreign Language, 16*(1), 1–19.

Yasuda, S. (2004). Revising strategies in ESL academic writing: A case study of Japanese postgraduate student writers. *Journal of Asian Pacific Communication, 14*(1), 91–112.

Yngve, V. H. (1970). On getting a word in edgewise. *Papers from the Sixth Regional Meeting*, 567–578. Chicago, IL: Chicago Linguistics Circle.

Zamel, V. (1992). Writing one's way into reading. *TESOL Quarterly, 26*(3), 463–485.

Zarafshan, M., & Ardeshiri, M. (2012). Relationship between emotional intelligence, language learning strategies and English proficiency among Iranian EFL university students. *Journal of Educational & Instructional Studies in the World, 2*(3), 5–14.

Zhang, J., Beckmann, N., & Beckmann, J. F. (2018). To talk or not to talk: A review of situational antecedents of willingness to communicate in the second language classroom. *System, 72*, 226–239.

Zhang, L. J., Gu, P. Y., & Hu, G. (2008). A cognitive perspective on Singaporean primary school pupils' use of reading strategies in learning to read in English. *British Journal of Educational Psychology, 78*(2), 245–271.

SLA in Plain English

Understanding and Applying SLA for Teachers of English as a Second or Foreign Language

From Practice to Theory

초판 인쇄 2020년 8월 24일
초판 발행 2020년 8월 31일

저자 Dennis Murphy Odo
디자인 박지영
발행인 차정인
펴낸곳 부산대학교출판문화원

출판등록 제1983-000001호 1938. 11. 10.
부산광역시 금정구 부산대학로 63번길 2 (우편번호 46241)
대표전화 051-510-1932 팩시밀리 051-512-7812
https://press.pusan.ac.kr

ISBN 978-89-7316-673-2 (93740)
CIP2020034842